Structural Turkic Language Contacts

Structural Factors in Turkic Language Contacts

Lars Johanson

Taylor & Francis Group

LONDON AND NEW YORK

First Published in 2002
by Curzon Press

Published 2013 by Routledge
2 Park Square, Milton Park, Abingdon, Oxfordshire OX14 4RN
711 Third Avenue, New York, NY 10017

Routledge is an imprint of the Taylor and Francis Group, an informa business

First issued in paperback 2015

Based on a paper presented 2 February 1991 in a meeting of the
Wissenschaftliche Gesellschaft of the Johann Wolfgang Goethe University at
Frankfurt am Main.

English translation © Vanessa Karam 2002 from a revised version of
Strukturelle Faktoren in türkischen Sprachkontakten (= *Sitzungsberichte
der Wissenschaftlichen Gesellschaft an der J. W. Goethe-Universität
Frankfurt am Main*, 29:5), Stuttgart: © Steiner Verlag 1992.

The support of the Institute for the Study of Languages and Cultures of Asia
and Africa, Tokyo University of Foreign Studies, is gratefully acknowledged.

Typeset in Times by LaserScript Ltd, Mitcham, Surrey

All rights reserved. No part of this book may be reprinted or
reproduced or utilised in any form or by any electronic,
mechanical, or other means, now known or hereafter
invented, including photocopying and recording, or in any
information storage or retrieval system, without permission in
writing from the publishers.

British Library Cataloguing in Publication Data
A catalogue record of this book is available from the British Library

Library of Congress Cataloguing in Publication Data
A catalogue record for this book has been requested

ISBN 978-0-7007-1182-6 (hbk)
ISBN 978-1-138-98307-6 (pbk)

Contents

Introduction *by Bernard Comrie*   vii

Chapter 1 Code Copying in Turkic Language Contacts
1.1.	Questions	1
1.2.	Turkic language contacts	3
1.3.	Code copying	8
1.3.1.	*Global copies*	11
1.3.2.	*Selective copies*	13
1.3.3.	*Mixed copies*	18
1.4.	Turkic characteristics	19

Chapter 2 The Role of Structural Factors
2.1.	Suggested restrictions	35
2.2.	Scales of stability	37
2.3.	Attractiveness	41
2.4.	Attractive features	44
2.5.	Social factors	49
2.6.	Structuredness	51
2.7.	Relative attractiveness	53
2.8.	Differences between languages	58
2.9.	Deep influence	59
2.10.	Types of influence involved in language maintenance and language shift	65

CHAPTER 3 STRUCTURAL COPYING IN VARIOUS LINGUISTIC DOMAINS
3.1.	Turkic–non-Turkic convergence	73
3.2.	Phonological features	75
3.3.	Word structure	79
3.3.1.	*Verbal inflection*	87
3.3.2.	*Postverbial constructions*	91
3.4.	Grammatical categories	97
3.5.	Syntactic combinational patterns	105
3.5.1.	*Word order patterns*	111
3.5.2.	*Clause subordination*	116
3.5.3.	*Constituent clauses and copied clause-combining patterns*	121
3.5.4.	*Implications of the copied patterns*	129
3.5.5.	*Attractiveness of leftbranching clause subordination*	134

CHAPTER 4 GENERAL AND AREAL TENDENCIES
4.1.	General tendencies	139
4.2.	Sources of areal tendencies	143
4.3.	Early leveling of Turkic?	149
4.4.	Similarities in the most stable substructures	152

NOTES	157
REFERENCES	163
INDEX	179

INTRODUCTION

BERNARD COMRIE

Recent years have seen an upsurge of interest in the phenomena of language contact and in the application of new methods to the investigation of this phenomenon, ranging from such general works as Thomason & Kaufman (1988) to detailed specific studies on such phenomena as code-switching and creole genesis. In the present work, Lars Johanson examines contributions that can be made to the general debate, in particular concerning structural factors in language contact, by examining contacts between Turkic and non-Turkic languages. As the author notes, Turkic languages are likely to present particularly rich sources of data for the study of language contact, given the number and diversity of languages with which they have been in contact, including both Indo-European languages (especially Iranian and, in more recent times, Slavic languages) and non-Indo-European languages (such as Arabic) – not to mention such recent widespread phenomena as interaction between Turkish and Western European languages as Turkish-speakers have sought economic opportunities in Western Europe. These contacts have been sufficiently intensive and long-lasting to produce such phenomena as Turkic languages some of whose grammatical components are almost totally modeled on non-Turkic patterns (e.g. Slavic influence on Karaim, Persian influence on Kashkay), and non-Turkic languages including grammatical components similarly patterned after Turkic (e.g. Turkic influence on the Greek dialects that were spoken in Central Anatolia).

In this book, Johanson's emphasis is on structural factors, but this does not mean that social factors are ignored. In particular, the author makes a distinction between 'adoption', where a structure is taken over into the language in question from another language, and 'imposition', whereby a population speaking A as its primary language carries over some features of A into its variety of B. Johanson employs the useful term 'copying' to subsume both kinds of contact, with a distinction between global copying, where the whole of the form and function of a structure is copied, and selective copying, which is similar to the traditional 'calquing', for instance copying of a structural pattern but using indigenous morphemes. Striking examples of selective copying, involving the copying of patterns but not of morphemes, are provided by the Turkic-like tense-aspect-mood system of northern Tajik and the Persian-like tense-aspect-mood system of Kashkay. In addition, the author notes repeatedly that under appropriate social circumstances, in particular contact that is sufficiently intense and sufficiently long-lasting, almost any feature from one language can ultimately be copied into another. In other words, social factors can overcome structural obstacles to copying. Indeed, the interplay of structural and social factors brings us to the heart of Johanson's argumentation: The likelihood of a particular structure being copied into another language is determined in part by social factors (such as the prestige of the language from which the structure is to be copied), in part by structural factors, the latter subsumed under the general heading of 'attractiveness'. Thus an attractive property of a language is quite likely to be copied into another even in the absence of overwhelming social pressure, but the presence of such strong pressure can ultimately foster the copying even of the most unattractive structures. Both attractiveness and social prestige are, of course, ultimately continua rather than discrete oppositions.

If language A has copied some structure from language B, then in principle the following explanations are possible: the structure in question might have been attractive; or the social influence of language B on language A might have been sufficient to overcome the unattractiveness of the structure; or indeed attractiveness and social influence might have both been at work. If one simply considers examples in isolation, then there is no principled way of distinguishing among these cases. But Johanson shows, by examining a range of instances of copying between Turkic and non-Turkic languages, that it is possible in many instances to distinguish among them, and to come up with plausible hypotheses about what features are structurally attractive, in part also by taking into account material concerning copying that does not involve Turkic languages. In the case of copying from Turkic, the situation is further complicated by the fact that many aspects of Turkic structure turn out, once one has examined copying across a range of language contact situations, to be attractive, which makes it particularly important to justify, in each particular instance, whether copying from Turkic is to be attributed to attractiveness or social prestige.

A good illustration of this is provided by Johanson using two striking features of Turkic morphology: first, its agglutinative nature (low level of fusion, in Sapir's terminology), i.e. the fact that there is basically one-one correspondence between grammatical categories and their exponents, and second, its highly synthetic nature (high level of synthesis, again using Sapir's terminology), i.e. the fact that a given word can contain a large number of morphemes. Now, copying of bound morphology is in general known to be relatively unattractive, but there are nonetheless clear instances of non-Turkic languages copying bound morphemes from Turkic languages, including both derivational morphemes like the agentive nominalizer *-či* copied into Tajik, and inflectional morphemes, e.g. case suffixes copied into some varieties of Tajik and person–number inflections copied into some varieties of Anatolian Greek. But what one does not find is copying of the degree of synthesis that characterizes most Turkic languages, i.e. even those non-Turkic languages that have copied Turkic affixes have not copied the possibility of stringing together long sequences of such affixes. And even within the set of individual affixes, there are striking differences, with those most liable to copying being those that are most peripheral, such as the already cited case suffixes and person–

number suffixes. By contrast, the suffixes standing closest to the stem of a Turkic verb, namely those expressing actionality and diathesis, are most impervious to copying. In this way, one can establish degrees of attractiveness independent of social factors.

One area that particularly clearly shows Johanson's meticulousness in handling his methodology is his treatment of nonfinite constructions in Turkic, these being the basic Turkic analogs of subordinate clauses in many of the languages with which Turkic has been in contact (in particular, Indo-European languages). Many earlier researchers have been inclined to write nonfinite constructions off as unattractive, and indeed Turkic languages have shown a propensity for borrowing conjunctions from languages with which they have been in contact. (But, as Johanson argues persuasively, these elements are often integrated into Turkic syntax in a way quite different from their behavior as subordinating conjunctions in the donor language; Johanson calls them 'free junctors' in Turkic languages.) However, some of the nonfinite constructions of Turkic languages have proven themselves to be remarkably stable within Turkic, in particular gerundial (converbal) constructions of the type 'entering the room, he sat down' versus the more standard Indo-European 'he entered the room and sat down'. In addition, Turkic gerundial constructions have been copied into Tajik, using Tajik participial forms to correspond to the Turkic gerund. Turkic relative clauses, being both prenominal (leftbranching) and nonfinite, have been particularly open to characterization as unattractive by other researchers, but Johanson is careful to present a balanced account. While the massively complex Turkic relative clauses that are possible, even if not all that often used (especially in the spoken language), have not been copied into other languages, simpler instances of nonfinite preposed relative clauses have been copied.

Another area where great care is needed, and shown by Johanson, is where copying from another language affects not so much the acquisition of a new structure as a shift in the use of existing structures. Word order is one area where this shows itself particularly clearly. Most Turkic languages are basically head-final, in particular verb-final within the clause, but 'leakage' of constituents to the right of the verb is permitted under appropriate pragmatic conditions. In some of the languages under the strongest influence of European languages, in particular Karaim and Gagauz, this contact has led to the abandoning of basic verb-final word order in favor of subject–verb–object. In other words, shifts in word order are particularly likely under foreign influence. In other cases, copied word order patterns are clearly innovations, as when prepositions are borrowed from Slavic into Karaim, and as in the possessive construction of northern varieties of Tajik: *muallim-ä kitåb-aš* literally 'teacher-of book-his', as in Turkic, rather than the pattern found in other varieties of Persian–Tajik 'book-particle teacher'. Such examples show, incidentally, that it is perfectly possible for a language to copy structures that might appear to be 'typologically inconsistent' with the rest of its structure.

The last few pages of this monograph introduce some interesting applications of Johanson's conclusions to other areas. For instance, if it is indeed the case that Turkic languages show an unusual preponderance of attractive features, an obvious question to ask is why this should be so. Johanson suggests that this may be the result of koinéization in the history of the Turkic languages, i.e. with contact among Turkic (and some non-Turkic) languages over an extended period leading to continued reinforcement of more attractive structures. Turning to the controversy surrounding the external genetic relations of Turkic languages within Altaic, Johanson suggests that the conservatism of Turkic verb structure – stable even in as de-Turkicized a language as Karaim – and in particular the extreme resistance to copying of the positions closest to the verbal stem might provide a more reliable tool than many of those used in the past to test whether there are indeed shared elements that testify to genetic relatedness, rather than intensive and long-lasting language contact, among the groups of languages that would constitute Altaic.

In sum, Johanson's work is a careful and insightful contribution to the general literature on language contact, in addition to its narrower interest for students of Turkic languages. Many false generalizations that still all too frequently find their way into the literature on language contact are laid bare, and the methodology used by the author in evaluating particular instances of language contact involving Turkic languages can be used with profit by all students of language contact.

Chapter 1

CODE COPYING IN TURKIC LANGUAGE CONTACTS

1.1. Questions

The influence that languages can exert on one another when they come into contact has long been a subject of linguistic debate: What can change, how far can the influence go, what factors inhibit contact-induced change? Language contact research is still far from able to clearly answer questions even so general in nature. Most investigations to date have been limited to cataloguing and describing contact-related change. Nevertheless, recent decades have witnessed some progress. In particular, a number of earlier, extremely generalizing theories have been disproved. Reductionist theses, which limit the influence to individual factors, have largely given way to the realization that the linguistic outcome of language encounters is determined by a rather complex interplay of causes. Nonetheless, diachronic linguistics still lacks theoretically sound and empirically proven hypotheses to accommodate the processes in question.

Based on Turkic language material, the present study sets out to examine the significance of certain factors in contact-induced change. Focus is placed on the extent to which the structural characteristics of contact languages foster or inhibit such change, and on how structural factors assert themselves against the nonlinguistic factors present in the contact situation. The findings can claim general relevance beyond the material examined and are thus not exclusively directed towards Turcologists. Only a small number of the abundant contact phenomena documented to date will serve as examples here. I will also avoid an overly eclectic assortment of data in order to draw a distinct picture of the principles involved in contact-induced language change. The discussion will be strictly confined to direct, nonlexical influence from spoken language, and be conducted exclusively from the point of view of the aspects mentioned above. A number of important issues concerning linguistic variation cannot be addressed here, e.g. which variety of a donor language a 'foreign' element comes from and which variety of a recipient language it is copied into. And we can only take a glance at the questions surrounding borrowing, the effect of substratum languages, koinéization, etc.

My ideas are based on several assumptions and terminological definitions which can be outlined as follows: The method I employ views each individual language as a historically developed creative technique *sui generis* that develops, applies and alters the rules of linguistic production. Technical elements that generate language change can be 'borrowed' from contact languages. For the purpose of description, I have chosen to analyze languages as *products*: In this concrete sense, I speak of new *language facts* which, in certain circumstances, even seem to 'replace' old ones. Thus I conceive of contact-related language facts as elements that have been 'copied' into the respective recipient language; see 1.3 below for the concept of code copying. I assume that one contact language can *socially dominate* another. 'A' designates the socially dominated, 'B' the socially dominant code. In addition, it is to be expected that linguistic features can be *structurally dominant*. Their dominance is at least partially determined by the typological relations between the contact languages and the structures within them. In view of the behavior of Turkic elements in contact with, e.g., Indo-European languages, one might tentatively consider whether certain structural features are *attractive* in the absolute sense that they especially lend themselves to copying. I shall discuss some preliminary observations concerning this question, among others, the speculations

(i) that structural features can be attractive per se,

(ii) that their attractiveness is relativized by the typological relations between the given contact languages, and
(iii) that social factors ultimately determine the extent to which attractiveness leads to influence.

Finally, I will address certain diachronic implications, e.g. the question of Turkic linguistic genealogy.

The discussion is based on the premise that contact-induced influence presupposes a certain degree of bilingualism. In the copying of linguistic elements, *two interacting types of influence* are to be distinguished which affect A speakers as follows:

(1) *B influences their A.*
(2) *A influences their B.*

The result of influence type 1 is called *adoption*, that of influence type 2 *imposition*. One possible consequence of strong social dominance is *language shift* – the relinquishing of the socially weak A code in favor of the socially strong B code.

Even after a group of A speakers has shifted to B, the result of their imposition (influence type 2) may continue to operate as a *substratum influence* on their B.

1.2. Turkic language contacts

The Turkic languages, interrelated on the linguistic family tree and more or less distant from one another as a result of divergent developments, are fascinating due to their uniformity, on the one hand, and their diversity, on the other (Johanson & Csató 1998). Their exact genetic relations, including the question whether they belong to an Altaic language family – with Mongolic and Tungusic, perhaps also with Korean and Japanese – continues to be controversial. Today, the Turkic languages extend from Bosnia to China, and from southern Persia to the Arctic Ocean. In a core area encompassing Asia Minor, northern Persia, Transcaucasia, and Western and Eastern Turkestan, we find the languages Turkish,

Azerbaijanian, Turkmen, Uzbek, Kirgiz, Kazakh, Uyghur and others. North of this area, among others, Tatar and the Siberian Turkic languages such as Yakut (Sakha) are spoken. In addition, there are other areas in China, Afghanistan, Iran, Iraq and on the Balkans where Turkic languages are found. For decades Turkish has also been spoken by large immigrant groups in Western Europe, especially in Germany.

Two aspects of the linguistic history of the Turkic languages deserve special mention: their numerous contacts with other languages and their aggressive character (Johanson 1988a). Turkic speakers have often acted as intermediaries in cultural border zones – between the Far East and the West, between the Iranian and the Slavic world, in the border regions between the Islamic and the Byzantine empires, etc. In numerous contacts with Iranian, Mongolic, Uralic and Slavic languages, to name a few, Turkic languages have served both as 'donors' and 'recipients'. Turkic speakers readily adopted loanwords, the sedentary peoples especially from Arabic–Persian, the nomads from Mongolic. And more than a little Turkic lexical stock has entered other languages. Some nonlexical influences will be discussed below.

The historical divergence of the Turkic languages is characterized by contact in other ways as well. As a result of the great mobility of the Turkic peoples, the boundaries of their linguistic areas were also constantly shifting. This geographical discontinuity prevents us today from assigning them to a coherent language chain such as the one Hugo Schuchardt once attempted to establish for the Romance languages from Sicily to Portugal. In Turkic, primary differentiations underwent subsequent areal changes, and new, genetically independent areal-typological continuities emerged. Although the numerous far-reaching expansions of Turkic rule did not always coincide with an extension of Turkic linguistic territory, the Turkic languages did conquer an enormous area overall. As a result, many of them have also been subject to complex substratum processes. Some languages show pronounced structural discontinuity because they developed in special socio-communicative conditions. This is particularly true of the period of the Mongol incursion, which also led to various kinds of leveling processes.

A mere glance at Turkic language encounters to date reveals that the *social factors* of the contact situation have greatly determined the direction, type, scope and depth of the influence. The relevant factors seem, however, to have varied and interacted in very complex ways. Evidently, the copying of linguistic elements was governed by conscious and unconscious motives, such as the desire to adapt to politico-economic exigencies and gain prestige by emulating the linguistic behavior of admired social groups. Often we lack the detailed information about social conditions necessary for evaluating linguistic influence.[1] Questions concerning social attitudes, which are generally difficult to judge, cannot be answered at all for many Turkic language contact situations.

Political, economic, cultural and numerical superiority as well as firm roots in the contact area are important factors of social dominance. Groups possessing several of these factors have usually exerted strong linguistic influence on others. Clearly asymmetrical dominance conditions have always seemed to favor the influence of B on A. However, no single factor has probably ever been crucial or sufficient for such influence, not even social superiority. Jakobson (1938) asserts that the effect one language can have on the phonological structure of another does not presuppose the political, social or cultural dominance of the nation speaking the former. This well-known statement should apply to other linguistic domains as well.

Turkic-speaking groups were not always politically dominant in situations where their languages exerted influence. Numerous Turkic migrations leading to increased linguistic influence were peaceful or defensive in nature. On the other hand, at times, politically dominant but numerically and culturally inferior Turkic groups adopted the languages of their non-Turkic subjects. In certain multilingual contexts, dominance was distributed unevenly, with a Turkic language governing specific areas of life and a non-Turkic one governing others.

The *intensity and duration of contact* are further important factors determining the extent and quality of bilingualism, both crucial aspects of linguistic influence. In cases of profound influence, a significant number of A speakers always seem to have been bilingual at least to some degree. Contact intensity refers to the variety and closeness of social contacts, with influence particularly thriving in mixed communities. Contact duration designates the time period available to the development of bilingualism and the conventionalization of innovations. Turkic language contacts resulting in profound change were never episodic, but rather the effect of sustained bilingualism. As a rule, the depth of the influence appears to correlate with the intensity and duration of the language contact.

The scope of the present study precludes an indepth analysis of such factors and circumstances as is prerequisite to any comprehensive examination of the conditions of linguistic influence. I must restrict this investigation to a number of exemplary cases: among them, unequivocal instances of high contact intensity, long contact duration and clearly asymmetrical dominance conditions.

An example of *non-Turkic dominance* is found in Karaim, a Turkic language whose few remaining native speakers now live in Lithuania, the Ukraine and Poland. For half a millennium, this language has evolved in isolation from other Turkic languages, mainly in Polish and Ukrainian surroundings, where Slavic spoken languages have influenced it intensely (see Csató 2000). Since the Karaim are Karaites of Turkic origin, their language also contains older influence from written Hebrew. An example of *Turkic dominance* is found in the Inner Anatolian Greek dialect group in Anatolia. This group developed under the similarly prolonged, overwhelming political and social dominance of Ottoman Turkish-speaking groups in small communities isolated from one another and was therefore subject to an unusually high degree of foreign influence (Dawkins 1916, for the social relationships, see pp. 1–38).[2] The above are prime examples of extreme asymmetry, high contact intensity, long contact duration, and the widespread and qualified bilingualism of the A speakers, accompanied by profound A change. The respective B structures were not subject to comparable influence, remaining stable instead.[3] In both cases, comprehensive language shift also occurred, namely from A to B only.

Another intense and lasting, but less asymmetrical example of language contact resulting in intense structural influence is the

Turkic–Iranian contact situation in Western Turkestan. There, close, more balanced relationships, e.g. numerous linguistically mixed communities, led to the widespread qualified bilingualism of both groups and linguistic influence in both directions. In particular, the northern Tajik dialects were Turkicized, while the Uzbek urban dialects were Iranicized.

The examples listed above are well known and often discussed in the sociolinguistic as well as the general linguistic literature. (A portion of the relevant literature will occasionally be taken into account below.) The following languages are also especially interesting: Khalaj, spoken in central Iran, which exhibits heavy Persian influence without having in turn influenced the neighboring Iranian dialects; Kashkay, spoken in southern Iran, one of the most heavily Iranicized Turkic varieties; Finno-Ugric-influenced Chuvash, spoken in the Volga basin, and in the same area, Mari (Cheremis), a Finno-Ugric language influenced by the neighboring Turkic languages Chuvash and Tatar. Afghan Uzbek, northern Persian Azerbaijanian, Gagauz and a number of Balkan Turkic varieties are other Turkic languages that have been significantly influenced by Iranian or Slavic. One of the Balkan Turkic varieties is the so-called Koranes (or *xorāxanē*) variety of Turkish which – often alongside Romani and Macedonian – is spoken by the Roma living in northern Macedonia (Matras 1990). Eastern peripheral Turkic languages such as Yakut (Sakha), Dolgan, Sayan Turkic, Yellow Uyghur and Salar display an abundance of contact-induced phenomena, some of which will feature as examples in this study.

Various Slavic and Mongolic varieties are noteworthy non-Turkic contact languages. Additionally, Tajik, mentioned above, is a remarkable instance of intense, long-term Modern Persian–Turkic language contact. Overall, the results of Persian–Turkic contact deserve attention. Similarly, the Inner Anatolian Greek dialect group constitutes a special case within the evolution of Modern Greek spoken in Anatolia. The more archaic Pontic dialects, however, show less heavy influence from Turkish (Oikonomides 1958). The role of Kurdish varieties in language contact in Anatolia is also of great interest, but unfortunately still rather obscure. Armenian plays an intriguing role as well; typologically it has rather distanced itself from its Indo-European roots. Western Armenian existed for at least 700 years as a minority language in Turkish-dominated Anatolia, and its speakers were usually bilingual. Furthermore, much too little is known about the contact-related development of the Caucasian languages spoken in the vicinity of Turkic; see, among others, Džangidze's (1978) description of a Georgian dialect influenced by Azerbaijanian. Finally, Ladino deserves consideration, i.e., the Sephardic koiné which evolved in the seventeenth century, and Istanbul Ladino (Faingold 1989).

1.3. Code copying

The analysis of linguistic influence phenomena presupposes certain basic theoretical concepts. What follows is a brief sketch of my code-copying model, which is conceived of as the basis for a coherent description of language contact phenomena and a point of departure for typological comparisons (cf. Johanson 1993b; 1999a; 1999b). It diverges in essential points from the classical models developed by Weinreich (1953) and Haugen (e.g. 1972; 1973).

A number of basic terms employed by traditional contact linguistics imply metaphors which have often distorted the analysis of contact-induced phenomena. The term 'borrowing' as such is already misleading. Nothing is actually borrowed in language contact: the 'donor language' is not robbed of any element, and the 'recipient language' does not acquire anything that is identical to an element in the donor language. The same potential misunderstanding is inherent in the term 'transfer'. I have avoided the term 'interference' because of the often negative connotations it conveys today. The influence types described in 1.1, adoption and imposition, are processes for which the designation *copying* would seem more adequate.

To alter the creative production rules of a language, material can be copied from a contact language. From the point of view of the analysis of the linguistic product as an object, the best metaphor for describing this contact-related process is the idea of elements of a foreign code being copied into the code of the recipient language.

The influence resulting from Turkic contact situations can be analyzed as various kinds of *intraclausal code copying*. One language constitutes the basic code, the other, the model code from which elements (units, structures) are copied. Thus my model disregards cases of *alternation* or *code switching*, i.e., the alternating use of several codes. The foreign elements merely serve as models and are *never identical* to the copies inserted into the basic code. Since each language constitutes a unique creative technique, the copy consequently belongs to a different system than its original. According to this interpretation, copying is neither a switch from the basic code to the foreign code nor a fusion of the two.

In the following discussion, which is essentially limited to *adoption* (see 1.1),

A designates the socially dominated language acting as the basic code; and
B the socially dominant language from whose code elements are copied.

The copying process can be *global* and/or *selective*. In global copying, a B pattern is copied into an A basic-code clause in its entirety, i.e., as a block of material, combinational, semantic and frequential structural properties. In selective copying, discussed below, the model consists only of selected structural properties of a B block, i.e., characteristics of a material, combinational, semantic and/or frequential kind.

The differences between the original and the copy can often be defined in terms of the substitution of certain properties for others. The results range from reproduction (close similarity to the model) to sweeping change and creative reshaping. The degree of similarity is not a direct reflection of the speaker's competence in B; hence, adjustments performed on the copy are not necessarily a sign of deficient B acquisition. Often, but certainly not always, differences can be viewed as modifications that allow copies to adapt to the basic code and thus reduce structural conflicts between the codes.[4] The copied elements are adapted to A elements, with which they are identified. The result can only be analyzed 'contrastively', in terms of an adaptational measure, if we are familiar with the model's precise variety of origin. Often the adjustment can be interpreted as an *over-* or *underdifferentiation* resulting from the A and B equivalents' divergent features. On the one hand, a distinction absent or uncommon in A can be made in the copy because it is usual or obligatory in B and therefore deemed appropriate in A as well. On the other hand, an otherwise common or obligatory distinction in A might be suppressed because it is missing or uncommon in B and therefore considered superfluous in A. *Reinforcement by analogy* is frequent in all areas, i.e., the giving of preference to units and other elements which the contact languages appear to 'have in common', in other words, elements identified as close correspondences of one another. Such adaptational tendencies result in different kinds of convergence between A and B in phonology, morphology, semantics and syntax.[5]

Concerning the *use* of code copies, preliminary distinctions are required in at least four dimensions. The first dimension is the distinction between the use of a copy as an innovation in discourse (so-called 'interference' on the performance level) and its systematic use in language (change on the competence level). The second dimension involves distinctions concerning the frequency with which copies and copy types are used ('text frequency'). I will occasionally employ the cover term 'habitualization' to designate these first two dimensions. The third dimension concerns the distinction between individual copies restricted to concrete elements and generalized copies (types, general patterns). The fourth dimension – 'conventionalization' – concerns the quantitative differentiation of how widespread the copy is in the linguistic community (i.e. the number of individuals using it systematically).

The habitualization and frequency of code copies depend on a complex interplay of social and psychological factors. 'Integration', the conventionalization of copies in the linguistic community, passes through various stages of social acceptance (including acceptance by monolingual speakers). Some decisive factors in this process are whether such a copy is subjectively regarded as part of A – no longer 'foreign' or belonging to B[6] – and whether or not the copy suppresses its A equivalent. The present study must neglect these important issues and can only marginally address the complicated questions surrounding the successive phases in the diachronic development of copies and 'generations' of copies.

1.3.1. Global copies

In global copying, the original, whose material shape is copied, can be morphemically simple or complex, free or bound, and can encompass one or more words. An example of a bound morpheme is Ottoman -*āt* (in *gidišāt*, 'the course of events'), copied from Arabic; compare derivational suffixes such as English -*able* (as in *eatable*[7]), copied from Old French. The clausal frame provided by the basic code includes combinational patterns and function units. The global copy is inserted into an *equivalence position* deemed appropriate for an A equivalent, i.e., an A unit largely equivalent to the copy. The equivalence of the copy and the respective A unit is based on the speaker's subjective assessment; hence, insertions can occur where no actual typological equivalence obtains. Normally, the global copy takes on the grammatical A morphology, i.e. the necessary sentence-hierarchic function units of the basic clausal frame – relators connecting constituents and marking their structural functions within the sentence. Grammatical relators are, for example, prepositions and postpositions (pre- and postpositive relational particles), free junctors (conjunctions) and other particles, case affixes, junctors in the form of predicators (cf. 1.4), etc.

This type of 'integration' cannot be interpreted as the switching from one code to another, because the basic-code clause provides the very frame for insertion. Nor can it be viewed as a form of 'substitution', since function units that have not been copied from the model obviously cannot be replaced.

However, grammatical relators can also be replaced by global copies. For instance, Central Anatolian dialects of Modern Greek show copies of Turkish function words, e.g. *ičün* 'for, because of', the interrogative particle *mi*, etc., northern Tajik has case suffixes copied from Uzbek such as -*gä*, -*dä*, and -*dän*.

Copies of complex B blocks may also be treated as simple, unanalyzed units in A. Thus we encounter complex copied units containing affixes but functioning as primary stems – for instance, Ottoman *fuqarā* 'pauper', the copy of an Arabic plural form. And we can observe how sentence-hierarchic B function units copied as part of a block become functionally redundant in A. Prepositional B phrases copied in their entirety can be marked in the basic-code clause by postpositive function units – relators such as case suffixes and postpositions – without a resulting duplication of function marking. (Regarding the Iranian Azerbaijanian type *xårič äz šährdä* 'outside the city', see 3.5.1. below.)

Material restructuring usually encompasses phonic as well as phonotactic adaptation (such as Altay Turkic *ostolmo* 'post, pole' < Russian *stolb*) and often entails morphological reshaping; for the material restructuring of loanwords see, e.g., Menges 1947: 89 ff.; Johanson 1986a. Combinational and semantic features are also altered, often by means of adaptation to an A equivalent with which the relevant block is identified. In certain cases the adaptation can go so far that global copying produces *new expressions for old meanings*: Languages can possess relatively stable concepts, e.g. grammatical functions, for which new exponents are created in this way.

As noted, the differences between original and copy can involve their semantic and combinational properties. Frequently, the use of a globally copied B unit follows A patterns. This is true not only of lexical items, but also of copied grammatical function units. For example, the Zyryan coordinating conjunction *i* 'and', copied from Russian, is not used according to the Russian pattern but is enclitic instead (Schlachter 1974). In terms of the frequency of its use, the copy often considerably deviates from its original, adaptation to an A equivalent occurring in this respect also.

An adaptational strategy of another kind is *morphological reshaping*, whereby the copies are morphosyntactically classified and prepared for insertion into specific A positions where they can combine with A morphology. I consciously avoid the traditional term 'morphological integration', as it usually also designates phenomena relating to insertion into the basic-code frame.

As a rule, of course, the more morphological classes and inflectional patterns language A contains, the more extensive are its modification strategies. For example, in Anatolian Greek dialects, globally copied Turkish lexical items were assigned to Greek classes and combined with the respective affixes in order to accommodate Greek inflectional patterns: e.g. nouns such as *ojáqï* 'stove' (< *ojaq*) and adjectives such as *čipláxïs* 'naked' (< *čiplaq*) (Sílli dialect; Dawkins 1916: 43). Adjectives too acquired gender morphology, e.g. masc. *bašqá-s* 'other' (< *bašqá), fem. bašqá-ssa*, neut. *bašqá* (Dawkins 1916: 48). By means of A suffixes, copies of B verbal stems were reshaped into A verbal stems, e.g. *düšün-d-üz-* 'think' (Dawkins 1916: 67).

Morphological similarities between A and B may facilitate the accommodation.[8] In Turkic (as in Persian), verbal stems are often formed by using copies of B verbal nouns (infinitives, participles, etc.). In Karaim, for instance, copies of Slavic infinitives are reshaped into verbal stems by means of the auxiliary verb *ät'-* 'do', e.g. *bit'ät'-* (in western Ukrainian Karaim > *bit-*) 'strike'. Interestingly, Tajik copies of Turkic verbal stems are sometimes rendered syntactically functional by attaching the participial element *-miš,* also copied from Turkic, e.g. *tugulmiš kärdän* 'be born'; cf. Uzbek *tuγ-il-* 'be born', Persian *kärdän* 'do, make'; see Doerfer 1967: 67–9. On the same method in other Iranian languages and some Caucasian languages, see Doerfer 1993. The element *-d-* (past tense stem) plays a similar role in copies attested in Greek and other Balkan languages.

1.3.2. Selective copies

In selective copying, only certain structural properties of B blocks serve as the model and are copied onto A units. This leads, *inter alia*, to phonological, semantic and syntactic influence. As a consequence, A units display material, combinational, semantic and frequential qualities stemming from B patterns.

An example of *material* selective copying is when phonetic properties of B blocks, i.e. segments and patterns – including accent patterns – typical of B are copied onto A units. Historically, Turkic languages have copied a number of phonetic features, not least of all phonotactic patterns, e.g. from Iranian and Finno-Ugric, and adapted them to the Turkic phonological systems (Johanson 1986a; 1993a). The distribution of sounds was altered, e.g. by extending their occurrence to new positions in words, thereby creating new syllable types. Reproductive global copies played a crucial role in this, effecting systematic structural change beyond their own domain. It is assumed, for instance, that a phonemization of /dž/ took place in Bulgarian under Ottoman influence. This consonant segment may have already been present as an allophone in certain environments before being phonemized under the influence of Ottoman global copies. Grannes (1988: 13) suggests that before the introduction of a large number of Turkic loanwords, /dž/ was merely an allophone of /č/ before voiced consonants.

A preponderance of oral global copies seems to boost the effect of phonetic selective copying. Many Turkic languages that have extensively copied auditively mediated Russian words display general phonetic convergence with Russian. (For Russian influence on Turkic phonetics, see Baskakov 1960: 28.) Of course, this type of influence is absent in cases where A speakers have primarily or exclusively come into contact with the B language in written form. Thus by virtue of their contact with the culturally dominant, highly prestigious Arabic literary language, the Islamic Turkic languages acquired a vast amount of globally copied lexical items without any significant concomitant phonetic selective copying.

Selective copying can be restricted to *nonmaterial* aspects. Note that my interpretation of this issue differs sharply from Haugen's. It seems misleading to refer also to nonmaterial (nonphonic) copying as substitution, when in reality no global copying has taken place, and therefore no phonic features existed to begin with which could have been replaced.

In some instances only semantic features are copied from B blocks onto A equivalents. So-called loan semantics usually involves the process of copying a single (e.g. metaphorical) semantic component of a B block onto an already approximately synonymous A unit (compare English *star* > Turkish *yıldız* '[movie] star'). This semantic influence often stems from difficulties caused by the differences between synonyms, i.e. from semantic over- and underdifferentiation. One source of such difficulties is visible in the complicated equivalencies between Tatar and Russian verbs of movement, such as *bar-* = *idti* 'go', *exat'* 'go by vehicle', *idti* = *bar-* 'go', *kil-* 'come', etc. Since Turkish *al-* corresponds to a number of German verbs (*nehmen* 'take', *bekommen* 'receive', *kaufen* 'buy', *leihen* 'borrow', etc.), many Turks living in Germany tend to use additional specifications (*satın al-* 'buy', *ödünç al-* 'borrow', etc.). The circumstance that a lexical field is less differentiated in B than in A might invite speakers to copy these underdifferentiations onto respective A units. Then, as a result of mistaken identity, an A unit is used in contexts where another unit would be appropriate; consider stylistic errors in the use of synonyms, such as Yugoslavian Turkic *sïra* 'row', which is occasionally used in the sense of 'order' under the influence of Serbo-Croatian *red* (Teodosijeviç 1985). The copying of less differentiated B distinctions leads to the suspension of A distinctions. Thus instead of differentiating between *qol* 'arm' and *älig, äl* 'hand', Turkic languages in prolonged, close contact with Mongolic employ only one of these units to denote both 'arm' and 'hand' (compare Mongolian *γar* 'arm, hand'); in other words, the respective oppositions have been suspended. For issues of this nature, see Brands 1973; cf. Johanson 1974c.

Combinational B qualities can also be copied onto A units, i.e. features of external combinability as well as internal lexical and clausal combinational patterns. This 'loan syntax' is manifested in the structural forms of words, word groups, phrases and clause types, sentence hierarchy, valency, diathesis, word order patterns, syntactically defined word classes, word-internal morpheme order, the relationship between juxtaposition and fusion, the relationship between synthetic and analytic structure, etc. Often, semantic and combinational B properties are copied onto A units.

Combinational copying occurs individually and in generalized form. Examples of individual instances are so-called 'loan translations', e.g. Uzbek *üstqurma* 'superstructure' < Russian *nadstrojka*. In many contact situations, phraseological stereotypes are imitated. When a concrete B complex has a concrete translation equivalent in A, semantic and combinational properties of part of the B complex can be copied onto an A unit which is equivalent to it in other contexts. These copied semantic and combinational features then become part of the A complex. In the case of Crimean Tatar *diqqat ayïr-* 'pay attention', under the influence of the equivalent Russian block *udelit' vnimanie,* the combinability of *udelit'* 'allot' has been copied onto its normal equivalent *ayïr-* 'divide off'. Hence, *ayïr-* can be used in this expression in the place of *et-* or *ber-* (Memetov 1986: 19). Semantic and combinational copies which imitate the internal semantic syntax of a B block are traditionally referred to as loan translations, those outside the lexicon as calques, e.g. Turkish *kıraldan fazla kıralcı* < French *plus royaliste que le roi.*

Copied combinational patterns of words and clauses can also be generalized as a means of constructing new syntagmatic types. Some contact languages of Turkic have copied the type noun + auxiliary verb *et-* 'do, make' in order to form verbal stems from nouns, e.g. Anatolian Greek *poíen émbre* 'he [made order =] ordered' (cf. Turkish *emretti*). We can often observe B influence on valency, government and case syntax (choice of case and pre-/postpositions). In some Turkic languages, verbs such as *min-* 'mount' or *paydalan-* 'exploit', which govern the dative and ablative cases respectively, can also be used transitively as a result of Russian influence (see Baskakov 1960: 30).

The copying of combinational and semantic properties can expand or reduce formal inventories and create, reshape or remove distributional classes such as word classes. In this connection, it has often been claimed that certain Turkic languages have emulated the model of Russian adjective endings and developed corresponding suffix classes of their own. An example of a similar selectively copied bound marker is the neologistic Turkish suffix *-(s)el,* which imitates the semantic-combinational pattern of the old globally copied 'nisbe ending' (*-i*).

Combinational copying often leads to over- or underdifferentiation, for instance, over- or undermarking with respect to functional units (number, case and possessive markers, articles, anaphora, etc.). Under the influence of a less differentiated B system of syntactic patterns, the corresponding inventory of A models may be reduced, restricting its ability to convey certain nuances. The circumstance that Turkish immigrants in Germany tend not to exploit the rich word order devices of Turkish (e.g. for modifying the sentence perspective) might be attributed to a syntactic underdifferentiation resulting from German influence. Copied combinational patterns can also alter the degree of a given unit's complexity, for example causing the simplification of complex A units. In Turkic diaspora (immigrant) varieties, grammatical reduction phenomena are not rare, especially within the complex verbal morphology. We shall return to this topic in chapter 3.

Selective copies are also subject to alteration by way of substitution and other kinds of reshaping. Combinational and semantic copying can produce considerable differences between the original and the copy, especially as a result of adaptation to the A system. Concerning the copied lexicon, the traditional distinction between 'loan translation' and 'loan transfer' relates to the proximity between the semantic-combinational copy and its original: in the case of 'loan transfers', the distance between the two is greater, while 'loan translations' are relatively faithful reproductions of the original. Complex elements such as compound nouns often display typologically determined, subtle differences between original and copy in terms of how the compound is marked or whether its structure is analytic or synthetic; see for example Turkish *zirve toplantısı* < English *summit conference*; Uzbek *qurållaniš påygasi* 'arms race' < Russian *gonka vooruženija*; Turkish *kamuoyu* 'public opinion' < Ottoman *äfkār-i̇ ᶜumumiyä* < French *opinion publique*.

Generalized copied combinations, such as sentence-syntactic patterns, are altered in similar ways. Many Turkic languages display clauses which appear to be reproductive copies of postpositive complement and relative clauses that have been equipped with finite verbs and are introduced by subjunctors (subordinative conjunctions or relative words [see 3.5.3]). But there are often essential differences between the original patterns and their imitations, at least partially brought about by their adaptation to the A systems. Turkic emulations of Indo-European hypotaxis are subject to numerous constraints, making their structural equivalence to Indo-

European constituent clauses rather doubtful. (For the limitations of this 'replica syntax', see Johanson 1975a; cf. 1969: 179; 1976c: 589; 1996b; 1997.) By identifying combinational copies with already existing A patterns, the copies can be adapted semantically, allowing certain A functions to remain relatively stable even though they have acquired new forms of expression.

Frequential patterns of B blocks can also be copied onto A units. This is a consequence of the reinforcement by analogy mentioned above, which gives preference to features which the contact languages seem to have in common. Frequential copying may cause an increased or reduced use of anaphoric units, number morphemes, conjunctions, etc. Indo-European-influenced Turkic languages, for example, tend towards an increased use of conjunctions. Occasionally, Turkish immigrants in Germany demonstrate an exaggerated use of *ve* 'and' under the influence of German *und*. They are also said to employ the plural more frequently than in standard Turkish for the same reason: Yıldız cites examples such as *Problemlerim olmadı* 'I didn't have any problems', where one would normally expect the singular (Yıldız 1986: 44, 83). (For the individualizing function of the Turkic plural, see Johanson 1977.)

In some Turkic languages that have experienced prolonged and intensive contact with Indo-European languages, certain generalized copies of clausal patterns, and word structure and word order patterns became nativized a long time ago. The genuinely Turkic types coexisting with them have consequently become less frequent. Thus Reichl, for example, assumes that in Afghan Uzbek 'the imitation of the Persian subordinate clause has led to a decrease of participial and gerundival constructions' (Reichl 1983: 490).

1.3.3. Mixed copies

In addition to purely global and selective code copies, we also observe *mixed copies*, i.e. combinational copies containing at least one global copy, such as lexically mixed copies ('loanblends' in Haugen's terminology), e.g. Uzbek *yarimavtomat* 'half-automaton' < Russian *poluavtomat* (Mardanov 1983). In the sentence syntax, a copied combinational pattern is often linked to a globally copied grammatical function marker. A copied synthetic possessive construction can include a copied possessive suffix, and a copied relative clause construction can contain a copied relative pronoun. Moreover, a combinational pattern imitating a certain type of complement clause may also use a copied conjunction, e.g. *ki* in Turkish *Anladım ki gelmez* 'I realized that she wouldn't come'.

From a diachronic perspective, mixed copies often represent a transitional stage between complex global copies and purely combinational copies. We frequently encounter complex, creative constructions that go back to various copying processes and presuppose the ability to analyze the B originals, copy them or parts of them and synthetically reorder them. The related details cannot be addressed here.

Mixed copies too differ more or less from their originals. Structural equality between the two is categorically out of the question. We often find distinct differences in Turkic mixed copies modeled on Indo-European hypotactical types and subordinative conjunctions. One doubt that arises is whether these constructions are also subordinative in Turkic and, therefore, whether the globally copied functional elements (such as *ki*) really are subjunctors.

1.4. Turkic characteristics

Of the various types of intraclausal code copying described above, selective copying and certain structural aspects of global copying are of particular interest to us here. In order to assess the results of Turkic language encounters in terms of the structural properties that are copied, one must first determine which properties typical of the Turkic languages are absent or occur to a lesser degree in their contact languages, the Indo-European ones in particular. What follows is a preliminary survey based on a number of characteristics – including several rather superficial, albeit remarkable, phenomena – *without any attempt at a thorough, detailed analysis*. The eclectic, by no means exhaustive, list comprises characteristics of lexical and phonological structure as well as properties of the semantically relevant syntax and morphosyntax. As a rule, I will describe the feature in question as succinctly as possible; some cases, however, require a more detailed examination. Most examples have been selected from Turkish, although they possess basic validity for other Turkic languages as well. For the various attempts at describing these and related Turkic phenomena, see Johanson 1990a.

Many of the features described below belong to the fundamental typological characteristics of the Turkic languages. Contact-induced change often takes place in these very areas. Not seldom, however, the properties are regarded as common features of the Altaic and even Ural-Altaic languages; numerous structural traits are also found, for example, in Korean, Japanese, Gilyak, Dravidian, etc.

As for my use of the morphosyntactic terms which follow, I regard a Turkic *predication* as being minimally comprised of a *[subject] + predicate*, e.g. Turkish *[Siz] bugün geliyorsunuz* 'You are coming today'.[9] The predicate itself consists of at least a *predicate core*, e.g. *gel-* 'come'. Predications take the shape of various types of clauses, usually equipped with *predicators*, e.g. *-iyorsunuz*. A predicator can contain a *subject marker* signaling person and number of the first actant of the predication, e.g. *-sunuz* (see Johanson 1990b).

1. *Synthetic structure*. The typical structure of Turkic is highly synthetic. The Turkic languages display numerous bound formal categories of word formation,[10] declination and conjugation. Their respective morphemes have extremely generalized contents – a typical trait of grammaticalization – and consequently cover a wide range of applications. Numerous word formation morphemes as well as plural, possessive and case morphemes can be affixed to nominal stems. Verbal stems can combine with a highly complex system of morphemes, e.g. of actionality (manner of action), voice (such as causative, passive, medial and other diatheses), possibility, negation, aspect, mood, tense, interrogation, subject marker (person, number[11]). Certain morphemes serve to nominalize or adverbialize verbal stems (and thus infinitize predications; see point 18; 3.5.2 below). This process generates, above all, highly synthetic verb forms. In most contact languages of Turkic, the situation is different: while number, case and, in some instances, actionality (which

directly modifies the content of the verbal lexeme) are expressed synthetically, categories such as possessive, passive, causative, negation, mood and evidentiality are not.

2. *Suffixes.* Bound units are postpositive, i.e. they are suffixes, not prefixes, infixes or replacive units. This is one of the characteristics Turkic shares with the Altaic, Uralic and Dravidian languages. In accordance with the typological regularities observed by Greenberg, postpositive nominal and verbal inflection correlates with left-branching sentence syntax (see point 16 below).

3. *Juxtaposition.* Another characteristic of Turkic word structure is the juxtaposition of morphemes separated by distinct boundaries, i.e. having a low degree of fusion. This device, traditionally termed 'agglutination',[12] creates transparency in the sense of easily segmentable structures and regularity by providing a largely 1:1 relationship between expression and content. (This functional unambiguity of the suffixes should not, however, be confused with 'monofunctionality', see Johanson 1969: 175; 1974a: 89.) Languages in contact with Turkic are often of a more fusioning type and have affixes that are more firmly tied to their morphological surroundings.

4. *Limited and predictable variation of morphemes.* In their respective environments, Turkic morphemes have a small number of not highly variable, mostly predictable (phonologically, rarely lexically, determined) allomorphs. Thus there is no basis for a division into declinations and conjugations.

5. *Syllabicity of the suffixes.* The suffixes frequently – yet by no means always – encompass at least one syllable each; in other words, they can be pronounced in isolation; compare the Turkish genitive suffix *-nin* and the plural suffix *-ler* in *Ali'nin* and *ördekler* with the nonsyllabic markers in English *Ali's* and *ducks*.

6. *Successive suffix modification.* The suffixes are usually organized in such a way that each one semantically modifies the entire lexical segment preceding it (Johanson 1974a). Thus the position of the suffixes within the modification structure – in the sense of distributional *suffix ranks* – is quite clearly reflected by their relative distance from the primary stem.

My analysis of the constituent order in the morphological word is based on the following premise: In the morphological word, a segment X can lexicosyntactically depend on one (simple or complex) basic segment, segment Y, whereby only Y can serve as the head of X, but not vice versa. Thus in Turkish *evde* 'in the house' and *evlerimizde* 'in our houses' the case suffix *-de* is dependent on the basic segments *ev* 'house' and *evlerimiz* 'our houses', respectively. Constituents form classes according to their ability to occupy the various relative positions within the word (*suffix ranks*, see 3.3).

On the other hand, one segment can semantically modify another. The modifier and the modificate together make up the domain of modification. With respect to lexicosyntactic order, many languages display a tendency towards *head-orientedness*. Lexical constituents usually stay within their domains, i.e. they do not stand apart from the elements they modify. This 'natural' order thus reflects the structure of the domain and the constituent's relative proximity in terms of semantic modification. At the same time, this principle interacts with other ordering patterns and is in itself too simplistic to fully accommodate the complexity of the language facts. Nevertheless, lexicosyntactically speaking, Turkic morphology seems to be heavily head-oriented: the primary stem occupies the initial position in the word, with the following suffixes as a rule modifying the entire preceding segment. The suffixes are iteratively encapsulated, as depicted by $(((ev \Leftarrow ler) \Leftarrow imiz) \Leftarrow de)$. The area to which a certain suffix potentially applies increases with its distance from the primary stem. However, these successive modificational relations do not imply that the relative positions represent differing degrees of semantic relevance for the primary stem, and that the suffixes thus more or less 'directly' modify the primary stem according to their distance from it (cf. Bybee 1985).

Generally,[13] Turkic suffixes are arranged as follows: units modifying the primary stem are usually located closest to it. Thus derivational suffixes precede inflectional ones. The normal sequence of nominal inflection suffixes is plural followed by possessive and then case suffixes,[14] e.g. Turkish *ev-ler-imiz-de* 'in our houses' ('house' + plur. + poss.1.p.pl. + locative). Plural suffixes directly modify the preceding stem for number; possessive suffixes signal the person and number of an entity expressed as the possessor of the preceding item; case suffixes indicate the sentence-hierarchic relationships of the entire antecedent segment. The productive classes of suffixes attached to verbal primary stems occur in the following order: actionality, diathesis, negation, aspect/mood, tense, subject marker, e.g. Turkish *kov-ala-n-ma-mış-t-ık* 'we had not been pursued' ('chase away' + iterative + passive + negation + aspect/mood + tense + subject marker 1.p.pl.). The slot filled by 'thematic stems', based on aspect/mood suffixes, in the finite forms can be occupied by various participial, verbal noun and converbial suffixes (see point 18) in the *nonfinite* verb forms, not every one of which admits a subject marker.

Actionality modifies the action expressed by the lexical stem. Today, however, this suffix class is rather meagerly represented, lacking productive members in many contemporary Turkic languages (cf. point 27). Diatheses (medial, reflexive, reciprocal, passive, causative) also semantically modify the preceding segment, but they alter valency as well. In other words, they influence the number and roles of the actants and, for example, change the relation of a potential subject to the predicate core. Diathetic suffixes are word formation units with language-specific meanings; at the same time, they constitute the core of their respective sentence-hierarchic diathetic system (Johanson 1990b). The verbal negation suffix usually negates the entire preceding actional expression, but it can vary its modificates without changing its position in the suffix chain (see Johanson 1971: 241–2). Aspect and mood do not modify the action itself, but rather provide various viewpoints on it, specifically in terms of the limits of the inherent event (Johanson 1971; 1994; 1996a; 2000c) and of the speaker's attitude towards it. Tense localizes the viewpoints temporally. The most peripheral units of verbal inflection, the subject markers, represent the first actant, thereby contributing to the modification of the whole predicate (Johanson 1990b).

7. *'Loosely connected' suffixes.* Some suffixes can modify an entire coordinative construction, even though they are merely attached to its final element. This applies especially to plural, case and possessive suffixes, nonpossessive subject markers and suffixed variants of the copula particles (such as Turkish *-(y)dI* 'was'); e.g.

Turkish *sağ ve soldakiler* = (*sağ ve sol*)-*da-ki-ler* 'those on the right and those on the left side'; *görmüş ve duymuslardı* = (*görmüş ve duymuş*)-*lar-dı* 'they had seen and heard it'. If at all, most languages in contact with Turkic display similar phenomena only in word formation and compounding. Many Turkic suffixes too lack this feature, e.g. *(*gör ve duy*)-*muş*.

Regarding the formal aspects of morphology, the difference can be explained by the fact that in the example cited last, the suffix is less autonomous, while the cohesion between the stem and the suffix is greater. Suffixes of the former category, on the other hand, though in principle bound elements, display an autonomy much like that of enclitics. In the example *sağ ve soldakiler* the degree of cohesion between the stem *sağ* and the suffix chain -*da-ki-ler* is extremely low. In such cases, Doerfer (1963: 86) speaks of more or less 'loose' or 'firm' suffix attachment. For cases where the suffixes refer to coordinations, Kissling (1960: 115) uses the quite practical and catchy, but factually misleading, term 'Suffixabwurf' [suffix deletion]. The circumstance that I give preference to Doerfer's terminology is not meant to produce similar misunderstandings, and his terms are only used in the sense indicated above.

8. *Enclitic particles.* Turkic also has enclitic particles, free grammatical units with a strongly generalizing function, e.g. postpositions that have not yet evolved into suffixes or, although they have suffixed variants, display phonological peculiarities (unaccentability, partially developed sound harmony); see, e.g., Johanson 1974a, 1981.

9. *Morphologically less distinct adjective categories.* The category of adjective as a morphological word class is less explicit than in a number of contact languages (see, e.g., Johanson 1990a: 186 ff.)

10. *Suffixless indefinite case.* In the nominal declination, the nominal stem is suffixless and acts as the indefinite case (among others, as a subject and object case; however cf. point 32).

11. *Comparison patterns.* Comparison in the sense of gradation is often constructed according to the pattern: standard of comparison + ablative suffix + property compared (roughly: 'X-from big' = 'bigger than X'). The word for the property compared is in the basic form and, therefore, not a formal comparative.

12. *Compound nouns.* The prevailing type of compound nouns follows the possessive pattern: noun + noun possessive suffix 3.p., e.g. Turkish *el çantası* 'handbag'.

13. *Genitive construction.* Genitive constructions (possessor + possessed entity) mostly adhere to the combinational pattern: genitive attribute + head possessive suffix 3.p., e.g. Turkish *öğretmen-in kitab-ı* 'the teacher's book' (roughly: 'the teacher's his/her book').

14. *Absence of agreement marking on adjective attributes.* Agreement marking is rather restricted in Turkic, mostly reserved to subject–predicate core agreement in person and number. Thus adjective attributes and other determining elements are not inflected for case, gender or number.

15. *The singular after cardinal numbers.* The limited agreement marking also implies that nouns are generally not plural-marked when their plurality is expressed by quantifiers such as cardinal numbers (e.g. Turkish *üç kuş* 'three birds').

16. *Leftbranching sentence syntax.* Beyond the lexical boundaries, a *rectum-regens norm* governs lexical constituents, whereby the syntactically dependent element (*rectum*) precedes its head (*regens*); in other words, the subordinate constituent is *prepositive*. This norm has also been referred to as the 'basic syntactic law of the Altaic languages' (the determining element precedes the element which it determines'); it applies to Japanese, Korean, Dravidian, etc. as well. Although the norm often corresponds to the modification structure, it should not be categorically identified with it (see point 17).

As the head of the predication, the predicate core generally occupies the final position in the clause. Thus as a rule, complements as well as free adverbials (valency-independent satellites) precede the predicate core. Likewise, adjective, genitive and participial attributes come before their head in the nominal phrase, and quantifiers, etc. precede the adjective in the respective adjective phrase. When different types of modifiers are used, the normal sequence is demonstrative pronoun + cardinal number + adjective attribute, e.g. Turkish *bu üç mavi kuş* 'these three blue birds'.

In his studies on word order universals, Greenberg (1966: 79) classified Turkic as 'the rigid subtype' of the so-called SOV languages. In reality, however, what we find here is for the most part a norm ('unmarked word order') with systematic deviations of a pragmatic nature, motivated in particular by the sentence perspective (see Johanson 1977; Erguvanlı 1984). The predicate core especially can occupy a position in the phrase other than the final one. In embedded clauses, constituent order is usually less free than in main clauses; the dependent can be connected to its head by means of a relator (junctor, etc.). The abovementioned postpositions can operate as grammatical relators. They occupy the final position in their postpositional phrases, where they morphosyntactically constitute the basic segment (head). They form a common constituent with the preceding nominal phrase, the dependent, linking it to its head.

17. *Successive modification of the constituents of the sentence.* The arrangement of units in the Turkic sentence-syntactic chain also quite clearly reflects semantic relationships. A syntactically dependent constituent often also semantically modifies the head. In this *head-oriented* modification structure, the clausal constituents remain located within their domains, i.e. they are not separated from their modificates. In many cases, we encounter a successive arrangement, an iterative encapsulation, whereby an individual constituent modifies the entire constituent complex following it; observe, for example, the sequential relations between the prenominal modifications in *(bu⇒ (üç⇒ (mavi⇒ (kuş))))*. The area to which a modification potentially applies increases with its distance from the head noun; if we imagine the sequence, beginning from the head noun (HN), as D1, D2, D3..., Dn, then D1 defines HN, D2 defines HN+D1, D3 defines HN+D1+D2, and so forth (see Seiler 1988: 11 ff.). This is the mirror image of the successive modification performed by the suffixes within lexical boundaries. Thus the word-hierarchic head-orientedness correlates to a sentence-hierarchic head-orientedness. For the Turkic 'rightbranching' word and 'leftbranching' sentence, see Johanson 1974a. Undoubtedly, other languages too exhibit a tendency toward this 'natural' ordering; however, in Turkic it is developed with an extraordinary

degree of consistency. Nevertheless, due to interaction with other ordering principles, some of them pragmatic in nature, deviations frequently occur.

18. *Syntax of clause embedding.* Turkic embedded clauses behave syntactically and morphologically unlike main clauses. Instead of constituent clauses that resemble main clauses, employing conjunctions or relative words, Turkic uses a special kind of infinitization of predications (so-called 'word groups with clause value' or 'quasi-propositions'; Deny 1921: 853). In these infinitizations, the predicate cores are equipped with morphemes that function as predicators and can act as subject markers, but possess other aspect-mood-tense inventories than main clause predicators.

Nominal action clauses are constructed from verbal noun forms – action nouns and verbal abstracts. For the most part, they act as complement clauses, denoting actions and themselves serving as actants in a subordinative predication. The pattern is: Turkish *evin yandığı* 'the house's its burning' = 'that the house is burning'. There are also 'short' complement clauses of this type, based on verbal nouns (often governed by modal lexemes). Because they are referentially identical to the first actant, these verbal nouns do not carry subject markers in the shape of personal suffixes, e.g. *gelmek* 'come' in Turkish *Ali gelmek istiyor* 'Ali wants to come'.

Adverbial action clauses, which function as free adverbials, and not as actants in the subordinative predication, are based on deverbal adverbials, so-called converbs. The pattern is: Turkish *[ev] yanarak* '[the house] burning'. When they semantically modify their head, they are called *satellites*. (See Johanson 1995.)

Relative clauses, actor clauses, can operate as adjectives, in the role of attributes, and as nouns, without a head noun. These clauses employ deverbal adjective forms, i.e. participles. The pattern is: Turkish *yanan evler* 'burning houses' = 'houses that are burning'.

These constituent clauses also follow the *rectum-regens* norm and are thus prepositive. They are synthetic in the sense that their predicators (the suffixes on the nonfinite predicate cores) usually act as junctors themselves.

19. *Few free junctors.* The tendencies described so far imply that Turkic has few free subjunctors, i.e. subordinative particles or

grammatical constituents that introduce or conclude embedded clauses. There is no genuine Turkic relative pronoun, and hardly any noncopied sudordinative conjunctions exist. The overall number of free junctors (conjunctions and similar relators) is remarkably low, particularly in older language stages. Genuine Turkic conjunctors (linking relata of equal rank) are also largely absent. (For free Turkic subjunctors of the *diye* type, see point 20.)

20. *Converbs of the verbs of speech as quotation particles and purposive subjunctors.* In the Turkic languages, the converbs of the verbs of speech *te-*, *de-*, etc. 'say', i.e. *dep*, *deyü*, *diye*, *tese*, etc. 'saying', act as postpositive quotation particles, marking embedded direct speech and thought. They can also function as free postpositive subjunctors (constituent clause-final conjunctions) which mark purpose clauses and causal clauses (used to explain actions by quoting the thoughts of their performers). Consider, for example, satellite clauses of purpose containing an optative predicate core, such as Turkish *ev yansın diye* 'so that the house should burn' ('the house shall burn saying').

21. *Postpositions.* In accordance with its leftbranching sentence syntax, Turkic employs postpositions instead of prepositions. Prepositions and postpositions are pre- and postpositive *relational particles* ('adpositions'). Pre- and postpositional phrases are closely equivalent to one another in respect of their combinational properties. According to Joseph Greenberg's well-known universals, however, postpositions are more natural for an SOV language than prepositions.

Morphosyntactically, postpositions form the heads of the preceding nominal phrases. From the point of view of the semantically relevant syntax, however, they constitute grammatical relators, sentence-hierarchic function markers, specifically, subjunctors. Like case markers, these subjunctors signal the sentence-hierarchic functions of the antecedent nominal phrase, linking it as a dependent to its head. Turkic postpositions are constantly being renewed by means of the grammaticalization of independent lexemes; Slobin (1986: 288) describes this process as a major historical tendency of Turkic languages. This renewal process reverses the modification pattern from that of a sentence-hierarchic head-orientedness to a word-hierarchic one: from *((ev-in* ⇒ *iç-i-ⁿ)* ⇐ *-de)* 'in the interior of the house' to *(ev[in]* ⇐ *içinde)* 'in the house' (Johanson 1974a). Postpositions can evolve into suffixes and, on the way to suffixation, often exhibit phonological peculiarities such as unaccentability, initial stages of sound harmony, etc. (Johanson 1981).

22. *Genitive subject.* In infinitizations employing verbal nouns, the subject can be in the genitive (e.g. Turkish *evin yanması* 'the house's its burning').

23. *Cases cover wide functional area.* The Turkic languages are characterized by simple, loose-knit, rather undifferentiated case systems that make use of few distinctions and signal rather general and nonspecific relations. Consequently, each Turkic case covers a broad functional area, e.g. the Turkish locative *-de* 'in, on, at, etc.' Necessary specifications are realized by other means, postpositions especially.

24. *Predications indicating possession* are formed using constructions of the type: [possessor + genitive +] possessed item + possessive suffix + 'exist', e.g. Turkish *para-m var* 'I have money' ('money-my exists').

25. *Complex verbal systems.* As noted, the Turkic languages have complex, close-knit verbal systems containing a large number of grammatical categories. Thus particularly in the elaborate aspect-tense system, the functional load of an individual unit is often lighter than that of its counterpart in a contact language.

26. *Indirective forms.* The wide array of verbal categories includes evidential items of the indirective type, denoting that a narrated event is stated in an indirect way, by reference to its reception by a conscious subject, for instance, indirect postterminal forms such as Turkish *Ali gelmiş* 'Ali [apparently, obviously] has arrived' (for the concept of postterminality, see 3.4). They refer to the evidential dimension, wherein the speaker qualifies the reported event in terms of his or her knowledge or awareness of it. The modification signaled by indirective forms is open to various readings. Depending on the source of the respective information, it can be construed as hearsay, conclusion based on results, evidence, perception, etc. (Johanson 1971: 280 ff.; 1994; 2000a).

27. *Postverbs*. A typical feature of many Turkic languages is the expression of actionality – e.g. of the descriptive or phase-specifying type (Johanson 1991g) – by means of actional postverbial constructions, i.e. combinations of verbal lexemes (chiefly converbs) and certain verbs with generalizing meanings, e.g. Turkish *Ali yazıp duruyor* 'Ali is writing continuously'. I use the term postverb analogously to the term preverb, which denotes the functionally equivalent verbal prefixes found in Germanic, Slavic and other languages.[15] Morphosyntactically, the last verb in the compound is the head of the preceding one; in terms of the semantically relevant syntax, however, it acts as a grammatical function marker semantically modifying the preceding actional phrase. Thus the modificational relations are reversed from sentence-hierarchic head-orientedness to word-hierarchic head-orientedness: from *((yaz-ıp ⇒ dur-)* 'stand (while) writing' to *(yaz- ⇐ (-ıp dur-))* 'continuously write' (Johanson 1974a). This process is yet another example of the grammaticalization of independent lexemes. In these postverbs based on a converbial suffix + 'auxiliary verb', the final element has usually not yet fully merged with the preceding verb; however, phonologically it often represents a transitional stage on the path to suffixation. Postverbial constructions can evolve into aspectotemporal forms (Johanson 1976a; 1976b).

28. *Restricted use of anaphora*. Compared to some of its contact languages, Turkic shows relatively inexplicit pronominal reference, i.e. the use of anaphora for actants whose referents are recoverable from the immediate discourse, the context and/or the situation.[16] This makes subjectless main clauses possible, e.g. Turkish *Geliyor* '[He, she, it] is coming'. Subject pronouns usually introduce new topics. (This is generally the case in Turkish, for instance, unless the pronoun *follows* the predicate core.) This absence of marking is usually permitted beyond the boundaries of the main clause. Other actants too can go unexpressed, however, not as a rule in cases where the predication in question introduces the discourse. I avoid the term 'pro-drop' commonly used in generativist literature to refer to the absence of marking, because this term presupposes that the respective pro-elements are actually present in a deeper structure. For subjectless sentences, also see Johanson 1990b.

29. *Interrogative suffix*. In yes/no questions a special interrogative element (*mi* and the like) is suffixed to the constituent whose content is in question, e.g. Turkish *Ali mi geliyor?* 'Is Ali coming (or who is coming)?'. When the content of an entire main clause is the matter of interrogation, the suffix follows the predicate core, e.g. *Ali geliyor mu?* 'Is Ali coming (or isn't he)?'.

30. *Absence of gender*. Unlike a number of its contact languages, Turkic has no classifiers of grammatical gender. Hence, gender does not play a role in grammatical agreement. In addition, with the exception of units copied from other languages, Turkic does not have the synthetic means of expressing lexical feminine forms.

31. *Absence of a definite article*. No Turkic language has systematically developed a definite article.

32. *Specificity through accusative marking*. In most Turkic languages, a direct object immediately preceding the predicate core can be marked with the accusative for specificity, e.g. Turkish *Ali, kız-ı gördü* 'Ali girl-acc. saw' = 'Ali saw the girl'; *Ali, bir kız-ı gördü* 'Ali a girl-acc. saw' = 'Ali saw a certain girl' (see Johanson 1977).

33. *Specificity through genitive marking*. Similarly, in some Turkic languages, a genitive subject in constituent clauses can signal specificity (Johanson 1977).

34. *Use of the dative in causative syntax*. In causatives based on transitive verbs, the first actant of the transitive verb is expressed by a dative complement, e.g. Turkish *mektubu Ali'ye yazdırdım* 'I had Ali write the letter'.

35. *Reduplicative compounds*. Another feature typical of Turkic is reduplication, i.e. the repetition of a lexeme in a consonant-initial form (*m-*, *b-*, *p-*, etc.) to express 'and the like', e.g. Turkish *kitap mitap* 'books and the like' (*kitap* 'book'), Uzbek *nån pån* 'bread and other baked goods' (*nån* 'bread').

36. *Reduplicative intensive forms*. Prepositive reduplication syllables produce intensive forms of adjectives, e.g. Turkish *kara* 'black', *kapkara* 'totally black'.

37. *Typical vowels*. [ö] and [ü] are characteristic vowels not found in most languages in contact with Turkic. Some contact languages also lack [ï].

38. *Tendency towards monophthongs.* A predilection for monophthongs, in other words, an aversion against diphthongs, is a typically Turkic trait.

39. *Vowel length.* Distinctive vowel length is atypical of most contemporary Turkic languages. Long vowels mostly occur as a result of contraction.

40. *Atypical sounds.* Among others, the following sounds are atypical of Turkic: nasal vowels, pharyngealized and glottal plosive consonants. There are few fricatives; e.g. [f], [v], [ž] and [θ] are atypical. The affricates [č] and [dž] occur, for example, whereas [ts] and [dz] are atypical.

41. *Constraints in initial position.* It is characteristic of Turkic words that they have no liquids and only a few fricatives in initial position. Some atypical initial sounds are [l], [m], [n], [r] and [z].

42. *Front vs. nonfront distinction.* The distinction front vs. back plays a significant role in Turkic phonology; for example, syllables are classified as being [+front] or [−front] (see Johanson 1991e; 1993c).

43. *Sound harmony.* A pronounced tendency towards sound harmony manifested by the systematic suspension of phonological features in suffix syllables is typical of Turkic. In this context, vowels in a word harmonize with one another in terms of frontness vs. backness and in some cases roundedness vs. unroundedness.

44. *Aversion against consonant clusters.* Restrictions apply to the structure of syllables, displayed by an extreme aversion against certain consonant clusters in particular positions. As a rule, a syllable contains a maximum of two succeeding consonants in final position, if one of them is a liquid, nasal or sibilant. Thus up to three consonants can occur at morpheme boundaries. Global copies with inadmissible consonant clusters (including affricates) are often reshaped according to Turkic phonotactic rules, e.g. by means of a prosthetic, epenthetic or epithetic vowel, by deletion (syncope, apocope, but rarely aphesis) or by metathesis.

45. *Consonant assimilation.* All Turkic languages – some of them to a very high degree – feature the assimilation of neighboring consonants, e.g. Kazakh *at* 'horse' + plural (*-lar*, etc.) = *attar*.

46. *Word-final voice reduction.* Turkic languages generally display reduced voicing of lenis obstruents in word-final position, e.g. Turkish [ad̥] 'name'.

Chapter 2

THE ROLE OF STRUCTURAL FACTORS

2.1. Suggested restrictions

Now that we have taken a look at a number of structural properties typical of the Turkic languages, let us turn to the question of the general constraints possibly affecting the copying of these and similar features. Surprisingly, until today, it is occasionally claimed that nonlexical structural features cannot be copied at all or, at best, only with great difficulty. Linguists doubt whether grammatical structures can be influenced. According to Oksaar, there are 'no clear cases that would permit a generalization of statements that grammatical paradigms, bound morphemes, word order etc. can be subject to interference' (Oksaar 1972: 492). Givón simply states that languages 'do not borrow grammar' and that their speakers prefer to use 'universal grammar' rather than breaking up morphosyntactic patterns as a result of borrowing (Givón 1979: 25 ff.). As we have seen, such claims are readily refuted by Turkic language data, for one.

At times, it is asserted that only superficial elements but no underlying 'deeper' grammatical structures can be copied. Sapir (1921: 203 ff.), for example, believed to detect only superficial morphological influence in contact situations. To this day, universal restrictions are said to apply to bound morphemes, such as Poplack's (1981) 'free morpheme constraint' in so-called code switching. (For other universal grammatical restrictions posited for code switching, see 2.7 below.) Weinreich perceived at least no 'transfer of a full grammatical paradigm, with its formant morphemes' (Weinreich 1953: 43–4). Occasionally it is also stated that copying practically never includes syntactic models (Lewandowski 1976: 177) and that foreign syntactic patterns do not endure over time. However, none of the suggested structural restrictions proves sound, with the exception perhaps of Weinreich's aforementioned constraint; we shall return to it below (see 3.3). As pioneers such as Schuchardt realized long ago, contact-induced language change occurs in all domains of language structure and can be very profound. Properties of grammatical structure can in fact be copied: various kinds of phonological rules, including accent patterns, word formation and inflectional elements, sentence-syntactic function markers, word order patterns, etc. (see Thomason & Kaufman 1988).

Universal restrictions of an implicational nature have also been suggested. The most well-known of these states that structural influence presupposes lexical influence. Indeed, the overall consensus is that nonlexical elements (bound morphemes, phonological, combinational and semantic features) are not copied unless lexical or phraseological global copies already exist (see, among others, Whitney 1881; Haugen 1950a, Moravcsik 1978: 110; Comrie 1981b: 202–3). Thus, word formation and inflectional units would first be copied together with loanwords, subsequently becoming productive themselves. Jakobson (1938), however, contends that lexical copies are not prerequisite to phonological structural influence.

Another assumption makes *structural similarity* between the relevant areas in the contact languages a precondition for structural influence. Meillet (1921: 87) claims that, e.g., grammatical borrowing can only occur between very similar systems. In that case, one would not expect Turkic–Indo-European language contact to have generated much structural influence, since, as we have seen, the two systems differ considerably in terms of phonetic, lexical and clausal structure. But grammatical elements (including grammatical categories) are in fact also transferred between unrelated and typologically divergent languages. Even B elements which are structurally quite unlike their A equivalents can be copied. In

Karaim and Anatolian-Greek dialects, for instance, influence is by no means restricted to areas where the respective contact languages are typologically similar. What we do encounter there are far-reaching changes in the phonological, morphological and syntactic structure. (For Karaim, see Csató 1996.)

There is another, more subtle assumption that an A language only accepts those structural B elements corresponding to its own internal developmental *tendencies* (Jakobson 1938). Thus it is often claimed that changes occur in accordance with the A system's potential for innovation, and that a language which adopts certain foreign structural elements must therefore already have had the tendency to develop in that direction ('native drift'). Although such hypotheses may contain a kernel of truth, attempts at descriptions based on them often prove vague or circular. That the development of a language should depend on 'the prevailing (or on some aimed-for) typology' is, according to Hoenigswald, 'a statement the dimness of which is excused only by our difficulties with the sociolinguistic underpinnings of directionality, areal and chronological' (Hoenigswald 1989: 351).

The invalidness of these proposed universal restrictions, however, by no means precludes the possibility that typological similarity between contact languages in particular areas may promote influence. We shall return to this point.

2.2. Scales of stability

Linguistic elements possess a certain degree of stability, i.e. features that impede influence and change. Experience shows that some elements are copied earlier and more easily than others. Which qualities are more likely to change in a contact situation, and which are more resistant? Should we assume differing degrees of susceptibility at least from the point of view of probability theory? Early on, contact linguistics believed to discern differences in stability among various linguistic domains. Numerous attempts have been made to set up scales of transferability. As early as 1881, Whitney listed linguistic elements on a scale according to the ease with which he believed they were borrowed. A similar aim was pursued by Haugen's 'scale of adoptability' which 'somehow [...] correlated to the structural organization' (Haugen 1950b: 224). Weinreich (1953: 35), however, correctly pointed out the hypothetical nature of this scale. While most attempts of this sort are restricted either to adoption or to imposition (see 1.1), van Coetsem's (1988) proposed stability gradient takes both types into account, although only in the area of phonological influence. To my knowledge, so far no comprehensive, more exact stability hierarchy or scale of susceptibility has been developed that grades linguistic elements and areas of both influence types according to their structural characteristics. For Thomason & Kaufman's (1988) scale, which correlates social and structural factors with one another, see 2.5 below.

How often an element occurs in speech – its text frequency[1] – is often seen as a factor contributing to differences in stability. Frequently performed speech habits are said to be more firmly entrenched than others and less susceptible to influence; the more often a linguistic element is used, the more difficult it is to replace (Haugen 1950b; 1969). It is true that a seldom used A element may be unstable in that a speaker, especially when speaking rapidly, may not immediately recall it and therefore replace it with an actively mastered B equivalent. A speaker's degree of familiarity with an A element might be a result of its text frequency. Infrequent use, on the other hand, does not necessarily mean that the given element is unknown.[2] It would appear that high or low frequency is not the *cause* of stability/instability, but rather results from the same social and structural conditions which promote or impede stability.

The top of the susceptibility scales is occupied by those elements which, empirically speaking, are copied the soonest and most readily, while those which are copied the latest and with the most difficulty are situated at the very bottom. Of course, the order cannot be identical for the two types of influence. More probably, scales applying to adoption are inverted for imposition. In other words, that which is imposed easily and early on is adopted later and with much more difficulty, and vice versa. A speakers tend to retain more stable A areas in A and to impose them onto B. Thus, stability hinders adoption and, conversely, fosters imposition. The decisive factor for scales of stability is the type of contact influence to which they are applied.

Generalizations asserting, for example, that grammatical forms are more susceptible to 'interference' than lexical ones (Juhász 1970: 127) are misleading; this statement *only* takes imposition into account. The Finno-Ugric–Russian contact phenomena described by Bátori (1979), which are very similar to Turkic–Russian ones, are a typical example of the reverse set of circumstances: The Russian spoken by Finno-Ugric bilinguals shows heavy phonological and syntactic influence, while the primary influence on their Finno-Ugric is lexical.

With regard to adoption – the type of influence to which the present study is primarily devoted – we can empirically set up approximative scales beginning with content words and ending with heavy morphosyntactic influence. I refer to the influence on the lower end of such a scale as *deep influence*. The lexicon is generally considered to be the most unstable linguistic area; it is most easily influenced in all contact situations, even in the absence of widespread bilingualism. (See, e.g., Dauzat 1938; Haugen 1950b: 223 ff.; Weinreich 1953: 35 ff.; Martinet 1955: 78–9; Hockett 1958: 265–6; Mackey 1970: 200–1.) Cultural and functional communicative factors give precedence to the global copying of free blocks, i. e. content units not belonging to the basic lexical stock. Nouns are most easily copied, followed by other word classes.

There is no consensus concerning the order in which the remaining units and elements are copied. According to Whitney (1881), the lexicon is followed by suffixes, inflectional elements and, finally, sounds; cf. Haugen 1950b: 'Nouns are most easily borrowed, then the various other parts of speech, then suffixes, then inflections, then sounds.' Many contact linguists regard phonology as the most resistant area (e.g. Hetzer 1983: 26); others deem morphology, particularly inflectional morphology, the most stable. Uhlenbeck (1981: 167), who contends that the degree to which rules apply differs from one linguistic area to another, assumes that stability increases along the semantics-syntax-morphology line, with the opportunities for 'linguistic creativity' decreasing accordingly.

However, Thomason (1980) has clearly exposed the weaknesses of the 'superstable morphology hypothesis'.

The investigations carried out to date permit only very vague statements about the general tendencies of linguistic copying processes. Numerous studies indicate that interjections and formulaic expressions are quite susceptible to global copying. As noted, various features of globally copied blocks are more or less modified in the recipient language. Selective copying – the adoption of selected features – usually occurs later on. The selective copying of semantic properties, however, frequently ranks rather high on the scales. Certain unbound grammatical function units (conjunctions, adverbs, pre- and postpositions, particles, personal and demonstrative pronouns) may also be copied at a relatively early stage. Initially, bound units are usually copied as parts of complex blocks, and word formation units are copied before functional ones. As a rule, the *productive* use of bound functional units sets in late. New phonotactic features, e.g. altered syllable structure, may develop as a result of combinational copying. Similarly, sentence syntax (word order, constituent clauses) can also be subject to influence. The following types of influence occupy relatively low positions on the scales: copies of new grammatical categories (such as case, aspect, tense, mood), copies of sounds, copies of lexical syntax (word-internal combinational patterns, tendencies towards fusion, juxtaposition, etc.), profound morphosyntactic change (e.g. in the diathetic system), copies of entire grammatical paradigms (with globally copied B markers), and global copies from the basic lexicon.

All of these generalizations of empirical findings may apply *grosso modo* to many Turkic contact situations and might therefore serve as a point of departure in this investigation. Nevertheless, they cannot form a universal scale without including additional structural factors as well as social conditions. Not only are they approximations, but, strictly speaking, as such also misleading; we shall return to their limited reliability.

2.3. Attractiveness

Why are certain elements more susceptible to copying than others? As noted above, one must consider the possibility that some linguistic qualities per se promote or impede influence. Not seldom, general structural factors have been proposed and schemata created in the attempt to predict the structural conditions affecting contact-induced change.

In particular, there has been an ongoing debate over the question whether certain structures are more *natural* than others. Early on, hypotheses were formulated which attributed more or less compulsory tendencies of linguistic development to features of the human anatomy, physiology and psychology. Thus, for example, reduced energy exertion was discussed in the context of articulatory ease as one cause of linguistic change. A number of general phonetic tendencies were explained as stemming from articulatory or perceptual difficulties. Later, certain natural tendencies connected with mental processes were posited, which, however, remain elusive, as the cerebral structures involved are less easy to observe than the features of the articulatory and auditory organs. Today we know for a fact, for example, that linguistic elements differ from one another in terms of their perceptibility and that they require processing techniques of varying degrees of cognitive complexity. Based on the relative ease or difficulty of perception and production, psycholinguistics and language acquisition research distinguish structures which are more or less 'marked'.

One approach has been to formulate general principles of acquisition and interpretation models that can claim universal validity, Slobin's (1973; 1985) 'operating principles' of first language acquisition being a well-known example. Numerous studies on learner language systems, which develop during second language acquisition, contend that less 'marked' elements are acquired sooner than others. Many linguists have attempted to devise hierarchies of 'naturalness' or 'markedness' and to establish corresponding general regularities. Such regularities are seen, especially by universalists of the generativist bent, to be the product of congenital biological mechanisms interacting with sociological and psychological restrictions.

Now, cognitive and perceptive principles regulating language acquisition and use could prove relevant to the stability of linguistic elements. If certain linguistic elements are processed more easily than others, one might conclude that they are also relatively easily copied from one language into another, while the opposite would apply to elements more difficult to process. Changes observed in many contact-related processes – also, e.g., in koinéization and creolization – can indeed often be regarded as simplifications that alter or remove 'unwieldy' structures. Slobin has been particularly resolute in correlating diachronic language stability/instability with early/late acquisition: he equates those parts of grammar most susceptible to change – e.g. as a result of copying from other languages – with parts that are acquired late and are relatively difficult to process (Slobin 1977; 1982; 1986).

Predictions on stability based on universalistic naturalness theses, however, are frequently vague, simplifying and even circular. Often, clear criteria for defining the degree of 'markedness' are missing. The yardstick varies according to the researcher's respective conception of grammar; in many instances, the evaluation is limited to selected areas. Some language acquisition researchers even go to the extreme of designating late acquisition as a criterion of 'markedness'. In language typology, 'marked' often just means 'less common' and, in that sense, is the opposite of frequency of occurrence; an element is considered more 'marked', the less often it is expected to occur and, consequently, the more attention its actual use attracts. The term 'marked' is additionally ambiguous as it is still used in its original meaning, namely for relations within linguistic oppositions (see, e.g., Jakobson 1932).

Many aspects of this complex issue remain obscure. One primary problem lies in the fact that relative ease of language production does not always coincide with relative ease of perception. Simplifying tendencies frequently compete with clarifying ones (see, e.g., Johanson 1979b: 135 ff.). Languages are constantly 'unburdening' themselves, while simultaneously acquiring the means necessary for maintaining their efficiency. Opportunities for simplification are limited since the distinctions required for communication must be upheld. Turkic language history bears witness to the fact that contact-induced language change by no means always results in simplification. Perhaps as a consequence of higher structural principles, foreign influence can even complicate certain structures.[3] Due to the intricate interactions in the system as a whole, individual change often has diverse and far-reaching effects. Simplification in one area (e.g. phonology) may complicate another area interacting with it (e.g. morphology). Thus, 'natural' tendencies often produce irregularities, systemic asymmetries (Martinet 1955: 97 ff.; 1960: 215–6) harboring a constant potential for renewed language change. In addition, various psychological and social factors, such as the tendency towards elements with higher status, can result in complication.[4]

All other dynamic processes leading to the development of new language systems – child language, fusion, creolization, koinéization, etc. – display similar tendencies, namely, the elimination or alteration of 'marked' structures. These tendencies, however, are not always identical. 'Natural' processes within child language, for instance, do not necessarily correspond to processes of historical language change. Elements that are acquired easily by children and appear stable may actually be particularly susceptible to the modifications of general language change.[5] Boeschoten explicitly criticizes certain attempts 'to link developmental sequences observed in the speech of children acquiring Turkish with trends of diachronic change exhibited by Turkic languages in general and contact situations' (Boeschoten 1990a: 141–2).

Despite these serious reservations, we shall proceed on the tentative assumption that certain structural properties can be dominant or *attractive* in the sense that they are favored relatively often in, e.g., language acquistion, contact-induced influence and other types of language change. I refer not so much to universals that are absolute and without exception, but rather to those existing as tendencies (see Greenberg 1963; Comrie 1981b: 19). Some of these tendencies may play a greater role in the case of imposition than in the case of adoption, which is the focus of this study.

2.4. Attractive features

There is a substantial literature, which is anything but unequivocal, addressing the question of which linguistic qualities are more or less attractive. I can give but a general impression of the findings here.

There is overall agreement that *analytic* constructions belong to the psycholinguistically favored structures attractive to global copying. Highly synthetic structures are said to be avoided, while a small number of syllables (one or two) in the morphological word is preferred. The abovementioned complex Turkic verb system with its abundance of bound morphemes is a prime example of extreme synthesis. Apparently, when an analytic structure is available (e.g. for comparative constructions), it is often favored over a synthetic alternative. Analytic ('syntactic') means of expression are more likely to replace synthetic ('morphological') ones than vice versa. Many languages, for example, have replaced possessive suffixes by analytic constructions. Nonetheless, there are sufficient examples of the opposite development. A number of languages in contact with Turkic have developed possessive suffixes which at times replaced analytic constructions (see below). The analytic expression of a function is not necessarily more attractive than its synthetic counterpart. As Weinreich stresses, 'it is not morphology itself that is marked and unlikely to be transferred from one language to another; rather, it is certain common features of morphological structure that often, but not always, make morphology hard to learn' (Weinreich 1953: 57).

The degree of cohesion which individual morphemes possess may differ within synthetic structures as well. Some units are less 'firmly' attached than others. It is possible that this kind of increased autonomy and mobility is attractive and enables a unit which, in principle, is a bound unit to be copied. One of the typically Turkic characteristics listed above was the optional omission, among others, of plural, case or possessive suffixes on nonfinal constituents of a coordination (1.4, point 7).[6]

Many Turkic suffixes have been shown to originate from the incorporation of an unbound lexeme into its neighbor in the syntactic chain. This type of process usually comprises numerous intermediate stages, where material changes occur in terms of shape, intonation, sound harmony, etc. (see Johanson 1974a; 1981). There exist a number of enclitic particles, free units, that do not yet possess the cohesiveness of suffixes although they already exhibit certain phonological traits typical of suffixes. Less 'firm' attachment may represent a particular phase in the development towards the highest degree of cohesion. We shall return to the question below whether this feature fosters copiability.

Easily recognizable, straightforward relationships between content and expression are considered especially attractive. According to Slobin (1980), language learners prefer 'metaphorical transparency' between meaning and form as well as 1:1 relationships between linguistic forms and semantic configurations ('mapping transparency'). Andersen sees the '1:1 principle' as the result of cognitive processing constraints inherent in the acquisition and use of natural languages (Andersen 1984: 79; 1989: 386). This principle would explain some cases which, although not classifiable as simplifications, represent something similar. Studies on language acquisition, language change and the development of pidgin and creole languages clearly reveal a certain penchant towards transparency. Slobin (1980) maintains that, on the other hand, languages are constantly drifting away from transparency, obscuring the correspondences between meaning and form.

Transparency of categories and unequivocal relationships between semantic elements and their exponents are morphosyntactic factors which facilitate not only learning. Language copying too seems to be largely guided by principles of 'simplifying' transparency. Thus, clearly delineated elements of an 'agglutinating' morphology are more attractive than the morphemes of inflectional languages, which are more closely bound to their surroundings. Juxtaposition, where morpheme boundaries remain conspicuous, is attractive, whereas fusion, which causes segmentation problems, is less so. Furthermore, relatively invariant allomorphy is attractive (see Weinreich 1953: 41; cf. Comrie 1981b: 203), i.e. the relatively constant phonic shape of a morpheme in various environments; all too numerous and irregular variants make a morpheme difficult to identify. The syllabicity of an affix, the possibility of pronouncing it in isolation, is probably an attractive feature as well. Examining the acquistion of Turkish as a first language, Slobin (1986) emphasizes that children have mastered the entire system of agglutinating nominal morphology before the age of 2. This stands in contrast to the acquisition of corresponding areas in Indo-European languages: 'whatever the language, the full means of expressing case relations are never mastered in an Indo-European language by age 2, as they are in Turkish' (Slobin 1986: 275; cf. Aksu-Koç & Slobin 1985; Boeschoten 1990a). The Turkic case suffixes – which are regular, transparent, easily acquired and formed synthetically by means of juxtaposition – correspondingly prove stable in language contact: hardly susceptible to influence, they even lend themselves to global copying.

Perceptibility is an important feature of attractiveness. Let us tentatively assume that the peripheral positions within the morphological word enhance perceptibility. Thus we would expect a bound unit that often occupies an initial or final position to be perceptually especially salient and, therefore, to invite copying to a greater extent than other bound elements. Because they virtually always occupy peripheral positions in the nominal morphology, the Turkic case suffixes, discussed below, exemplify how frequent peripheral positioning promotes saliency.

Another attractive feature is 'natural' constituent structure, i.e. the ordering of units within the word and sentence, which, by virtue of the relative proximity of the constituents to one another, reflects semantic modification structures. Other factors of semantic structure may be of relevance too. As in the selection of material during second language acquisition, cognitive representation also seems to play an important role in the copying of B material. Modern psycholinguistics can surely provide valuable insight into this area. Certain semantic structures prove to be more stable than others.[7] As far as grammatical categories are concerned, the more stable ones are categories whose meaning is relatively broad and nonspecific (cf. the Turkic case and verbal suffixes discussed above). Thanks to their many functions, these widely applicable and communicatively rich categories also usually occur frequently. Slobin has repeatedly called attention to the stability of certain semantic categories of Turkic, for instance elements in the nominal and verbal inflection (e.g. Slobin 1986: 288).

Semantically *essential* distinctions, such as those of cases and aspect-tenses, tend to be more stable than more arbitrary, less informative ones. When contact-induced influence results in the loss of morphological categories, it is predominantly agreement and gender marking that are affected. The absence of inflectional agreement (e.g. of adjective attributes) and of grammatical gender might even be considered attractive, since it undoubtedly constitutes simplification. Concerning the considerable linguistic changes in diaspora Yugoslavian spoken by children, Đurovič (1988) observes that usually the 'most redundant' elements of the language system are susceptible to influence, whereas mood and aspect oppositions are rarely disrupted. In a study on German language acquisition of adolescent Turks living in Germany, Pfaff (1987) discovered that the nominative vs. accusative distinction is upheld more consistently than the gender distinctions. She links this finding to the fact that while case marking is semantically motivated, grammatical gender marking is not. According to Andersen (1989: 392), this argument supports the aforementioned '1:1 principle'.

Occasionally it is assumed that the *degree of abstraction* of a grammatical meaning somehow affects its attractiveness and, therefore, the stability of the category to which it belongs. Thus it is frequently claimed that a linguistic element is more difficult to replace, the less conscious the speaker is of it (Haugen 1950b). This circumstance is attributed to the semantic structure of the given element. Elements with abstract contents not directly relating to perceptible phenomena – such as elements expressing grammatical relations of which the speaker is not readily conscious – are said to be relatively stable. More concrete semantic elements, by contrast, would be more susceptible to influence. If this is true of adoption, then the reverse should be true of imposition. Juhász (1970: 128) observes that the more conscious speakers are of a native language element, the less likely the corresponding foreign language element is to 'interfere' with it, and vice versa. Thus, more concrete semantic elements of the first language would influence the second language less, while more abstract grammatical ones would influence it all the more.

Another claim is that contact-induced influence frequently leads to simpler syntactic structures overall. Many diaspora varieties, for example, display noticeable tendencies to simplify sentence structure (loss of complex structures). According to Wurm (1987), recent foreign influence on Turkish, some of which is German in origin – transmitted, among others, by emigrants returning to Turkey – has led to syntactic simplification, especially among the younger generation. Because leftbranching Turkic clause subordination (see 1.4, point 18 above) is generally considered cumbersome, its replacement by postpositive constructions is viewed as a simplification (see 3.5.3 below).

We might also expect more or less attractive features in the phonological domain. This is evidenced by certain frequently encountered preferences, such as favored chronological sequences during language acquisition and the replacement of certain qualities by others in the course of creolization and koinéization. These developmental phenomena include a preference for less substantial vowel and consonant systems; vowels such as [a], [i], [u] are favored over [ö], [ü], [ï]. Similarly, short vowels have priority over long vowels, oral vowels over nasal ones, monophthongs over diphthongs, initial plosives over initial fricatives, affricates and liquids, etc.

One way language demonstrates efficiency is by avoiding certain awkward combinations by means of phonic adaptation when joining segments, i.e. by omitting certain inessential phonetic features. This type of simplification evidently creates more attractive structures; the consonant assimilations found in numerous languages are one example of this process. The Turkic type of sound harmony, consisting in the suspension of certain phonological oppositions, e.g. [± front], in suffix syllables can also be considered attractive (as it is similarly simplifying). Consonant clusters, on the other hand, are often awkward and are more or less simplified in all known languages. Alternating sequences of consonants and vowels seem to accommodate the human speech organ. The voice reduction of word-final obstruents may also be considered 'natural' in this sense.

2.5. Social factors

In order to predict the conditions in which the different types of contact-induced change take place, I believe much more sophisticated analytical means are needed than the ones used to date. Nor is the tentatively conceived notion of attractiveness very helpful in this general form.

Of course, social factors must also be taken into consideration. As noted, such factors have greatly determined the direction, type, extent and depth of influence in Turkic language contact situations. True, attitudes (such as the willingness to adapt and the desire to gain prestige) are difficult to determine and evaluate. Nonetheless, even basic information about objective social conditions makes clear that the depth of linguistic influence correlates with certain intricately interacting social factors. Experience with Turkic language contact situations has shown that in instances of strong social B dominance (political, economic, cultural, numerical superiority; firm roots in the contact area), prolonged contact, high contact intensity and the widespread qualified bilingualism it facilitates, profound changes within A and/or comprehensive language shift from A to B take place. It is crucial to make the most differentiated assessment possible by applying the relevant criteria to the social situation in question. With reference to the far-reaching contact-induced developments in some Turkic languages, Boeschoten rightly points to 'the setting of the language contact in each case', remarking that 'it seems obvious that the idiosyncratic developments in Gagauz, Karaim, Uzbek and Azeri cannot be accounted for by the typological characteristics of the contact languages involved, or by psycholinguistic mechanisms, alone' (Boeschoten 1990a: 142).

Weinreich (1953) and subsequent similar studies deal with the interaction between social and structural factors in various contact situations. There have been attempts to generalize these interactions also and to define the regularities connected with them. For the most part, however, such analyses only operate on the basis of a limited number of social categories. Thus P. Kiparsky (1973) merely distinguishes between 'casual contact' and 'extensive bilingualism'.

Thomason & Kaufman (1988), on the other hand, try to devise more precise scales that correlate a large number of social and structural factors with one another. In particular, they differentiate between several degrees of contact intensity: 1. casual contact; 2. slightly more intense contact; 3. more intense contact; 4. strong cultural pressure; 5. very strong cultural pressure (Thomason & Kaufman 1988: esp. 50, 74–6, 115–46).

One may question whether it is actually possible to set up scales which are both sensitive and able to claim universal validity. In my view, these kinds of generalizing empirical observations at best allow us to posit certain rules of thumb: In instances of casual contact (where all A speakers need not be familiar with B) only lexical global copying is likely. When contact is more intense, the result will depend on the type of bilingualism. Comprehensive structural copying presumes qualified, active, longer-term bilingualism for at least a portion of the A speakers who speak B fluently and use it regularly as a means of communication. Furthermore, the following general observation is of relevance here: The lower an element is located on a stability scale of adoption, the greater the social pressure must be in order for it to be copied. In their general form, the calculations in question hardly offer more in the way of insight.

In addition, it is frequently asserted that, compared to the language-inherent 'causes' of language change, the social 'causes' always remain superficial: They cannot themselves effect change, but only trigger or accelerate tendencies already existing in the language. Bickerton even claims: 'At the level of *parole*, social forces do have an effect on language; at the level of *langue*, they hardly ever do' (Bickerton 1980: 125). Let me stress once again that I do not consider any of the structural factors described above nor any social conditions to be the *causes* of language change; I merely regard them as circumstances which potentially promote or prohibit influence.

2.6. Structuredness

There is a problematic issue associated with the concept of structure. Very often it is claimed that stability depends on the degree of *structuredness*, i.e. the degree of integration in the network of relationships within a subsystem whose elements interact in a complex way. Thomason & Kaufmann (1988: ch. 4–5), too, contend that an element is the more 'structured', the lower it ranks on a stability scale of adoption.

However, the role that structuredness plays in connection with stability is far from clear. The problem has two basic aspects:

1. Is a *B element* less copiable, the more structure it displays? Experience rather indicates that even essential B structures can be ignored by the copying process, and that various B qualities can be replaced by A qualities. Even from a B morphology that less explicitly represents the relationship between content and expression (with obscure morpheme boundaries and irregular allomorphs), entire sequences and even individual salient morphs can be copied and used regardless of the complex relationships obtaining in the originals. In this way, for instance, some Turkic languages have appropriated the genitive or plural forms of Russian nouns as primary stems. Haugen observes: 'But if it is true [...] that the more structural a feature is, the less likely it is to be borrowed, it will be evident that a corollary is that the effects of borrowing on structure are likely to be small' (Haugen 1950b: 226). This conclusion proves to be empirically false.
2. Is an *A element* less likely to be influenced or replaced by a B element, the more structure it possesses? There is a long-standing assumption that stability depends foremost on the structural organization of the 'recipient language', and that the susceptibility of one of its elements to influence decreases with increasing systemic integration. Thus the most structured subsystems are also considered to be the most stable ones. Whitney noted that 'whatever is more formal or structural in character remains in that degree free from the intrusion of foreign material' (Whitney 1881). According to Tesnière (1939: 85),

susceptibility diminishes with increasing structural integration. Haugen's 'scale of adoptability' is also 'somehow [...] correlated to the structural organization' (Haugen 1950b: 224). Weinreich (1953: 35) suggests that less structured subsystems have relatively independent elements; this would explain how foreign elements can sometimes predominate in the lexicon, while structural elements tend to be stable. Givón regards copies as having a disruptive effect on an 'interlocking, highly nonarbitrary part of the system' (Givón 1979: 25 ff.). Therefore the decomposition of morphosyntactic A patterns as a result of copying would increase the 'markedness' of the A grammar.

The degree of *openness* of individual subsystems is likewise deemed a decisive factor of stability. Meillet (1921: 84) regards the adoption of new elements into closed systems such as phonology and morphosyntax as relatively difficult. There is the consensus that foreign elements are the more easily copied, the more *variation* the subsystem permits. The number of units in a particular area is not only thought to reflect its structural organization, but also to determine the frequency of these units. According to this view, phonemes, for example, are less likely to undergo alteration because a language possesses only a small number of phonemes, each of which is frequently repeated. The adoption of new elements into inflectional systems is considered problematic since these systems are relatively closed and usually highly structured.

Consequently, we can say with certainty of the adoption type of influence that pre-existing A structures offer more structural 'resistance' than the B structures destined for copying. If some grammatical B elements are more impervious to copying than others, this is due less to the elements themselves than to the degree of cohesion within the A frame into which the elements are copied. As the cohesion of morphemes within a word is greater than the cohesion of the words within a phrase, global copies of B morphemes would often be difficult to insert into A words.

Therefore Haugen's above-cited objection does not quite get to the gist of the problem. Instead we might state: If the susceptibility of A elements diminishes with the increased degree of their structuredness, we should conclude that 'borrowing' has no significant impact on linguistic structures. But this conclusion is easy to refute empirically too. The validity of the *structuredness = stability* equation, even in this unspecific form, remains to be proven.

2.7. Relative attractiveness

In my opinion, neither general notions of attractiveness nor undifferentiated concepts of structuredness suffice to even roughly determine the role of structural factors involved in the various types of contact-induced language change. Neither simplistic structural calculations nor general references to natural or congenital tendencies are useful for predicting the results of language contact. One is hard-pressed to find A structures that absolutely obviate the copying of certain B structures. Even generally 'attractive' structures, which are known to be copied more readily than others, may be lost under foreign influence. And unattractive structures might be retained even though heavy B influence would seem to invite their abandonment. General principles governing influence can have diverse structural effects: The schemata must be relativized.

An initial differentiation might be made between that which is adopted and that which is lost. As noted, the absence of an identifiable equivalent in B can lead to the loss of an original A distinction. Reinforcement by analogy gives preference to the contact languages' 'common' features while suppressing structures 'absent' in B. Which elements are relinquished in A as a result of a lacking contrast in B is also unpredictable. The contact-induced *loss* of elements seems to be even more unpredictable than the contact-induced *adoption* of new ones.

In particular, the schemata must be relativized in such a way that they take the typological relationships between corresponding A and B structures into account. The different ways in which tendencies of attractiveness can manifest themselves are also determined by these relationships. A possible hierarchy of contact-induced influences should at least be based on a concept of *relative attractiveness*. The probability of influence appears to depend greatly on this concept.

General structures that are largely analogous in A and B have long been suspected to facilitate contact-induced influence. Typological proximity seems to play an important role in both types of influence (1 and 2). Typological similarity promotes copying because the process itself is based on the (subjective) *perception of interlingual equivalence*. B elements serving as models are thereby identified with A elements in respect of certain characteristics. In phonology, morphology, semantics and syntax, we often observe that B elements appearing to have close correspondences in A are more susceptible to copying. 'Common' surface structures provide an especially favorable frame for copying. Combinational patterns that basically correspond in A and B offer equivalence positions for the insertion of B copies into the A frame (see 1.3.1 above). When the typological distance between the contact languages is greater, fewer equivalence positions inviting insertion are present.

It thus becomes apparent that many a linguistic feature described earlier is not more or less attractive (or 'marked') per se, but rather only in relation to corresponding substructures in the contact language. Weinreich (1953: 33) emphasizes the importance of structural congruency especially for facilitating morphological influence. Relatively independent elements of less structured subsystems (see 2.6 above) and elements whose functionality is rather straightforward are much more likely to correspond to elements of the respective contact language than relatively dependent and multifunctional elements. Hence, structures whose morphemes display clear boundaries and are free, mobile, invariant and functionally simple (see 2.4 above) would offer the most favorable conditions for the interactions of code copying. The generally meager participation of bound and functionally more complex elements in these processes, however, does not result from their being bound or functionally complex. Rather it is due to the low probability of their having typologically corresponding substructures in the contact language.

It follows from these considerations that global copying will be eased, for example, when a grammatical B category is fairly analogous to an A category and both can be expressed analytically, by means of free forms. Thus a free copy of a free B unit often replaces a free A unit. The free copy of the free B unit may also replace a bound A unit. It is less likely, but entirely possible, for a bound B morpheme constituting part of a synthetic B expression, e.g. an affix, to be extracted from its word-internal combinational pattern and, as a bound copy, to replace a bound A unit. This process occurs most easily when A and B display similar word-internal combinational patterns. Moreover, the copy of a bound B unit might also be used freely and replace a free A unit, or the copy of a free B unit might become bound and replace a bound A unit. The three remaining theoretical possibilities are less likely.

Similar observations can be made for imposition. This type of influence is easier when the interacting units are relatively analogous. Formerly, however, it was often assumed that greater distance favored this type of influence. Auburger (1983: 5-6) maintains that very similar languages tend to display a greater 'frequency of interference' and greater 'unavoidability of interference' than less similar ones.[8] The so-called interlanguages, which develop during second language acquisition, prefer free, invariant, functionally simple morphemes that are congruent in the first and second language (Andersen 1989: 389). Eckman (1977) calls attention to the problems encountered with 'marked' elements of the target language that lack correspondences in the first language. According to the 'alternation hypothesis' (Jansen, Lalleman & Muysken 1981), when the target language has two alternative structures, second language learners tend to overgeneralize the structure having a parallel in their first language and to avoid the other. This is an example of the aforementioned adaptational tendencies of reinforcement by analogy: By means of the copying of frequential features, preference is given to elements that the contact languages 'have in common'. Germans learning Turkish, e.g., show a propensity towards prepositive possessive constructions of a pattern common to German and Turkish (*bizim köy, unser Dorf* 'our village'). By contrast, Turks hardly ever impose postpositive possessive constructions onto their German (although the type *köyümüz* 'our village' is the normal one in Turkish) because German lacks a corresponding pattern.

The typological distance between contact languages must be defined contrastively, especially in terms of the structuredness of their subsystems, which has a significant effect on the contact results. Pfaff (1979) established that 'code switching' also favors structures shared by some or all of the participating languages. But these tendencies should not be considered absolute. In particular, they by no means hinder B elements that are incongruent or incompatible with the respective A structure from being copied into A (cf. Bickerton 1981: 50). Thus a number of universal grammatical restrictions posited for 'code switching' are invalid, e.g. Poplack's (1980) so-called equivalence constraint, which only allows code switching in positions before and after which both languages have the same word order. Appel & Muysken (1987: 123 ff.) employ general principles of 'linearity', i.e. the tendency to retain linear order, and of 'dependence', i.e. the impossibility for code switching to take place between two units, one of which grammatically depends on the other. Here, again, we are dealing with mere tendencies connected with relative attractiveness. Furthermore, the problematic assumption mentioned above, claiming that a language prefers to copy elements that correspond to its internal developmental tendencies, does not necessarily rule out that the language might also undergo other changes.

If typological proximity indeed played such a decisive role in copying, not much in the way of mutual influence between Turkic and its mostly differently structured neighboring languages could be expected. Thus, for instance, if phonological influence depended on closely corresponding phonological structures, one would be more inclined to predict the often substantial discrepancy between Turkic and its contact languages to counteract that type of influence. We have seen that little structural similarity exists in several areas, such as word classes, e.g. between Turkic and Greek, or the structure of compounds, e.g. between Turkic and Russian, etc. Other congruent combinational patterns are usually also absent, for example patterns that would encourage A roots to assume inflectional affixes copied from B. Suffix languages such as Turkic are less given to copying prefixes, and vice versa. A comparable case of typologically relativized attractiveness is the circumstance that postpositional languages do not easily copy prepositions, and prepositional languages are reluctant to copy postpositions. Pre- and postpositional phrases are closely equivalent in terms of their external combinational patterns, but their internal combinational patterns are incompatible (with regard to the position of the relational particles). Several languages in contact with Turkic exhibit a higher degree of fusioning, so their affixes are more tightly bound to their environments than Turkic ones. Morphosyntactic relationships, such as the inventories of grammatical units, are also usually too divergent to render the global copying of whole B categories (e.g. case) probable.

Nevertheless, as we shall see, cases continuously crop up that would seem to violate the principle of typologically relativized attractiveness. In my view, however, what is essential for understanding contact-induced influence is the realization that objective structural equivalence is not an absolute condition for copying. Experience with actual Turkic contact situations has shown that elements lacking close correspondences in the respective contact language may be copied as well. Although structural affinity may facilitate the process, what ultimately affects copying is the *subjective perception of equivalence.* If, on the one hand, certain linguistic features can be considered 'attractive' because they empirically prove to be relatively successful in the copying process, on the other hand, their attractiveness is relativized by subjectively determined specific A – B equivalencies (although these are often based on genuine structural similarity).

Consequently, copying is also possible even when, due to greater typological distance, there are few equivalence positions encouraging insertion. However, in the process, A copies often emerge which flagrantly violate the structural features of the B original. The thorough alteration of B structures enables these copies to function in the A grammar. Sometimes this process is described as the 'suspension of the B grammar'. According to my understanding, however, copies *always* function inside the A grammar, so that the B grammar is suspended by definition. As mentioned, 'violations' of the B structure need not be an indication of inadequate B acquisition (see Johanson 1993b). Below, we shall return to cases where features are copied despite objective structural incompatibility and the structural features of B are significantly altered.

2.8. Differences between languages

Do typologically induced differences exist that would make certain languages per se more resistant to influence than others? The susceptibility of Turkic, especially Ottoman Turkish, to foreign influence has been the object of frequent speculation. However, so far no such systematic differences between languages have been convincingly demonstrated. At best, one might assume that languages which are mainly juxtaposing copy foreign elements into their combinational patterns with relative ease, whereas morphological patterns with less transparent relationships between content and expression have more difficulty incorporating individual copies into their complex relational networks. In particular, there are considerable differences with regard to the *morphological adaptation* of the copies (see 1.3.1 above). In languages of the Turkic type, this process is much easier than in languages featuring large amounts of morphological classes and inflectional patterns.

Languages also differ distinctly in terms of the relationship between global and selective copying. Some languages, e.g. English and Classical Ottoman, are 'heterogeneous' in that they tend strongly towards global copying when creating expressions for new terms; other languages are more inclined to copy semantic qualities onto indigenous material.[9] However, as V. Kiparsky points out, these differences depend not on the linguistic structure of the language, but rather on the sociopolitical attitudes of its speakers (see Vočadlo 1938: 176).

In addition, languages and varieties can surely be said to differ in their choice of attractive structures – for one, in their tendency to adjust foreign elements to their own systems. Classical Ottoman, which was developed by scholars of diverse linguistic and historical backgrounds, is an example of a language particularly reluctant to perform such adaptations. For many centuries it remained a socially 'marked' variety with relatively unattractive structures, characterized, among other things, by so-called compartmentalization, with certain foreign (Arabic and Persian) elements making up a separate subsystem. Portions of the lexicon consisting of relatively faithfully reproduced global copies were structurally irregular; for example, they deviated from the norm with regard to sound harmony.[10] Thus by way of omitting certain adaptational techniques, etymological knowledge about these units led them to be characterized as [+ foreign]. Such cases of special treatment also result primarily from the social attitudes of the language users.

2.9. Deep influence

Even though it may be possible to devise hierarchies of contact-induced influence based on relativized *scales of attractiveness*, the way the values are realized undoubtedly remains highly dependent on social factors. Only sociolinguistics can provide differentiated information on the correlations between various degrees of contact duration and intensity, on the one hand, and disparate contact results, on the other. In the absence of such precise data, the most the observation of Turkic language contacts permits is this very general conclusion: The less 'relatively attractive' an element is, the more favorable the social conditions must be in order for it to be copied.

Can favorable social factors overcome even resistance against structural elements ranking low on the relativized attractiveness scale? Thomason & Kaufman (1988: 72) point out that under exceptionally advantageous social circumstances elements can be copied which typologically deviate from their counterparts in the recipient language. Karaim, Inner Anatolian Greek and northern Tajik are prime examples of how languages, reacting to immense social pressures, can profoundly change by adopting typologically very divergent elements. Karaim displays amazingly far-reaching phonetic and syntactic influence; its clausal structure has been heavily de-Turkicized. Central Anatolian Greek has copied, among other things, Turkish phonic qualities, word formation patterns, syntactic patterns, inflectional morphology and even parts of the basic lexicon (see Dawkins 1916). In the intense but socioculturally more balanced Turkic–Iranian contact situation in Western Turkestan, northern Tajik dialects were heavily Turkicized, while Uzbek urban dialects were Iranicized – especially in their phonology and syntax. Such instances of profound change (affecting articulation, sound structure, lexical structure, grammatical categories, syntax, etc.) renew the question of where, if they exist at all, the limits to structural influence are. There is no documented case where structural change appears to follow only the tendencies dictated by the typology of the individual recipient language.

These observations need some additional explanation. Profound change, which is undoubtedly induced by social factors, additionally involves structural aspects that are relevant to its explanation. One of these has to do with the duration of contact and concerns the *successive character of the learning processes.*

When two languages are typologically very close, intense contact between them may relatively quickly lead to considerable convergence. However, conditions for strong convergence may also develop between originally quite divergent languages. In this light, I shall now briefly discuss a number of issues concerning the successive phases in the diachronic development of copies and 'generations' of copies.

Many results of code copying are ephemeral, restricted to the sphere of discourse, and remain below the integration thresholds of habitualization and conventionalization. Others are longer-lived and have real diachronic effects on the language: They enjoy widespread systematic use in the speech community, become established as parts of new norms and may even end up replacing their A equivalents.

This kind of integration process usually presupposes a certain length of contact. Each copy from B that becomes an integral part of A creates more similarity between the two codes. This similarity, in turn, encourages renewed copying. Thus the results of earlier processes provide the basis for new ones: older copies pave the way for new copies. The circumstance that even a very convergent development may begin and continue without any major typological changes is often overlooked.

The prerequisites for convergence are established, above all, by the copying of combinational patterns that produce new equivalence positions. Patterns which reorder existing categories without otherwise changing them are copied with relative ease. Globally copied, whole, free lexical B forms lay the foundations not only for the copying of bound units, but also for the copying of lexical combinational patterns. The clausal frame of the basic code can also be changed by way of copied combinational patterns, thus creating new equivalence positions for potential global copies. Once conceived, an A alternative (e.g. an alternative word order) may be overgeneralized, i.e. reinforced by frequential copying. Individual, generalized structural copies often have a significant impact on other parts of the linguistic system. So far, however, the way that structural patterns and units interact in this respect has hardly been examined. There has also been little research into the implicative stages of contact-induced influence. In this context, the Azerbaijanian dialects spoken in Iran, with their multiple layers of influence, present interesting objects of investigation.

We can envisage *tendencies* which increase a language's susceptibility to certain kinds of influence. The language might possess a certain disposition preparing it to move in the respective direction. Such assumptions, however, become questionable when formulated as absolute restrictions. 'A change and B influence' may emanate from an already existing tendency towards change in A that is *accelerated* through contact with B. Successive creative processes can bring about increasing typological affinity, thereby effecting profound structural change overall. In other words, the processes are not only determined by social factors, but undeniably by linguistic ones as well.

Initially, an innovation is more or less 'socially marked' and may subsequently be more or less conventionalized while attaining various levels of social acceptance. What is important is the extent to which it is considered as belonging to A and no longer 'foreign' (belonging to B). Even a variety characterized by heavy copying can become the norm of a group, thus becoming a new 'socially unmarked' basic code. Every new norm can, in turn, be deviated from by new 'marked' copying. Therefore the basic code must be defined anew at each developmental stage. This means that for the evaluation of any copying process, knowledge of past copying processes is crucial (Johanson 1993b).

It is sometimes said of certain cases of heavy copying that, because no corresponding A tendencies were present, social dominance must have been particularly pronounced. This impression will inevitably arise when an early stage of overall development serves as the basis of comparison. At such a level, Anatolian Greek, for example, will have possessed only few Turkic characteristics. But 'tendencies' must be sought out at the A stage in which the new creative processes in question evolved. Often A structures that are susceptible to influence at a particular developmental stage have already become more similar to the respective B structures through previous developments. This successive adaptational process may increase convergence between A and B so that, eventually, deep influence can occur *without extreme degrees of social dominance or contact intensity*.

In situations of sustained asymmetrical dominance, language A becomes more similar to language B. Through a similar process of successively reinforced disposition, long-lasting and intense areal contacts can lead to structural convergence – in the sense of a so-called *Sprachbund* – between several originally rather dissimilar languages. One characteristic of areal-typological adaptation is combinational selective copying, which generates isomorphous patterns in the lexical and clausal syntax. We shall return to examples of such adaptational processes in the Central Asian (Uzbek–Tajik) and Balkan areals.

Which B elements A speakers select for copying partially depends on the level of their proficiency in B. The elements' accessibility varies, the A speakers' type and degree of familiarity with B often playing an important role. It appears, e.g., that bilingual A speakers copy B elements when they are 'ready' for them, i.e. when their level of B proficiency exhibits structures that resemble structures present on their level of A proficiency. B elements can then be copied more easily because, in this subjective sense, they have become more 'similar' to their A equivalents. Thus, differences between B elements in terms of their learnability play a certain role here. When there is sufficient time for bilingualism to develop, even B structures that are relatively difficult to acquire can be copied more easily. This circumstance obviously implies a *further relativization of the concept of attractiveness*.

As a consequence, in the course of successive copying, general differences in attractiveness become less significant. Consider Soper's comments on Turkic influence on Tajik and Persian influence on Kashkay: 'it may be that certain linguistic structures, because of some property of 'explicitness' in the form-to-meaning relationship, are borrowed more readily at stages of language contact in which the kind of extensive cross-language influence exhibited by Tajik and Qashqay has not occurred, but at the stage of considerable influence there may be no correlation between explicitness and the ability of a structure to be adopted by a recipient language' (Soper 1987: 411–2).

Certain B elements, thus, are not copied until the degree of influence exerted by B has developed structures conducive to further copying. As a rule, multiple layers of copying are discernible in the diachronic development of a language, e.g. older copies from periods of limited bilingualism in the A group and later copies from periods of improved bilingualism. Often this variation is most visible in the phonetic structure of copies. Many Turkic languages have doublets for Russian loanwords. Copies stemming from periods of less advanced bilingualism often show extreme phonetic adjustment to the A systems; later copies are usually less adapted. Whereas Russian words copied in pre-Revolutionary times were often 'deformed', later copies have mostly followed the Russian norm (Musaev 1984: 179–80). Rules for substituting consonants and avoiding consonant clusters (see above) were modified (Baskakov 1960: 29; cf. Wurm 1960: 54–5). Older forms reflecting a highly adapted pronunciation became obsolete, for example Karakalpak *källiyktip* < *kollektiv* or *kämuvnes* < *kommunist* (Baskakov 1960: 28).

The results of long-term successive influence may also be difficult to analyze due to the many possible layers. This is especially true when language A reflects a stage of development from which B, in certain areas, has long departed. Here, as well, the differences between a copy and its original can only be determined when the actual original is known. Faced with the type of successive layering mentioned, this task becomes particularly tricky. The debate concerning Turkic influence on Tajik has suffered from its orientation towards modern Uzbek. In reality, the convergent linguistic development began long before the emergence of Uzbek, so that much influence is actually very old. Thus, for example, the unit *-miš*, which is not a typical feature of contemporary Uzbek, must have been copied early on. The Tajik high-focal present tense, formed with *istådän* 'stand', is a copy of an older Turkic from with *tur-* 'stand', whereas an additional renewal of the present tense based on the verb *yat-* 'lie' has since taken place in Uzbek. (For the notion of focality, see 3.4 below.)

There is the additional question of how to measure and define 'deep influence'. First of all, we must distinguish between the number of influence-related phenomena and their text frequency. Second, we must define the depth of influence with respect to the varieties of a language. Despite numerous types of phenomena, influence might remain quantitatively limited and/or reserved to certain subsystems. Thus the notion of deep influence must be relativized by taking frequency of occurrence and the structures of varieties into account. An example: Thomason & Kaufman (1988: 93–4) depict Turkish influence on certain Anatolian Greek dialects as extremely strong. However, a number of phenomena resulting from Turkish influence, as reported by Dawkins (1916), are actually only sparsely attested in the texts. Hovdhaugen (1976: 149) therefore rejects the notion of Turkish having deeply influenced these varieties. He contends that the original morphological and syntactic structures of these dialects are well preserved and only slightly altered – tendencies towards agglutination, a reduction of the gender system, the adoption of Turkish word order, etc. never having replaced the inherited structure.[11]

2.10. Types of influence involved in language maintenance and language shift

What are the consequences of deep influence on genetic relations? Even extreme cases such as Karaim, Inner Anatolian Greek and northern Tajik have retained enough genuine features to still be identifiable as Turkic, Greek and Iranian, respectively. I shall not discuss here when such cases should cease to be considered 'daughter languages', i.e. branches on the respective genealogical tree; in other words, the question of how far contact-induced change can proceed without effecting a qualitative leap to nongenetic development. According to a rather widespread contention that has been the cause of much theoretical confusion, relatedness and 'borrowing' are not antithetical terms, but merely 'terms for different degrees and stages of one process', 'terms designating the same thing from different perspectives' (Setälä 1915: 11). By that token, what is to be considered 'copied material' in one phase must be considered 'genetic material', i.e. 'cognate' material in another. For example, Fokos-Fuchs (1962: 125) contends that when we encounter 'borrowings' from very early periods on a large scale – so large that the borrower's original language layer has been obscured – then the languages in question must be considered as having become related to each other. Based on this thesis, the author then enlists syntactic arguments in an attempt to prove Ural-Altaic kinship.

Obviously, genealogy cannot be reasonably discussed within such categories. Moreover, genetic relations no doubt represent only *one* aspect of a language's historical development. I shall ignore here whether 'relatedness' can evolve as describe above. Instead, the question is: Can a language be influenced to such an extent that its true genetic origins are no longer recognizable? As noted above, linguists have repeatedly called attention to certain supposedly inalienable elements and areas allegedly resisting influence (syntax, basic lexicon, inflectional morphology, etc.). If such stable elements actually exist, they would represent decisive criteria for genetic relatedness which could be used to determine whether the similarity between two languages is genetic or contact-induced. However, no element or single area appears stable enough to serve as a touchstone for genetic relatedness.

Certain elements which experience has shown to be relatively stable, with low positions on stability scales of adoption, may serve as indicators in many cases, although not as individual items but rather in constellations. Genetic relations can only be substantiated through traces of systematic correspondences in several areas. According to Weinreich, relatedness is established by 'the existence of cognates in the basic morphemic stock, with parallelism in allomorphic alternations as a powerful supplement' (Weinreich 1958: 376). But such traces may also have been effaced long ago. Older results of copying and kinship are often hard to distinguish from one another; the period when relatedness was still visible may lie too far in the past.

The absence of traces of systematic correspondences may also indicate a contact-induced nongenetic reorganization of linguistic properties. As seen, pronounced B dominance often entails heavy copying. Another possible consequence of strong B dominance is the failure to pass language A on, i.e. the relinquishing of A in favor of B. After an A group has undergone such a language shift, the result of their A → B imposition (see 1.1) may continue to act as a substratum influence in their variety of B.[12] Especially in cases of geographic or social distance from the main bulk of B speakers, substratum dialects of B can develop and establish themselves. Significantly large groups can also influence the varieties of original B speakers; this seems to be the case with the originally Turkic-speaking portion of the Slavic-speaking Bulgarians.[13]

It is often difficult to distinguish retrospectively between the results of heavy adoption (occurring in favorable conditions) and those of substratum influence in the sense of imposition. Does a given phenomenon go back to *adoption + language maintenance* or *imposition + language shift*? Frequently, structural differences are not discernible. Thus, A varieties may undergo deep phonological influence as a result of prolonged contact; and substratum dialects can contain remnants of the sound system of A. In both cases, the result will greatly depend on the level of the A group's knowledge of B, and hence usually on the contact duration. A → B imposition also occurs when the A group shifting to B has been bilingual for generations, but it is likely to be the stronger, the more imperfect their B skills were preceding the shift.

We encounter imposition especially in the domains of phonology and syntax. Substratum influence often takes place without comprehensive lexical global copying from A. The lexicon of the B variety may be subject to little influence from A, since it has priority over pronunciation and grammar for the purposes of communication. Thus, the lexicon may be composed differently than it is in the case of adoption. Probable instances of substratum influence are such cases, *inter alia*, where lexical influence, which always occupies the top position on influence scales of adoption, is sparse, whereas phenomena tending to rank lower on those scales predominate. For example, Samoyed lexical influence on South Siberian Turkic is modest, while, according to widespread opinion, a number of phonological peculiarities – Sayan Turkic glottalization, Tofan and Khakas nasalization of *y-* – are the result of Samoyed influence. (For glottalization, see Johanson 1986b.)

Thus, the question also arises whether the evidential (indirective) categories of the Bulgarian verb go back to early Turkic imposition or were copied from Ottoman Turkish in the course of long and intensive contact. The majority of the Turkic-speaking Bulgars who had crossed the lower Danube in 679 had apparently become Slavic-speaking by the 9th century. On the other hand, early linguistic Ottomanization took place on Bulgarian territory. So, both imposition + shift and adoption + maintenance are possible. One would tend to give preference to the first option, since it is less likely that Ottomanization could have exerted such strong linguistic pressure on the Slavic language to cause it to copy foreign grammatical categories. In fact, however, both cases probably occurred: first, the shift to Slavic coupled with early Turkic imposition, and, later, maintenance of Slavic with increasing Ottoman-Turkic adoption.

The Volga region with its phonological Finno-Ugric–Turkic contact phenomena – on the Turkic side in Chuvash, Tatar and Bashkir – presents similar problems (Johanson 2000b). Sometimes we know that a non-Turkic substratum is present, e.g. from southern

Samoyed and Yenisey-Ostyak in the South Siberian Turkic languages, e.g. Tofan. Dolgan, mostly considered a Yakut dialect, is, like other Yakut varieties, influenced by Mongolic and northern Tungusic, but also displays a component indicating a Samoyedic substratum. For a substratum dialect of the Turkic-speaking Roma living in the Balkans, see Matras 1990. By contrast, certain other cases of strong influence obviously are not substratum-related. For example, in the case of Karaim, no shift from Slavic to Turkic, and in the case of Inner Anatolian Greek, no shift from Turkic to Greek seems to have taken place. In both cases, the heavy B influence must be explained as the result of adoption + maintenance.

Dialects of the shift type spoken in relative isolation from other B varieties often tend to conserve certain characteristics and to impede the further development of B, probably in part due to imposition. The shape B had when it was taken on during the language shift is often maintained longer than in other B varieties. On the southeastern Black Sea coast we encounter various kinds of Turkish–Pontic Greek contact varieties: Greek-influenced Turkish varieties of the maintenance type and Turkish varieties that developed in relative isolation and contain Greek substratum. The varieties of the shift type – as well as the Turkish varieties of adjacent bilingual groups – frequently possess more archaic Turkic elements, e.g. in the morphonology, than the Greek-influenced varieties of the maintenance type (see Brendemoen 1992).

The difficulties in distinguishing the two types are also caused by the often rather systematic character of copying processes. According to Fokos-Fuchs (1962: 50), an abundance of syntactic correspondences, among others, are decisive indicators of genetic relatedness. However, one can frequently observe that syntactic changes resulting from copying – unlike changes to the lexicon – are closely interrelated and take place systematically. Strong syntactic influence is not a matter of coincidence; units are not selected individually for copying, but rather as parts of bundles of relationships. Soper demonstrates how, in the Kashkay verbal system, the copying of Persian subordinate clauses with prepositive junctors and finite verb forms accompanied by the loss of serialization devices due to the abandonment of the converbs 'have combined to produce a single effect, a remarkable parallelism between Qashqay and Persian syntax' (Soper 1987: 401).

Certain contact areas within the Turkic-speaking world exhibit the results of extremely complex processes. Innumerable Turkic dialects of Eastern Turkestan are clearly substratum-influenced, e.g. in the phonological domain, although the sources of this influence cannot be exactly determined. Nevertheless, some things are known, for example about Sogdian, which was influenced by Old Uyghur from the ninth century on (Johanson 1993d). The Sogdians, who, according to Maḥmūd al-Kašɣarī, were still bilingual in the eleventh century (see Dankoff & Kelly 1982: 83-4), were Turkicized shortly thereafter. Yaɣnåbī, a language that goes back to Sogdian and has survived in the Pamir region, still displays Old Uyghur loanwords. The process as a whole is characterized by the fact that Turkic offensively displaced Iranian from large geographical areas: 'Turkic dialects have virtually erased Iranian in northern Afghanistan and Central Asia except for the Tajiki enclave. The Turkicization of much of these areas began before the end of the first millennium AD and does not seem to have halted yet' (Windfuhr 1990: 523). As noted, the intensive Turkic–Persian contacts in Western Turkestan led to centuries of successive intersecting and overlapping processes of adoption + maintenance and imposition + shift in both directions. Northern Tajik bears very complex traces of these processes. The dialect group comprising the so-called 'Uzbek' dialects is based on Turkic varieties with heavy copying from Iranian (adoption + maintenance), Iranian–Turkic substratum varieties (imposition + shift), as well as various combinations of the two.

The situation is similar in other ancient cultural regions where diverse ethnic groups and languages intermingled. Crimea was a well-known melting pot of this kind. Another was Khwarezm on Lake Aral, an old center of Iranian language and culture that, from the eighth century onwards, was progressively Turkicized until the Khwarezmian language finally became extinct in the thirteenth or fourteenth century.[14] Here, we later encounter complex inner Turkic contact processes with Uzbek, Turkmen and Kazakh/Karakalpak elements. In Azerbaijan, too, manifold processes of adoption and imposition have been interacting for centuries in intricate ways.

Although heavy copying and language shift both occur in conditions of intensive, ongoing contact, the two must be carefully distinguished. Several of the most heavily influenced languages within the Turkic–Indo-European contact situation are facing extinction or have already disappeared. The Inner Anatolian Greek dialects described by Dawkins (1916) vanished for well-known political reasons. The existence of Karaim too has been threatened since World War Two; today, the language is hardly passed on in a normal way. (The so-called Eastern Karaim, who remained in Crimea, abandoned their language in favor of Crimean Tatar long ago.) A further interesting example is the Sephardic Ladino koiné which developed during the seventeenth century. After contact with the basic codes Spanish and Portuguese had ended, Turkic-relexified Ladino varieties evolved, among others. The demise of the Ladino spoken in the east of the Ottoman Empire began in the eighteenth century. In Turkey only very few speakers remain who have preserved an archaic Ladino variety, but this language is evidently not being passed on (Faingold 1989).

Attempts to portray the shift from A to B as a sort of gradual development from A to B brought on by progressively stronger structural influence must be rejected. This tendency can be discerned, for example, in Haugen's works (see, e.g., the 1972 collective volume). Even if structural change is intense, it should not be able to prevent a language from being passed on from one generation to the next. Languages do not cease to exist for structural reasons, e.g. because they have become overwhelmed by foreign elements, but rather because they are no longer handed down. The abovementioned languages did not cease to be functional as a result of 'mixing'. The decisive factors were social in nature. Nevertheless, functional reduction as a result of B dominance may diminish the speakers' competence to the point that their A displays conspicuous structural features, such as reduced formal inventories and oppositions (see Dorian's studies, e.g. 1981). Khalaj, a Turkic dialect spoken in central Iran that is heavily influenced by Persian and Azerbaijanian, may already exhibit such symptoms. That much can be gleaned from the descriptions of the rather unsystematic variations detected there (Doerfer 1988a; cf. Johanson 1991f).

Similar conditions prevail in the Mongolic Mogholī dialects spoken in Afghanistan (Weiers 1972; cf. Johanson 1974b).

Thus far, we have only considered contact results characterized by adoption + maintenance and imposition + shift. Sometimes a typologically different kind of contact result is claimed to exist, namely 'fusional', 'hybrid' or 'mixed' languages, comprising two components that are not integrated into one system. According to Faingold (1989), the Ladino dialect of Istanbul, in which a Spanish and a Portuguese component have coexisted for centuries without assimilating one another, may represent this type. The Eynu language spoken in Eastern Turkestan has been taken to be a 'hybrid', produced from two different languages. It is rather an Uyghur variety characterized by extreme lexical imposition of a former non-Turkic (Iranian) primary language on a Turkic basic code. Varieties of certain 'Abdal' groups in Uzbekistan, Afghanistan, Iran and Turkey combine, in a similar way, a local Turkic morphosyntax with a vocabulary that is partly of Persian and partly of unknown origin (see Tietze & Ladstätter 1994; Hayasi 2000).

Chapter 3

STRUCTURAL COPYING IN VARIOUS LINGUISTIC DOMAINS

3.1. Turkic–non-Turkic convergence

So far I have described a number of features typical of the Turkic languages, on the one hand, and discussed some supposedly generally attractive linguistic features and their relative significance for susceptibility in contact situations, on the other. As it turns out, the Turkic languages display a remarkably large amount of these putatively attractive qualities. This chapter will examine, on the basis of examples taken from various areas, what type of elements Turkic languages and some of their contact languages have been prone to copy from one another, i.e. which features have proven to be *relatively attractive.*

Both the foreign structural elements copied into Turkic and the Turkic elements serving as models for copying appear to be, for the most part, the kind of elements defined above as generally attractive. In other words, attractive qualities have usually been copied and unattractive ones replaced. Complicating elements have only been selected for copying in extremely rare cases. The copying process has foremost targeted 1:1 relationships between expression and content, as well as transparency, regularity and simplicity. This rule applies even to the longest lasting and most intense contact situations.

A number of instances of particularly pervasive convergence between Turkic and non-Turkic languages are worthy of special attention. This convergence seems to have been brought on almost exclusively by processes of simplification. The convergence of Karaim with Slavic and that of the Inner Anatolian Greek dialects with Turkic resulted from the acquisition of simplifying features from the respective contact language. It is interesting to compare these cases with those of Turkic–non-Turkic convergence in which attractive features, too, play a central role, although we lack sufficient knowledge of the modalities involved in the influence. Examples of this are the structural similarities between Turkic and languages such as Mongolian, Persian and Armenian.

Benzing (1954) says of the mutual influence of Turkic and Iranian languages that still virtually nothing is known of the linguistic effects borne of the ancient relations between Iranian peoples and Turks. Many questions remain unanswered to this day. What is apparent is a certain convergence that began early on. According to Doerfer (1967: 60), Persian has long tended towards the Turkic language type and, in some cases, has taken on an altogether un-Indo-European aspect. He states that the degree of convergence was already considerable in older Persian, especially in the syntactic domain, and that, since the Middle Persian period, Persian has increasingly moved towards a point of unification with Turkic. Windfuhr (1990: 530) stresses that Persian and the Persian dialects, especially in terms of their morphology, 'may be called the most atypical Iranian language', and that this process started during the late Old Persian period. Modern Persian does indeed have important typological characteristics in common with Turkic – numerous attractive features typical of the Turkic languages. The same is true of other western Iranian languages, especially the Kurdish ones. As noted, Modern Persian–Turkic convergence has progressed the furthest in northern Tajik, which Doerfer (1967: 57) describes as a Turkic language in *statu nascendi*. (For Iranian influence on Turkic cf. also Johanson 1986a; 1988c.)

How one assesses *Turkic–Mongolic* relations depends essentially on where one stands on the question of Altaic genetic relations. At any rate, relatively recent convergencies of certain Mongolic languages with Turkic can be observed. These, too, tend to involve the acquisition of attractive – typically Turkic – features.

The origins of countless Turkic-type features found in the Indo-European language Armenian remain obscure as well. Certain phonological and grammatical affinities with South Caucasian languages seem to be substratum-related (Deeters 1926, 1927). As for Western Armenian, after the Turkish conquest of Anatolia it became another minority language subject to prolonged Ottoman influence.

3.2. Phonological features

In most Turkic contact situations the phonological domain has retained attractive structures and/or simplified relatively awkward ones.

The result of global copying into Turkic often shows considerable differences between the original and the copy. The material change includes *phonic adaptation* to the basic code through the substitution of phonetic features. In words stemming from Persian, Arabic, Russian, Chinese, French, etc. certain less attractive phonic segments were replaced by their nearest equivalents in the respective Turkic phonological system. With respect to the vowels, diphthongs were replaced by monophthongs, nasal vowels by oral ones, reduced central vowels by high or low unreduced vowels, and (in later periods) long vowels by short ones. Consonant segments were also replaced (e.g. [f], [v], [ž], [θ], [ts] by [p], [b], [dž], [t], [č]; emphatic consonants by nonemphatic ones, etc.[1]), or they were simplified (e.g. [šč], [pf] to [š], [f], etc.), or they were dropped (e.g. [ᶜ]). As a result of these simplifications, the inventories of phonic segments have remained relatively restricted despite global copying from many different languages. Thus Turkish [h] corresponds to no less than three consonants ([x], [ḥ] and [h]) in words originating from Arabic (usually via intermediary Persian copies).

Frequently the material alteration also entails a phonotactic adaptation which creates more attractive structures. Initial liquids, fricatives and affricates are avoided, awkward consonant clusters are dissolved or simplified by means of assimilation, the voicing of final obstruents is reduced. The syllables of global copies are also classified according to the distinction [± front]. Contrary to widespread opinion, however, intersyllabic sound harmony – particularly vowel harmony – is clearly not one of the initial adaptational measures (see Johanson 1986a, 1989a, 1991e).

Since copying can also result in reproduction, i.e. close similarity to the model, certain sound qualities foreign to Turkic have been adopted and conventionalized as parts of relatively closely replicated global copies (Johanson 1986a). One example of this is [ž] in Iranian loanwords (Tietze 1952: 231).[2] As noted, more recent copies are less adapted than older ones. Phonotactic properties are also reproduced: According to Baskakov (1960: 29), Turkic languages in the Soviet Union developed new syllable types in this way. Wurm (1960: 54–5) emphasizes the strong resistance to such structures, predicting however that this resistance, influenced by systematic and intensive Russification, will diminish and eventually fade away. Similarly, McCarthy (1970: 177) anticipates that, by virtue of its 'great adaptability', Turkish will in future also be able to adopt /θ/ as a phoneme.

In intense, long-lasting contact situations, phonological B qualities, i.e. segments and patterns characteristic of B blocks, can be copied selectively onto A units and become generalized there. This further step towards the phonological convergence of A and B usually takes place under the influence of a large number of conventionalized global copies. However, as mentioned above, according to Jakobson (1938), lexical copies are not a prerequisite of this process. We have also seen that Iranian and Finno-Ugric phonic features that were copied into some Turkic languages have been modified and generalized there (see also Johanson 1993a). Moreover, Soviet Turcologists repeatedly stressed that Russian had exerted a similar phonological influence on certain Turkic languages. I have already noted the limited influence of Arabic in this respect. Menges (1983) considers the phonological opposition front vs. back to be one of the prehistoric Altaic or proto-Altaic influences on Slavic. In his opinion, later Turkic influence on individual Slavic languages was chiefly lexical and hardly altered their structure.

It should be noted, furthermore, that all the phonic restructuring never significantly raised the respective number of Turkic phonemes; the Turkic vowel and consonant systems have always remained relatively limited and simple. Unfortunately, the present study cannot deal with the interesting issues concerning distinctivity and phonemization.

Selective phonological copies, too, often prove to be copies of attractive qualities. Under Iranian and Slavic selective structural influence, especially the typically Turkic and, as was presumed, less attractive vowels [ö], [ü] and [ï] were altered. In urban Uzbek they approach [o], [u] and [i]. In Halich Karaim, [ö] and [ü] have been abandoned.[3] Tajik, in turn, lost its vowel length distinction 'most likely under the influence of Turkic, by the merger of the short and long high vowels and the rounding of long *a*' (Windfuhr 1990: 543–4). Simplifying Turkic influence may also have led to the replacement of the fricative [f] by the plosive [p] in Tajik dialects (see Doerfer 1967: 56). Simplifying Turkic influence on the consonant system of Inner Anatolian Greek is exemplified by the loss of [θ] and [ð] through fusion with [t] and [d] (Dawkins 1916: 44, 76–7; cf. Thomason & Kaufman 1988: 28). The abandoning of distinctions of this kind can be explained by a lack of contrast in B, i.e. the absence of B equivalents.

Phonotactic patterns were also copied, for example from Iranian and Finno-Ugric languages, and adapted to the Turkic systems, altering the combinability and distribution of certain sounds. It is quite possible that attractive Turkic phonotactic patterns also influenced some neighboring languages; consider, for instance, the Persian aversion towards initial consonant clusters.

Sound harmony in the sense of the systematic suspension of phonological features in suffix syllables has proven relatively attractive. Even under strong foreign influence, front vs. back harmony is not relinquished in Turkic. Uzbek, too, has retained it despite heavy Iranicization; for the effects of Iranicization on Turkic languages, see Johanson 1986a. What Uzbek did eliminate were 'marked' vowels such as [ö] and [ü], not however the sound harmony, which eases articulation and delineates word boundaries (Johanson 1993c). Comparable developments can be observed in Gagauz and Karaim. Similarly, among the Tungusic languages, Chinese-influenced Manchu has also preserved its sound harmony.

However, in Uzbek, Gagauz, Karaim and in Turkic languages of other areas (Eastern Turkestan, the Caucasus, Azerbaijan, etc.) *vowel harmony* is less well developed. It can usually not be determined whether the vowel harmony was abrogated under foreign influence (lack of contrast in Iranian, Slavic and other neighboring languages), or, what is sometimes more likely, whether its initial development was stunted. But vowel harmony has also shown its attractiveness in the proactive, 'aggressive' sense. In Inner Anatolian Greek dialects we encounter, e.g., copies of Turkish vowel harmony in Greek inflectional suffixes attached to globally copied Turkish stems, e.g. *bašladá* 'he begins', *düšündé* 'he thinks', *bašladúmi* 'we begin', *düšündúmi* 'we think' (dialect of Sílli; Dawkins 1916: 42–3). This illustrates the possibility for languages, in the course of intense and prolonged contact, to copy elements with which they entirely lack typological affinity.

The overall picture, however, is far from unequivocal. As a result of intense and long-lasting contacts, typologically alien elements, at times even those which would be considered less attractive, have been copied. Occasionally, Anatolian Greek dialects display [ö], [ü] and [ï], albeit usually in lexical copies from Turkish, sometimes, however, in native Greek stems and suffixes. Turkic consonants such as [č], [dž] and [š] have also been copied. In the Halich dialect of Karaim, post-alveolar fricatives have been replaced by alveolar ones: [č] > [ts], [š] > [s], [dž] > [dz], [ž] > [z]. A large number of Turkic languages and dialects in Eastern Turkestan, the Volga region, South Siberia, the Caucasus region, on the Black Sea coast of Turkey, etc. exhibit un-Turkic and relatively less attractive phonetic features, such as glottalization, pharyngealization, nasalization, etc. Many of these cases probably represent substratum varieties characterized by imposition.

Nonetheless, the results of intense and sustained contact are not the same everywhere. As noted above, unattractive structures are not necessarily dropped even when heavy B influence would seem to encourage their deletion. Thus, strong Iranian influence does not always lead to the loss of Turkic vowel distinctions. Kashkay, e.g., which in some ways is more Iranicized than urban Uzbek, still features /ü/ and /ö/ as phonemes. As pointed out earlier, the abandoning of structures due to a lack of contrast in the dominant language (absence of B equivalents) may be less predictable than the adoption of new ones.

3.3. Word structure

With regard to word structure, the typically Turkic juxtaposition, with its transparent morpheme boundaries, has proven to be an attractive combinational feature. Juxtaposition has gained ground in the Turkic languages themselves (e.g. through the regularization of pronominal paradigms) and exerted influence on other languages. Northern Tajik declination has almost entirely converged with that of Uzbek. Contemporary Armenian is essentially a juxtaposing language with a number of irregularities left over from an earlier inflectional system. Western Armenian strongly converges with Turkic inasmuch as it shows only faint traces of Old Armenian fusion (e.g. in the pronouns). As a result of Turkic influence, Cappadocian Greek exhibits juxtaposing tendencies in its declination, e.g. nom.pl. *nék-es* 'girl', gen.pl. *nék-ezyu* (Dawkins 1916: 114). Language-contact-induced tendencies towards fusion, on the other hand, are unknown.

Analytic structures often prove attractive and have replaced synthetic expressions in some foreign-influenced Turkic languages. Karaim has adopted analytic alternatives to some units of the complex Turkic synthetic verb system; e.g. the suffix of possibility can be substituted by a copied Slavic modal lexeme, *možna*, *mogät*, etc. 'one can, one may'. Persian-influenced Azerbaijanian dialects have analytic modal constructions of the type *eliyä bil-* + optative verb (Ritter 1921: 186). Whereas Turkic verbs are negated by means of bound elements, Finno-Ugric, Mongolic and Tungusic employ special verbs of negation. Chuvash has a negative particle *an*, derived from a Finno-Ugric verb of negation, e.g. *an śir!* 'don't write!' (compare *yazma!*); this is a mixed copy (combinational pattern plus global copy). The adoption process was probably facilitated by the circumstance that Chuvash already possessed similar adverbial particles. Copying is thus eased by the existence of analogous A structures. In this case, a free, functionally simple B morpheme replaced its categorically analogous A equivalent while largely maintaining its combinational features. This was accomplished by virtue of the existence of syntactically similar B units with comparable combinational patterns.

The above illustrates the necessity to typologically relativize the notion of attractiveness. Surface structures shared by two languages in contact foster copying. Opposite influence would appear less likely, i.e. the extracting of a bound negative marker from a morphologically complex verb form and its insertion into a language whose word-internal combinational patterns differ, and which normally expresses negation by means of a free particle. The Turkic marker of negation is not merely integrated into the verbal complex, but very firmly attached to it, as it occupies a relatively close position to the primary stem.

I mentioned above the varying degrees of cohesion within synthetic structures and asked whether copiability might be enhanced by greater autonomy and mobility in terms of a less 'firm' attachment of certain units which in principle are bound. The 'loose' affixation frequent in Altaic languages, which applies to plural, case and possessive suffixes, is not a characteristic shared by many languages in contact with Turkic (see 1.4, point 7). Doerfer (1963: 86) assumes that it was precisely this feature that enabled the Altaic case suffixes to spread from people to people.[4]

Turkic analytic structures have also been successful in language contact. For example, the Cappadocian Greek dialect examined by Dawkins (1916: 117) forms the superlative with the prepositive particle *en/an* copied from Ottoman, e.g. *én do méa* 'the greatest'; cf. *en büyük*. Interestingly, Turkic has also occasionally mediated analytic structures not Turkic in origin. The imitation of Indo-European relative clauses produced mixed copies containing globally copied relative pronouns – paraphrases comprised of relative junctors + Turkic demonstrative pronouns, e.g. *ki onda* 'at which' (compare Persian *ki dar ān*). These types of constructions have shown themselves to be attractive in Turkic–Slavic language contact on the Balkans, e.g. the southern Slavic paraphrase *što u njom*, copied from Ottoman, in place of the genuine Slavic *u kojom* (Menges 1987: 33–4).

Bound units with juxtaposing and moderately synthetic structures can also be considered attractive in a typologically relativized sense. Again, analogous substructures in A and B are important. Bound B units are more readily globally copied if the A code possesses an analogous synthetic morphological category, i.e. if equivalent A units exist whose combinational patterns roughly correspond to those of the B unit. Certain Turkic derivational suffixes have been globally copied into numerous contact languages, especially *-či* for agent nouns. By the same token, Turkic languages have copied many foreign derivational suffixes. Karaim takes this process to an extreme. It has adopted an abundance of Slavic derivational suffixes, including diminutive suffixes such as *-ik*.

Analogous combinational patterns facilitate global copying in both directions. For instance, in Iranian Turkic the comparative suffix *-raq* is often replaced by Persian *-tar* (e.g. Azerbaijanian *aztär* 'fewer, less'), whereas Tajik employs Turkic *-råq*. In this regard, however, Karaim again goes beyond normal typological equivalence by copying prefixes whose insertion presupposes un-Turkic combinational patterns. Thus the unit *nay-*, a superlative prefix, is a mixed copy (combinational pattern + global copy). The form *nayfaynraq* '(the) finest' (Pritsak 1959: 332) comprises a copied Slavic prefix which, by means of a copied Slavic combinational pattern, precedes a complex consisting of a primary stem copied from German followed by a Turkic suffix. The abovementioned, typically Turkic reduplicative compound (e.g. *kitap mitap* 'books and the like') has also been adopted by non-Turkic languages in the form of mixed copies; for the Balkan languages including Bulgarian, see Grannes 1988: 12 and 1978. The same is true of reduplicative constructions used to form intensive adjectives, e.g. Turkish *kapkara* 'completely black'; compare, for instance, the Mongolic type such as Khalkha *xab xara* or Tajik forms like *sip-siyå*. All of these cases involve derivational elements that produce only moderately complex synthetic structures and can be employed almost regardless of other bound units.

Not only Turkic word formation units prove attractive. The remaining Turkic nominal morphology comprising declination – the number, possessive and case suffixes – is acquired early and easily, remains remarkably stable nearly everywhere, and is occasionally copied into other languages. This is due in part to the transparency created by juxtaposition, the low allomorphical variation of the suffixes, the circumstance that the suffixes are not very firmly bound to their surroundings, the syllabicity of the suffixes, and the existence of typologically corresponding substructures in the contact languages.

The transparent, regular case system has proven exceptionally stable in contacts with other languages (Slobin 1986: 275). As mentioned, children acquire it early and master it effortlessly; it does not erode very quickly in diaspora situations, does not disintegrate during the initial phases of language loss. For the essentially intact case and number morphology of Turkish children living in northwestern Europe, see Pfaff 1988a and 1988b; Boeschoten 1990a. Apparently, one of the preconditions of stability and attractiveness is also a moderate degree of synthetic structure. Less transparent, more complex systems present more of a problem. The erosion of Turkic nominal inflectional morphology, e.g. case marking, seems to begin typically in *complex structures* (Pfaff 1988b: 71). A moderately synthetic structure can be stable and attractive if it remains juxtaposing.

Hence, global copies of Turkic inflectional suffixes have sometimes become productive in other languages. In the course of the pronounced movement of its case system towards the Turkic type, northern Tajik globally copied numerous suffixes (dative, ablative, locative, equative, terminative). Mongolic has much in common with Turkic in its declination especially, a fact which can be interpreted differently, depending on one's approach to the genealogical issue; see 4.4 below. A certain plural morpheme used in the Volga basin may represent a global copy, although the question of what language exerted the influence is controversial: Some researchers contend that the Volga Bulgar and Chuvash plural morpheme *-säm* is of Finno-Ugric origin (thus Adamović 1983). Conversely, the model for some similar Mari (Cheremis) plural markers (*šaměč*, etc.) is often assumed to be Chuvash (Bereczki 1988: 341).

We come across similar phenomena in the verbal system. Tajik, for example, has nonpredicative verbal nouns in *-miš,* modeled on the identical Turkic aspect-tense suffix. It has been claimed that the considerable Uzbek influence on the Tajik verbal system involved no globally copied Turkic grammatical function marker besides -*miš* and that, rather than being integrated into the verb system, even this one unit has remained a derivational suffix. (For the status of this morpheme in Uzbek, see 2.9 above.) Soper asserts that – despite the convergence of the basic Tajik and Kashkay verbal paradigms with the respective Uzbek and Persian ones – 'not one of the bound, inflectional morphemes used in the donor language was borrowed' (Soper 1987: 419 and 424). He sees in this a confirmation of Weinreich's (1953: 319) claim that this type of transfer is entirely unusual in the languages of the world. This argumentation casually dismisses the Uzbek case morphemes copied into northern Tajik dialects, on the grounds that they function as postpositions in the recipient language. But, whatever accommodation may have occurred here (see 1.3.1 above), there can be no doubt that in this case 'bound, inflectional morphemes used in the donor language' were indeed copied.

Central Anatolian Greek shows occasional global copies of Ottoman case suffixes. In some villages, the influence went much further, and even finite Turkic verb endings were copied, generalized and affixed to the Greek endings, e.g. *koimásti-niz* 'you sleep' (Dawkins 1916: 58, cf. 144). In the history of languages, this certainly represents a rare, unusually far-reaching innovation. However I would hesitate to portray these forms as entire, globally copied paradigms. Contrary to the view engendered by Thomason & Kaufman (1988), these forms do not contradict Weinreich's abovementioned dictum that 'the transfer of a full grammatical paradigm, with its formant morphemes, from one language to another has apparently never been recorded' (Weinreich 1953: 43–4).

We also encounter instances of selectively copied inflectional morphology, where semantic and combinational B features have been transferred onto A material. An example is the Iranian particle *ba, va,* used as a dative suffix in northern Tajik. For the astonishing selective copies of entire verbal paradigms, see 3.4 below.

The copying of combinational patterns can also create synthetic expressions for categories that already existed but were only formed analytically. In the concrete cases of interest to us, the course the influence has taken is not always clear. Nevertheless, we can see, for example, that most modern Mongolic dialects have possessive suffixes and thus converge with Turkic in this respect (Doerfer 1963: 88). By developing possessive suffixes, Persian has also moved closer to Turkic (Modern Persian *ketāb-e man* / *ketāb-am* 'my book'; cf. Turkish *kitab-ım*). Windfuhr remarks on the obvious Turkic influence on Tajik that 'the marked inversion of possessor head noun, *pedar-e man* > [*man*] *pedar* [*-am*] 'my father', has become the unmarked construction in Tajiki, again under the influence of Turkic' (Windfuhr 1990: 544). Armenian, too, has developed suffixed possessive pronouns, e.g. *girk^c-s* 'my book'. Following the Turkic pattern, Cappadocian Greek dialects used possessive suffixes, which partially replaced the analytic possessive construction, e.g. mixed copies such as *wawá-mas* 'our father' (cf. Turkish *babamız*; Dawkins 1916: 121).

One should not, however, automatically read Turkic influence into every tendency to form suffixes. Some Indo-European contact languages, for instance, display diathetic suffixes quite similar to their Turkic counterparts without necessarily having been influenced by them: some examples are the Persian causative suffix *-ān* (as in *xor-ān* 'let eat, feed'; cf. Turkish *ye-dir*); the Armenian causative suffix *-cn-*, which already existed in Old Armenian (Jensen 1959: 36), and the passive suffix *-u-* (e.g. *gə siruim* 'I am loved'; cf. Turkish *seviliyorum*), already present in Middle Armenian (Karst 1901: 292 ff.). As noted, parallel structures in Turkic contact languages may have had a reinforcing effect, e.g. by influencing the frequency of use and productivity of the suffixes in question.

In the documented cases of contact-induced suffix development, either with or without global copies, the end products exhibit an only moderately synthetic structure: the number of syllables remains limited. There is no indication that the highly synthetic structure characteristic of Turkic is attractive. 'Agglutination' per se cannot be considered a generally attractive feature. This vague, traditional term actually implies several features: juxtaposition, highly synthetic structure and predictable (phonologically motivated) morpheme variation. When present to a high degree, synthetic structure actually tends to be unattractive. Interestingly, highly synthetic combinational patterns have never been the object of transfer; the Turkic tendency has never set the direction of change in this respect. When it is claimed that 'agglutination' has a stabilizing effect and that the Turkic languages have managed to maintain their basic typological stability against an abundance of potentially disruptive external influences, in part thanks to a core of 'agglutinative' morphology (Slobin 1986: 288), then these qualities must, above all, be related to the technique of juxtaposition.

Certain placement features appear to play a role with respect to bound units. Inspite of the juxtaposing word formation devices typical of Turkic, the degree of cohesion between the morphemes within the word is considerably greater than within the clause. The Turkic suffixes occupy fixed positions; they are subject to an internal hierarchy and can be divided into distributional *suffix ranks* according to their relative distance from the primary stem. A rank is determined by the number of other ranks that can occur between it and the primary stem; the *innermost* and the *outermost* ranks constitute the extreme positions.

These kinds of combinational features are important structural qualities of the suffix and probably play an essential role in perception as well. The copiability of a bound unit seems to increase when it frequently occurs in outer positions of the morphological word. Suffixes of inner ranks rather seldom occur at the end of concrete word forms and are therefore less frequently copied. Frequent final positioning can make a suffix more salient, possibly encouraging copying. I have already mentioned Turkic case suffixes, which practically always occupy a peripheral position and are hence particularly salient. This principle also applies to the other aforementioned globally copied bound units. In prefixing languages, the initial position in the morphological word has a similar effect. We saw earlier how Karaim, despite its normally suffixing structure, even copies Slavic prefixes. Consider also the widespread feature of reduplication, which is based on the word-initial sound.

It is not always easy to interpret the processes involved in the copying of lexicosyntactic combinational patterns. These patterns seem to be susceptible to copying foremost in units that are less firmly attached, in the sense of the 'loosely connected' suffixes discussed above. This happens to be another feature shared by Modern Persian and Turkic, see, e.g., *bay u būstānhā* 'the gardens and parks' (Jensen 1931: 39); cf. Turkish *bağ ve bostanlar* (Doerfer 1967: 59).

Now, it appears that the order of plural and possessive suffixes was altered in Chuvash as a result of combinational copying. The common Turkic order plural + possessive + case (e.g. *äv-lär-im-dä* 'in my houses') corresponds to Chuvash possessive + plural + case (*kil-ĕm+sän-čä*). This may be a result of Finno-Ugric combinational influence. However, the influence question is closely connected with the question surrounding the origin of the suffix *-säm*.

If *-säm* was originally a globally copied foreign lexeme (whether an adjective denoting 'all, entire' or a noun meaning 'the entirety') that became suffixed in Chuvash or, earlier, in Volga Bulgar,[5] then combinational features originally copied along with this lexeme (such as **säm-i* 'the entirety thereof') may have continued to have an effect. But similar combinational features might naturally also be involved if *-säm* went back to a genuinely Turkic noun, perhaps **sām* '[total] number' (from *sā-* 'count'; compare Hungarian *szám* 'number').

What is the relationship between lexicosyntactic dependence and the modification structure when combinational patterns of the type described are copied? In Turkish *evlerimde* 'in my houses' (plural + possessive + case), the case suffix *-de* (as segment X) depends on *evlerim* 'my houses' (as basic segment Y), while the possessive suffix *-im* (= X) depends on *evler* (= Y). In Chuvash *kil-ĕm-sän-čä* (possessive + plural + case) the lexicosyntactic relations would appear to be altered: the plural suffix *sän-* (= X) is dependent on *kilĕm* (= Y). Does this also change the semantic modification structure? As noted, Turkic tends towards an order in which each suffix modifies the preceding part of the word. An example of this successive, head-oriented modification structure is: *(((ev ⇐ ler) ⇐ im) ⇐ de)*. In *kil-ĕm-sän-čä* the domains of modification seem to have changed, with *ĕm* denoting the possessor of *kil* and *kil-ĕm* being modified by *-sän*, i.e. *(((kil ⇐ ĕm ⇐ sän) ⇐ čä)*. The difference is insignificant; in particular, this modification structure can be said to be no less 'natural' than the common Turkic one. It is not always easy to decide whether the combinational pattern correlates to the modification structure. As for the order between plural and possessive, possible differences between the languages with respect to their concept of plurality may in principle be of importance; that issue cannot be dealt with here.

Generally speaking, it seems plausible that foreign combinational patterns which generate only minimal alterations of the type described are copied with relative ease. In some other languages, by contrast, we find lexicosyntactic patterns seeming to correspond less well to the modification structure: Mongolic and Tungusic have the combinational pattern plural + case + possessive, e.g. Mongolian *ger-üd-tür-minu* (Khalkha *ger-üd-te-min*), Evenki *jū-l-dū-v*. This is also the order in Western Armenian. In these cases, then, the discrepancy between the lexicosyntactic order and the modification structure seems more obvious: Here the case suffix is placed *inside* a complex whose *external* syntactic combinability it signalizes. The history of Turkic language contacts does not offer a single instance of the copying of such less 'natural' combinational patterns.

3.3.1. Verbal inflection

The complex Turkic verb forms present a special problem. Their highly synthetic combinational patterns do not invite copying. As for the morphemes they contain, the majority are rarely copied and are themselves quite impervious to influence.

The circumstance that the verbal morpheme chain does not provide a framework conducive to the interactions of copying is in part due to the mentioned preference for analogous structures. The many bound Turkic morphemes, e.g. for the causative, the passive, possibility, negation, mood and interrogation, correspond to free units in the contact languages, so that the existence of typologically equivalent substructures is improbable. Even languages otherwise participating in the copying process exhibit little common ground here. Turkic and Persian have few similarities in their conjugation systems. No movement towards the complicated Turkic verbal system has occurred that would rival the convergence with the attractive case system. The same is true of Turkic and Mongolic, which have much in common in their declensions. Their verbs, however, share no features indicative of convergence. In this respect, as Doerfer (1967: 63) contends, Turkic and Mongolic 'are typologically (and probably also genetically) worlds apart'; the tense suffixes of the two languages display nothing in common whatsoever (Doerfer 1963: 86). The Mongolic verb generally makes a more archaic impression than the Turkic verb. Below, we shall return to this significant fact and to the question whether these typological differences necessarily preclude common genetic roots. Despite convergent developments, Turkic and Western Armenian also have few similarities in their conjugations; the morphological structures involved are very divergent. The Western Armenian negative conjugation, which is reminiscent of the Turkic type, developed in Middle Armenian, i.e. before contact with Ottoman. Nor does the causative construction go back to Ottoman influence, as it already existed in Old Armenian.

Turkic verbal morphology is not only complicated because of its many categories, i.e. the fact that highly synthetic forms are potentially possible and that the speech chain quite often actually contains relatively complex forms. Its striking tenacity also derives from its extreme structuredness and the partially high degree of cohesion of its morphemes.

As for the suffix ranks, the primary stem is generally followed by suffixes for actionality, diathesis, possibility, negation, aspect, mood, tense, interrogation, person and number. Thus, the innermost ranks consist of suffixes forming secondary verbal stems. As noted, however, actionality markers, which are positioned close to the primary stem and modify the action denoted by the word stem (for inchoativity, intensity, iterativity, spontaneity, etc.), are relatively rare in modern Turkic languages; these old elements have largely been replaced by periphrastic auxiliary verb constructions (post-verbial constructions; see 3.3.2 below). By contrast, suffixes expressing passivity, reflexivity, mediality, intransitivity, causativity, reciprocity, etc. occur in all languages and varieties.

As actional and diathetic suffixes are located close to the primary stem, they rather seldom occur at the end of concrete word forms and are hardly ever copied or replaced. This is more easily accomplished in the outer ranks. For example, the Turkic interrogative particle *mi*, which is often word-final, has been copied into northern Tajik (Doerfer 1967: 25); earlier, I mentioned global copies of the same particle in Central Anatolian dialects of Modern Greek. Characteristically, the grammatical paradigm of personal suffixes copied into Cappadocian Greek also represents the most peripheral rank in the verbal structure. Moreover, the indigenous personal suffixes are peripheral as well, i.e., they have highly analogous equivalence positions. This is another example of typologically relativized attractiveness.

A morpheme might also be less attractive because its allomorphs are not exclusively determined by the phonology. In many Turkic languages, diathetic suffixes close to the primary stem display an otherwise atypical lexical dependence. Irregularities of this kind diminish transparency, obscure the clarity of categories and complicate the relationship between content and expression. These are obviously older forms that have not yet been regularized; the causative suffixes are particularly diverse in this regard (see Johanson 1978a; 1978b). Thus, the suffix immediately following the primary stem, once established in this position, is less likely to undergo phonological or analogical changes. This tendency may also contribute to the circumstance that morphemes of this type are less easily replaced by copies.

While, on the one hand, verbal suffixes close to the primary stem are sometimes less generalized in terms of their form, on the other hand, they display a high degree of semantic generalization and usually denote rather abstract concepts. Above, we saw that Turkic suffixes are chiefly ordered in such a way that each modifies the portion of the word preceding it, and that a suffix's position within the modification structure might therefore be reflected by its rank. Nearest to the primary stem are modifiers that modify the stem itself. As mentioned, the diatheses are not only lexical modifiers but also of central syntactic relevance as they determine the number and the roles of the actants. If the degree of semantic abstraction affects stability at all, then this should be another reason why the units adjacent to the primary stem, whose grammatical content often lies below the speaker's domain of consciousness, are less susceptible to influence. Occasionally, however, these forms can also be semantically dependent on the preceding stem and express less general, more specific, lexicalized meanings (e.g. Turkish *aldır-* 'take care of'; causative of *al-* 'take').

Another important question concerns cohesion within the synthetic structure. Some bound elements of Turkic morphology do not exhibit the kind of 'loose' attachment described above (see 1.4, point 7), and might consequently be more stable. As Doerfer (1963: 86) notes, tense suffixes, e.g., are more firmly attached than suffixes of the nominal morphology and cannot be omitted in paratactic constructions. The latter, however, is possible for nonpossessive subject markers and suffixed variants of copula particles. Diachronically, these were originally free pronouns (e.g. *-sin* < *sän* 'you') and forms of the verb *är-* 'be' (e.g. *ärdi* 'was') that were later suffixed, albeit mostly without achieving the accentability typical of most other suffixes.[6] As we have seen, 'more loosely attached' suffixes also seem to be more susceptible to copied lexicosyntactic combinational patterns. The more firmly attached ones – especially those of the verbal morphology, such as aspectual suffixes – exhibit a more rigid order less open to influence.

The Turkic interrogative marker (*mi*, etc.), which features the characteristics of both a suffix and a particle, is peripheral and very loosely attached. In certain Turkic varieties, e.g. Azerbaijanian and Kashkay, radical morphological simplification has taken place, completely eliminating this interrogative marker. Yes/no questions are merely marked by means of intonation, which is the norm in colloquial Persian. This is another example of influence brought on by the absence of a B equivalent.

Those verbal units that were globally or selectively copied in the most intense of contact situations also mostly possess the features that were described above as facilitating copying. Soper rejects Weinreich's assertion that 'the more explicit pattern' (with 'relatively free and invariant morphemes') (Weinreich 1953: 41) is usually copied and argues that 'both Tajik and Qashqay have acquired the major grammatical distinctions of the donor-language paradigm, no matter how explicit the morphemic representation was' (Soper 1987: 411). I do not agree with this view. The verbal paradigms selectively copied into these languages do not even change the respective grammatical system 'towards a less explicit form' in Weinreich's sense; furthermore, they also possess other abovementioned attractive structural features.

In summary, we can say that units located near the primary stem, such as Turkic causative morphemes, possess several features (mostly in the dimension of cohesion) that might inhibit their engaging in contact-induced interaction. In other languages, these bound and distinct units often correspond to unbound units or elements of lexicalized causatives (e.g. *bil-dir-* ≈ *let know, inform*), whose copies are less easily inserted into a highly synthetic, juxtaposing word structure. This is especially true of proximity to the primary stem, by virtue of which the respective unit rarely appears at the end of the word. The suffixes are not 'loose' in the sense described under 1.4, point 7. In addition, the position of the unit correlates to a close semantic connection with the lexical stem. The sentence-syntactically central, rather abstract grammatical content may also have a conservative effect. Allomorphic irregularities that have not yet been leveled contradict the principle of a 1:1 relationship between content and expression (Johanson 1978b). It is true that causatives, too, have been renewed in quite a few Turkic languages, i.e. they have been reinforced and clarified when their distinctiveness was threatened, e.g. by phonological developments (Johanson 1978a).[7] Nevertheless, the Turkic causative has remained a fairly stable category. For one thing, lexicalizations have not developed in such large numbers that the productivity of the morphological causative processes would appear to be at risk (cf. Bybee 1985: 19).

3.3.2. Postverbial constructions

Through the periods of Turkic language history known to us, we can observe a growing complexity of the morphological verb due to processes of grammaticalization and the suffixation of free lexemes. As noted, the suffixation process typically passes through intermediary stages, such as enclitics, units with suffixed variants, unaccentable, loosely attached, nonharmonic suffixes, etc. Recent developments of this kind have occurred in the area of postpositions, primarily, however, in the verb. Boeschoten must be alluding to this phenomenon when he states that 'one basic tendency of the diachronic development has been an increase in the degree of agglutination, particularly in verb inflection' (Boeschoten 1990a: 141).

The expansion of the synthetic structure by means of the successive incorporation of a lexeme into the syntactic chain of an adjacent lexeme begins with frequent collocation and conventionalization of the combination. This process is connected with a semantic generalization of the secondary unit; its content becomes broader, less specific. This does not necessarily imply semantic 'fusion', whatever is meant by the term, but merely a connection that lets the content of one unit modify the content of the other. Nor does the degree of formal integration – ranging from the loosest connection to complete incorporation – directly reflect the degree of semantic evolution. Such parallels merely represent a certain tendency and should not be taken for absolute in an attempt to harmonize or simplify the processes involved. Whether a category is expressed synthetically or analytically is also not determined by its position in the modification structure.

A development of this kind visible in many Turkic languages is that of the postverbial construction, i.e. the combination of a verbal lexeme with a following grammaticalized verb whose function is extremely generalized. The verbal lexeme typically appears in a converbial form. These complex verbal constructions usually denote actionality, e.g. phase specification. As a rule, both semantic elements, the lexical and the grammatical one, are expressed by free units that have not yet fused into one word. Nonetheless, these types represent a kind of intermediary stage on the way to suffixation. In some instances the expression has already reached the stage of lexeme + suffix, in others a merger into a single lexeme has additionally taken place (*alip käl-* > *äkkäl-* 'bring', etc., of which *al-* 'take', *käl-* 'come').

Postverbial constructions are based on a limited number of verbs whose normal predicative potential bars them from being further expanded. A combination as in *Ali yazıp duruyor* 'Ali is continuously writing' (from *yaz-* 'write' and *dur-* 'stand') constitutes a single predication; *duruyor* does not express a content of its own, but is only a grammatical form element that actionally modifies *yaz-*. Morphosyntactically, the second verb is the head of the first; in terms of the semantically relevant syntax, however, it modifies the preceding actional phrase. Thus, restructuring above all implies a reversal of the modificational relationships – the transition from a sentence-hierarchic to a word-hierarchic head-orientedness, from the 'leftbranching' clause to the 'rightbranching' word: from ((*yaz-ıp*) ⇒ *dur-*) 'stand writing' to (*yaz-* ⇐ (*-ıp dur-*)) 'continuously write' (see 1.4, point 21 above). However, similarly complex verbs can also be formed paratactically, i.e. with both the primary lexeme and the postverb in corresponding finite forms, e.g. *yazar durur* 'writes [and] stands' > 'is continuously writing'.

Actional postverbs modify the content of the preceding actional phrase descriptively, phase-specifically or perspectively. Postverbial constructions also generate aspect-tenses (see Johanson 1976a; 1976b; 1991g; 2000c; etc.), with the converbial suffix constituting part of the predicator, e.g. Altay Turkic (Oyrot) (*baz-* ⇐ ((*ip otur*) *di*)) 'he was leaving'. In this way, finite forms have developed that have, e.g., renewed the high-focal present or the perfect tense, for example *yaza turur* 'he stands there writing' >> *yaza* 'he is writing' or *yazıp turur* 'he stands there having written' >> *yazıp* 'he has written' (Johanson 1991d).

An Anatolian dialect described by Demir (1992) presents a fascinating phenomenon: Forms such as *ya'zip duru* 'he is continuously writing' (actionality) and *yazi"p duru* 'he is writing' (aspect-tense) are distinguished by means of intonation only. A construction such as *yazi"p durudu* 'he was writing' is to be analyzed as stem + intraterminality + anteriority, i.e. (*yaz-* ⇐ ((*ip dur-u[r])du*)) = standard Turkish *yaz-ı-yo-r-du*.

The combinational patterns of the postverbial constructions prove to be relatively attractive and have obviously become widespread as a result of language contacts. They are found in several older Iranian languages; Benzing (1954) points them out in Khwarezmian, which disappeared in the thirteenth to fourteenth century. These patterns are particularly abundant in contemporary northern Tajik. There, participial forms (preterite stem + *-ä*) are combined with a limited number of verbs performing various actional functions, e.g. *bäråmädän* 'come out', cf. Uzbek *čiq-*; *dådän* 'give', cf. *ber-*; *didän* 'see', cf. *kòr-*; *firiståmdän* 'send', cf. *yubår-*; *giriftän* 'take', cf. *ål-*; *guzäštän* 'go through', cf. *òt-*; *måndän* 'stay', cf. *qål-*; *pärtåftän* 'throw', cf. *tašla-*; *räftän* 'go', cf. *ket-*; *šudan* 'become-', cf. *bol-*. The various constructions of this kind, e.g. *šudä räft* ('becoming' + 'went'), *xurdä did* ('eating' + 'saw'), *kitåbrå xåndä baråmäd* ('reading the book' + 'came out') are undoubtedly selective copies of Uzbek models, e.g. *bolip ketdi* '[suddenly] became' ('becoming' + 'went') and *yeb kòrdi* 'tasted' ('eating' + 'saw'), *kitåbni oqip čiqti* 'read the book through' ('came out reading'). See, for instance, Borovkov 1952; Rastorgueva 1952, 1964; Doerfer 1967; Perry 1979; Soper 1987.

Mongolic also has similar patterns; e.g. Khalkha Mongolian developed the completive actional marker in *-čxa* relatively late: *ide-* 'eat', *ideji orxi-* 'throw while eating' > *idečxe-* 'eat up'. Among the Finno-Ugric languages, Mari uses postverbial constructions similarly to the neighboring Turkic languages Chuvash and Tatar (see Serebrennikov 1960: 180, 271). Turkish patterns with *dur-* and *yat-* were copied into Anatolian Greek. Dawkins comments: 'The use of *durmaq* 'to stop' and *yatmaq* 'to lie' to express continuous action is transferred to the corresponding Greek verbs' (Dawkins 1916: 199); he then presents examples from various Inner Anatolian Greek dialects, e.g. *érxumu ki kásumu* (dialect of Sílli) 'I am continually coming' (literally 'I come and sit'). Instead of a pattern employing the converb, this is evidently a complex verb of the mentioned paratactic type, in this case modeled on the pattern *gälir otururum 'I come [and] sit'.

As certain heavily Persian-influenced Turkic languages demonstrate, postverbial devices can also be lost. The loss of the *-ip* converb in Kashkay was accompanied by the erosion of the postverbials (Soper 1987: 396 ff.). The same is true of Khalaj: There, following colloquial Persian custom, the use of converbs is largely avoided (Doerfer 1988a: 130).

The Turkic postverbial constructions may be relatively recent forms. They occur less frequently in earlier known developmental stages than in later ones; even today they are rather sparsely represented in certain peripheral languages (e.g. Turkish). At least, they are unlikely to constitute old common Altaic linguistic stock. The many Tungusic actional markers do not fit very well into the patterns described above. In this context, Benzing (1953b [1988: 49]) remarks that even if one managed to identify some of them as cognates, the overwhelming majority would defy this analysis.

The Turkic postverbial combinational patterns may seem complicated and therefore unattractive. However, one should not overlook the fact that in their initial developmental stage they constitute an *analytic* method. A postverb such as -*ip dur*- functions as an extension of the verbal stem, carrying the remaining necessary grammatical morphology. Not even at later stages of grammaticalization do postverbs necessarily generate overly synthetic structures.

Since postverbial constructions are actional modifiers, they partially supplement and replace the old synthetic actional markers. Diachronically, one might suspect a connection between the decrease in old actional markers – long having been bound elements following the primary stem – and the development and spread of postverbial constructions.

In the sentence as in the word, units that operate together also tend to be located next to each other; cf. the first 'Behaghelian law', postulating that that which belongs closely together mentally is also placed closely together (Behaghel 1932: 4). The order of morphemes within a word may be the reflection of an earlier sequence of words within a sentence; cf. e.g. Givón 1971; Vennemann 1973. However, one should not regard such tendencies as absolute, along the lines of the recently popular motto that 'today's morphology is yesterday's syntax'. Morphology is subject to various kinds of structuring and is far from being entirely explicable as petrified clausal syntax. Yet, it may often be true that proximity to the primary stem of the word reflects earlier proximity to the verb within the sentence. Turkic postverbial constructions indicate that suffixes modifying the lexical stem may go back to free units that, prior to their incorporation, stood near the main verb and denoted actional concepts. The old actionality suffixes, too, may have once evolved from analytic constructions of the postverbial construction type. True, a connective element, such as a converbial suffix, is missing here; however, such an element can also be lost in the more recent postverbial constructions. In Khakas, for instance, formal changes have at times gone that far, e.g. *pas sal-* 'write down' ('write' + 'lie down' < **bas-ip sal-*); for the endingless deverbal adverb in Khalaj, see Doerfer 1988a: 134 ff. We shall return to this circumstance and to the fact that the Tungusic languages have retained numerous synthetically formed actional expressions, in connection with a number of diachronic issues.

Limited contact-induced interaction in the area of verbal inflection – the fact that not much is copied from or into Turkic – means that the very existence of the complicated, extremely elaborate Turkic verbal morphology can be seen as a sign of genetic continuity. As noted, a language may be so deeply influenced that its genetic origins are no longer discernible, i.e. that adoption + maintenance can no longer be distinguished from imposition + shift. No element of Turkic seems to be so stable that its retention would prove membership in the 'genealogical tree'. Nonetheless, next to similarities in the basic lexicon, systematic correspondences (or traces thereof) within the verbal morphology provide persuasive evidence of genetic relatedness to genuine Turkic languages: material and semantic similarities of the morpheme categories, corresponding allomorphic variations and preserved complex combinational patterns. A convincing argument for genetic continuity is when several elements known to be quite unsusceptible to influence are retained *together*.

Even in Karaim, which has otherwise succumbed to profound influence, the Turkic verbal system has remained essentially intact (Zajączkowski 1932; Csató 2000). In the Volga basin, home to complex copying and substratum processes, Chuvash, in some ways a peculiar language, has similarly and without exception retained the Turkic conjugation system and its patterns (see Johanson 1976b). I believe this circumstance to be an unmistakable sign that Chuvash is not a heavily Turkicized language, but a language belonging to the

Turkic genealogical tree (Benzing 1959: 696), even if it exhibits traces of Finno-Ugric imposition (Johanson 2000b).

The complex combinational techniques of the verbal system constitute one part of the Turkic language system that is mastered with difficulty and susceptible to disruption. Experience would lead us to expect simplifications in substratum dialects. In situations of language erosion, e.g. involving Turkish immigrant children[8] or the initial phases of language shift among adults, it seems to be this system precisely which is more prone to reduction than, say, the nominal inflection. Detailed investigations are lacking in this area. Nevertheless, it would appear that simplification is manifested, for example, by the reduced usage of certain categories (e.g. the indirective) and the avoidance, restructuring or simplification of certain morpheme complexes (pluperfect, conditional, forms containing negative and interrogative particles, etc.). Languages such as Karaim and Chuvash do not display much simplification of these complex structures.

3.4. Grammatical categories

In intense and prolonged encounters between Turkic and non-Turkic languages, the copying of semantic and combinational qualities has led to various changes in grammatical distinctions and categories. Often the given contact languages possessed otherwise quite unsimilar grammars. Sometimes the results are altered functions of pre-existing A units brought on by B influence. Sometimes they constitute the creation of new A forms patterned after the functions of B units.

Not only can distinctions develop or change due to copied combinational patterns, they can also disappear. When they do, a restriction to categories present in both contact languages takes place. This often commences with the reduced use of A categories absent in B, which, due to the lack of contrast, are felt to be superfluous. Mostly, the more arbitrary, semantically 'redundant' parts of the grammatical system are susceptible to this kind of erosion. However, the loss of categories does not always lead to a simplification of the A system. It has consequences – especially when semantically relevant categories are involved – for the functional load of the remaining categories and may also be compensated for by means of complications in other areas.

The Turkic languages display certain basic grammatical content-categories that, despite all diachronic developments, have remained remarkably stable inasmuch as they have been either subject to little change or renewed through the creation of new forms. The categories in question are semantically essential ones with a high degree of abstractness and applicability. Slobin (1986: 288) considers the fact that certain central and closely interacting concepts have remained stable and constantly been reformulated to be one of the main historical tendencies of Turkic. In a number of contributions, I have called attention to the formal renewal, e.g., of basic aspect-tense categories (Johanson 1971; 1991c; etc.). This mostly involves the perspective (viewpoint) notions of *intraterminality* (observing an event between its outer limits) and *postterminality* (observing an event after its relevant outer limit), the notion of *focality* (actional concentration on the intraterminal or postterminal viewpoint) as well as several cardinal categories based on these notions, e.g. more or less focal 'present tenses' and 'perfects'. For these notions and terms, see, *inter alia,* Johanson 1971; 1994; 1996a; 2000c. As noted, aspect-tense-mood-systems play a central role in terms of a language's semantically relevant syntax.

With respect to these categories, we can observe or presume certain convergent developments between Turkic and several of its contact languages. Menges (1983; 1987) considers ancient Altaic influence on Slavic (before the latter differentiated into individual historical languages) to be responsible not only for considerable losses in the verbal morphology, but also for the rise of a 'definite' vs. 'indefinite' opposition, which, he contends, resulted in the 'perfective' vs. 'imperfective' opposition of the Slavic verb. The formal aspects of the morphologies of the Persian and Turkic conjugation systems exhibit few correspondences; their conceptual aspect-tense-mood systems, on the other hand, show noticeable similarities, although these similarities cannot be attributed to concrete contact-induced influences. By contrast, there is clear evidence of a significant Uzbek impact on the Tajik aspect-tenses and moods.

We have seen that certain grammatical distinctions may be attractive because they are semantically essential, are abstract and cover a broad functional area. Examples of semantically relevant, communicatively rich functional categories are the Turkic forms of the evidential dimension, in which the speaker qualifies the event in terms of his or her knowledge or awareness of it (see 1.4, point 26 above). Indirective verbal categories (for indirect reference) – such as the indirect postterminal forms in *-miš or -gän* (e.g. Turkish *gelmiş* 'has (apparently) come') – signalize a special type of evidential modification. Such distinctions also exist in several languages neighboring on Turkic.

Thus the Bulgarian verb has indirective forms deriving from strong early Turkic substratum influence (imposition) and/or adoption from Ottoman in the course of long and intense contact (see Johanson 1971: 304–5; Bazin & Feuillet 1980; Grannes 1988: 13–14; Johanson 1996c and 1998a). Georgian perfect forms, too, have functions resembling those of the Turkic indirect postterminals (Vogt 1971: 191–2). The same is true of the Kurdish perfect forms (Bakaev 1973: 186). The Western Armenian perfect *kərer em* 'I have written' also has indirective nuances (Feydit 1948: 132); we shall briefly return to the question of their origin – possibly a result of Iranian influence – below.

The Persian perfect (*raft-e ast* 'has gone') also acts as an indirective simple past tense (see, e.g., Boyle 1966: 66–7). This applies to Afghan and Tajik Persian as well. Indirectivity is not restricted to the perfect, but rather, as is the case in Turkic, exists in other forms of the past, e.g. the imperfect *mi-raft-e ast* 'was apparently going'. Indirective forms already appear in early Modern Persian prose texts, most of which come from the East. Windfuhr observes: 'Their appearance in early texts, as well as their reappearance in contemporary standard Persian of Iran, can /.../ be explained by interference from Turkic /.../' (Windfuhr 1990: 544).

Here, once again, Tajik goes to extremes; the connection between the indirective semantic shift of the perfect (and other forms), and

Uzbek is obvious, e.g. *hämi roz åmädäs* 'he seems to have come today'. Turkic signals indirectivity not only in anterior forms; the indirective copula particles *iken/ekan* and *imiş/emiš* in Turkish and Uzbek, for example, are temporally indifferent. In this respect, too, Tajik closely follows the Turkic pattern: the form *mi-räft-ä äst* 'has already become tense-neutral' (Windfuhr 1990: 544).

Another example of pre-existing Tajik units taking on altered functions under Turkic influence is the future participle in *-äni* (cf. Uzbek *-måqči*). However, new Tajik forms that imitate the functions of Uzbek units have also emerged. In sum, what we find here is the extraordinary case of the copying of entire paradigms. Soper even postulates that — with the exception of the subjunctive, optative and imperative forms – 'the Tajik verb system has been modified so as to replicate nearly the entire Uzbek verb system' (Soper 1987: 90[9]). This gives renewed relevance to the question whether a language can in fact copy a structure so abstract as a paradigm, in other words, a complete system of distinctions: 'can a language "borrow" an inventory, and not just elements from that inventory?' (Soper 1987: 283.)

Tajik copies from the Uzbek aspect-tense system are in part based on *-gi* participles onto which features of the Uzbek *-gän* participles have been transferred. In this way, Uzbek influence has also led to the development of presumptive forms, e.g. *räftägist* (< *räftä-gi äst*) 's/he would seem to have gone, must have gone'; cf. Uzbek *ketgändir*, (spoken) Turkish *gitmiştir*. Other aspect-tense units are based on the verb *istådän*. One method of high-focal ('progressive') present tense renewal is the replication of the Uzbek pattern *-ib tur-ib-di* (converb + *tur-* 'stand' + converb + 'is') in the form *-ä iståd-ä äst* (participle + *iståd-* 'stand' + participle + 'is'), e.g. *kitåb-rå xånd-ä iståd-ä äst = kitåb-ni oqi-b tur-ib-di* 's/he is reading the book'. The existence of such forms also causes the functions of the less focal present (*mekunäd* 's/he does', etc.) to become more similar to those of the Turkic 'aorist' (*yapar*, etc.). The nonanterior forms in *-gi + äst* are said to convey presumptive nuances as well (Kerimova 1966: 223); accordingly, Tajik *xånä räftä iståd ägist* 'he must be on his way home' would compare to, e.g., Turkish *eve gidiyordur*.

Central Anatolian dialects of Modern Greek displayed at least one aspect-tense form resulting from Turkic influence: a 'pluperfect' consisting of aorist + copula of the 3.p.sg., apparently patterned after the Turkish type *geldim* (*geldin,* etc.) *idi* ('I came' + 'it was') (Dawkins 1916: 61, 147).

Turkic aspect-tense systems have been subject to considerable foreign influence as well. Kashkay is remarkable in this respect. It has copied the most important distinctions of the Persian verbal paradigm and has thereby changed considerably (much like northern Tajik). Commenting on the Kashkay aspect-tense-mood system, Soper even states that 'in many respects it corresponds one-to-one to the verb system of the donor language, Persian' (Soper 1987: 349). Thus we have a further example of the copying of entire paradigms.

A great number of exile varieties clearly evidence that even the essential categories of aspect-tense systems can succumb to influence. The Modern Greek spoken in the United States tends to abandon aspectual differentiations, a phenomenon which is attributed to the lack of contrast in the dominant language, English (Seaman 1972: 147 ff.). Many observers concur that the second generation of Turks living in Germany show signs of a reduction ('impoverishment') of the rich Turkish aspect-tense system. For example, use of the postterminal-indirect finite form *-miş* has diminished, a form lacking an equivalent in the German verbal system.

As repeatedly stressed, the Turkic case system has remained exceptionally stable. The advantages of this system, which is a central one in terms of the semantically relevant syntax, lie not only in its formal features, discussed above, but also in its loose-knit functionality (few distinctions, few specific relations, broad functional areas). The northern Tajik case system has closely approached the Turkic one. Among the Turkic case categories, on the other hand, the genitive has proven weakest, i.e. the most susceptible to influence. Its relative dispensability undoubtedly stems from the fact that in Turkic it is not a case governed by verbs, but rather functions in nominal phrases. (For genitive subjects and their susceptibility, see 3.5.4 below.) Thus in Uzbek the genitive has merged with the accusative; compare the similar situation in northern Tajik. In turn, the loss of the genitive in Yakut may have been prompted by Tungusic influence. Several similar phenomena in non-Turkic languages may also be contact-related. By dropping its nominative suffixes, Modern Persian has at least moved closer to Turkic. The older Mongolian differentiation between the nominative and indefinite case is blurred today; thus Mongolian, too, has approached Turkic (Doerfer 1963: 88).

We observe influences of a more subtle kind in the area of 'specificity'. Whereas Bulgarian and other Balkan languages display the contact-induced innovation of distinguishing definiteness by means of articles, no Turkic language has systematically developed a definite article. At times an increased use of demonstrative pronouns (*bu*, *o*, etc.) occurs; cf. the instances where Coman *ol* is used like an article (in the Codex Comanicus, compiled in the fourteenth century) or the circumstance that in Karaim religious texts which slavishly adhere to their Hebrew originals, a definite article (*ol* or *ošol ol*) renders Hebrew *hā*. Drimba (1973: 56) contends that the existence of a definite article is absolutely excluded in Turkic languages (cf. Johanson 1976c: 590).

On the other hand, marking of the direct object to signal 'specificity' has proven an attractive feature. One of the ways Modern Persian converges with Turkic is that nonspecificity remains unmarked, i.e. is expressed by the nominative. Like Turkic, Persian does not formally signal definiteness. Formerly, the Turkic accusative marking was considered to be just such a signal; however, Johanson 1977 already showed that rather than indicating 'definiteness', the accusative marking signals 'specificity'. Modern Persian *rā* (< *rādi* 'because of') presents a similar case, the earlier assumption being that it denoted 'definiteness' at least on direct objects. As Windfuhr remarks, this 'until recently' prevailing opinion must be revised: 'What is marked by *rā* is not definiteness, but topicalisation or specificity' (Windfuhr 1990: 534). The two languages are conspicuously similar in this respect. Both the Turkic accusative and Persian *rā* are compatible with expressions of 'indefiniteness' such as Turkish *bir* 'one' and Persian *-i* (< *aiwa* 'one'). Compare, e.g., *xāne-i āteš zadand* = *bir ev yaktılar* 'they burned a house down' with *xāne-i-rā āteš zadand* = *bir evi yaktılar* 'they burned a [certain] house down'. Northern Tajik has particularly closely reproduced the Uzbek specificity distinction.

In many Inner Anatolian and Pontic dialects of Anatolian Greek, the indefinite direct object is in the nominative; in some dialects the definite article is restricted to definite object forms. According to Hovdhaugen (1976: 148), these developments could be a result of Turkish influence. The same is probably true of an early Pontic Greek tendency to additionally mark subjects already marked by the definite article with the accusative.

Persian has also moved closer to Turkic in terms of the concept of plurality. In both languages the singular is an 'indefinite number' (Doerfer 1967: 59), meaning that an unmarked noun can refer to the singular or plural, e.g. *asb* = *at* 'horse, horses'. In Old Persian and in early Modern Persian, this generic use was limited to nonhuman referents (Windfuhr 1990: 541); in contemporary Modern Persian it has become generalized. Compare *Man ketāb lāzem dāram* with Turkish *Bana kitap lazım* I need a book/books'. Correspondingly, both languages use the plural in similar ways. The Turkic plural individualizes countable referents (*at-lar* '[individual] horses'; cf. *asb-hā*); on uncountables it acts reinforcingly (*su-lar* 'large amounts of water'; cf. *āb-hā*); see Johanson 1977.

As described above, the copying of combinational and semantic B features onto A units can also generate new distributional classes in the form of word classes. Turkic languages in which the syntactically defined word class of adjective is less distinct as a morphological word class than in some contact languages globally copied Persian, Arabic and Slavic elements to create explicit adjective forms, *-ī*, *-oviy*, *-skay*, etc. This pattern was also applied to create corresponding markers from Turkic material, e.g. the Turkish neologistic suffix *-(s)el* mentioned above. It is often asserted that certain Russian-influenced Turkic languages similarly tend to develop the adjective as a morphological word class by assigning the function of adjective formation to nominal derivational suffixes such as *-li*, *-lik*, *-siz* and *-gi* – replicating the pattern of Russian suffix classes. However, selective copying of this kind has not created a new word class, but, at best, more firmly established the adjective as a morphological category, thus increasing structural correspondences with certain non-Turkic languages. Examples of globally copied elements denoting other categories absent or not systematically represented in Turkic are lexical feminine forms such as Ottoman *muᶜallim-ä* 'female teacher' or Karaim *dost-qa* 'girlfriend'.

Grammatical gender is one of the less essential, semantically relatively empty distinctions. It is often dispensable as it can be eliminated without compensation. The role that Turkic played in connection with the loss of grammatical gender in Persian and Mongolian is still unclear. Older Mongolian still had a gender distinction (*ke'ebi* 'she spoke', *ke'ebe* 'he spoke'), which has disappeared in the modern Mongolic languages (Doerfer 1963: 87–8). Similar developments in Persian, where the Old Iranian distinction between masculine, feminine and neuter has vanished, have contributed to its typological convergence with Turkic. The loss of gender distinctions in Anatolian Greek was obviously brought on by Turkish influence (Dawkins 1916). All of these cases clearly represent simplifying changes. Experience has shown that gender systems are subject to considerable instability in exile situations. For the difficulty US Greeks have determining the genders of Greek nouns, see Seaman 1972: 176.

The personal suffixes of the verbs can also be eliminated under foreign influence. In the language of the Yellow Uyghurs and in Salar, both spoken in Chinese environments, the personal suffixes, and with them the distinctions between the persons as well as between singular and plural, have virtually disappeared from the finite verbs. But even this loss does not involve a semantically essential category. Personal suffixes are the most peripheral units of the verbal inflection and, as subject markers, represent the first actant of the predication, signaling its person and number. If the first actant is realized as the subject in the sentence, the personal suffix agrees with it, and therefore merely conveys redundant information. In the absence of personal suffixes, the subject compensates for the loss of information, e.g. Yellow Uyghur *men parmas* 'I do not go', Salar *men alïr* 'I take'.

Turkic language contact history presents not one case of an inessential, ineffective grammatical category being copied. Some

Turkic languages, specifically northeastern Turkic (Yakut, Tuvan, Tofan, Shor, Khakas, Altay Turkic, etc.), Turkmen and Bashkir dialects show an 'inclusive' vs. 'exclusive' opposition in the 1.p.pl. imperative. The inclusive is the marked form and usually takes the shape exclusive + personal element of the 2.p.pl. Contrary to certain assumptions, it is unlikely that these complicating and rather ineffective distinctions were copied from contact languages. Schönig (1987: 212) doubts they were, but in view of their formal disunity does not entirely exclude the possibility that the category was copied relatively late, at a time when the imperative paradigms had already begun to develop in different directions. This opposition may also be an old phenomenon that was lost relatively early in the majority of the Turkic dialects. It does not (any longer?) exist in East Old Turkic and Old Uyghur. Mongolian, too, has largely abolished its old distinction between 'exclusive' and 'inclusive' in the verb and seems to have converged with Turkic in this respect as well (see Doerfer 1963: 87).

3.5. Syntactic combinational patterns

Copies of syntactic combinational patterns occur on all syntactic levels and are often extremely successful. Well-known examples of the considerable impact of Latin on European languages are, e.g., constructions imitating the *accusativus cum infinitivo*, absolute constructions, and perfect forms modeled on the pattern *habeo* + postterminal participle. For the influence of German within the Hanseatic language contacts, see Ureland 1987; cf. Johanson 1989a. The syntax of Finno-Ugric languages such as Finnish and Hungarian has been heavily influenced by Indo-European. Moreover, the languages of the Balkan areal have been copying and spreading one another's syntactic combinational patterns for centuries. As stressed earlier, selective syntactic copying often occurs rather systematically, a single change frequently entailing others.

The degree of foreign influence on the syntax of the older Turkic literary languages is controversial. Certain translation texts are extreme, 'for the sake of the greatest possible accuracy stick[ing] closely to the original, all too often at the expense of the language into which the translation has been made' (Menges 1968: 182). The Old Uyghur translation literature already appears to mirror many foreign patterns. Some researchers even claim that the texts of the important Coman literary monument, the Codex Comanicus (fourteenth century), represent maladroit word-for-word translations. Others such as Drimba are of the opinion that Coman syntax is not particularly un-Turkic and that parallels of nearly every syntactic deviation can be found in other Turkic languages (Drimba 1973: 187; cf. Johanson 1976c). Particularly strong influence is visible in Karaim Bible translations, where 'the word order is exactly and literally that of Hebrew' (Menges 1968: 182). Some Turkic languages with a more extensive literary tradition, such as Chagatay and Ottoman, were subject to foreign influence from the outset.[10] Over the past century, the syntax of standard Turkish as used, e.g., by the mass media has been more heavily influenced by European languages (at first by French) than is commonly recognized. Russian has exerted a corresponding influence on a great number of eastern Turkic literary languages.

Copies of Persian syntactic combinational patterns have played a major role in many Turkic languages (see, e.g., Menges 1949; Reichl 1983). Many of them display old Persian influence that has been reinforced by newer, European (French, Russian, etc.) influence. In the relations between Uzbek and Tajik, the syntactic influence also runs in both directions. Next to Karaim, Daco-Rumanian- and Russian-influenced Gagauz syntax is considered to be extremely de-Turkicized (Pokrovskaja 1978; Menz 1999). According to Hetzer (1983: 26 ff.), the higher structural levels of Gagauz have been heavily affected by contact and follow the patterns of the surrounding Indo-European languages, whereas the Turkic character has been preserved on lower levels such as phonology and word structure. In oral contacts with, e.g., Bulgarians and Macedonians, many Balkan Turks have copied syntactic combinational patterns which are expressed by Turkic material (Pokrovskaja 1977).

Nonetheless, the issue of the Turkic languages' susceptibility to syntactic influence has remained controversial. Baskakov (1966: 23) believes that the syntax is relatively stable throughout: even in Gagauz and Karaim, he sees the typological change as being limited to partial shifts in no way infringing on common Turkic norms. The present state of knowledge allows only conjectures concerning numerous potential old contact-related phenomena. Menges (1983; 1987), for instance, assumes that certain syntactic constructions in Slavic, e.g. the use of the genitive with the negated object, are the results of old Altaic influence on those languages.

Below, we shall take a more detailed look at the exchange of syntactic qualities between Turkic and various contact languages. The picture which emerges is that, on the one hand, genuine Turkic syntax exhibits a large number of cumbersome features. On the other hand, the order of units within the syntactic chain of the Turkic sentence often very directly reflects semantic dependencies and thus comes very close to a 'natural' constituent structure.

Occasionally, syntactic similarities between Turkic and non-Turkic languages can be attributed with a great degree of certainty to a specific source of influence. This is the case, for example, when the Turkic type of predications indicating possession [possessor + genitive +] possessed item + possessive suffix + 'exists' appear in Iranian languages. In colloquial Persian they constitute an alternative to 'have'-predications, 'as long as no true possession is implied' (Windfuhr 1990: 535). In Tajik they are well attested, e.g. *puläm häy* 'I've got money' ('money-my is'), cf. Turkish *param var* (Borovkov 1952: 169). This is undeniably a copied Turkic pattern. In many other cases, however, it is impossible to trace the similarity back to influence moving in one or the other direction. Consider an example from the causative syntax: In Western Armenian, as in Turkic, when the causative is formed from a transitive verb, its first actant takes the dative case. Whether this widespread phenomenon (cf. French *faire faire quelque-chose à quelqu'un*) is contact-induced cannot be determined, especially since it already occurs in Old Armenian (Jensen 1959: 146).

The abovementioned pattern of comparison may represent a similar case, namely standard of comparison + ablative + property compared (in the basic form), i.e. X-from big = 'bigger than X'. This pattern appears to have enjoyed sweeping success; we find it in a number of languages in contact with Turkic. In one of the Western Armenian comparative patterns, the standard of comparison takes the ablative, while the property compared is optionally preceded by the adverb *aveli* 'more' (like *daha* in Turkish). Hovdhaugen (1976) suggests Turkish influence here. Modern Persian employs the preposition *az*, corresponding to the Turkic ablative, Bulgarian the preposition *ot*. Cappadocian Greek dialects show the typical Turkic pattern, e.g. *etá ap etó méγa ne* = 'this from this big is', which Dawkins compares to *šu bundan büyüktür*: 'In this the Turkish system is visible; the Greek άπ, άς replaces the Turkish abl. ending -*dan*' (Dawkins 1916: 116). All the same, patterns of this kind are so widespread that direct Turkic influence need not have generated them in each case. Grannes (1988: 15) observes that Turkic influence on the comparative constructions of the Balkan languages is unverifiable.

Sometimes, however, a pre-existing alternative construction is reinforced by foreign influence, while the frequency of use of the unsupported alternative diminishes accordingly. This is another example illustrating that the attractiveness of a language's means of expression is typologically relativized. Apparently, analytic structures are given preference over synthetic ones in this respect as well. Western Armenian (like Old Armenian before it) has the comparative particle *kan* 'as'. However, the colloquial language also employs the pattern described above, i.e. ablative + basic form of the adjective. Use of the latter would appear to have been at least greatly fostered by Turkic influence. An example of syntactic reinforcement by analogy that runs in the opposite direction is found in the occasional, similarly increased use of the analytic Hungarian construction, comparative form + *mint* 'as', at the expense of the synthetic construction, case (adessive/ablative) + comparative form. This phenomenon is visible among Hungarians living in linguistic surroundings where analogous constructions act as reinforcement, e.g. German *größer als Peter* = *nagyobb mint Péter* 'bigger than Peter'.

We have noted that agreement marking is relatively limited in Turkic; thus the adjective attribute and determiners show neither case, number nor gender inflection, e.g. Turkish *bu mavi kuşlardan* 'from these blue birds'. When adjectives are globally copied from languages whose adjective attributes are marked for agreement, frequently a single inflected form is selected and generalized, e.g. the nominative singular masculine form of Russian adjectives in some of the more eastern Turkic languages (Altay Turkic *social'nïy naukalar* 'social sciences'). We have also seen that the loss of morphological categories often involves agreement marking, a phenomenon that, due to its semantically inessential, redundant nature, is relatively unstable and can be eliminated without compensation. Whether contact-induced or not, such processes as a rule also lead to grammatical simplification. Several languages in contact with Turkic have given up earlier agreement marking on the adjective attribute and now have uninflecting generalized adjective forms. It is often impossible to judge whether these are selective copies of attractive Turkic patterns. Loss of agreement marking occurs in Persian, Mongolian, Western Armenian etc. Number agreement had already been dropped in Middle Persian. Doerfer contrasts the literary Mongolian nominal group *xo'as sayid ökid* 'pretty, noble girls' with Khalkha Mongolian *gua saịn oxid*, whose adjectives are as unalterable as Turkic ones (Doerfer 1963: 87; cf. Benzing 1953a: 3). While the Old Armenian adjective was usually inflected for case and number, Western Armenian has been simplified in this respect. Adjective agreement was also abandoned by many Inner Anatolian and Pontic dialects of Greek. In the Cappadocian dialect described by Dawkins, the adjective is nearly unchanging: 'This invariability of the adjective is a Turkism' (Dawkins 1916: 115).

A further example of limited agreement marking in Turkic is the circumstance that after cardinal numbers the singular is used instead of the plural, e.g. Turkish *üç kuş* 'three birds' (Johanson 1971: 32–3). Here again, Persian (since Middle Persian), Mongolian and Western Armenian converge with Turkic. Compare, for instance, older Mongolian *tabun kö'üt* 'five sons' with Khalkha *tawan xü* (Doerfer 1963: 87; cf. Benzing 1953a: 3). But contact-induced influence does not always lead to simplification. The semantically irrelevant feature of number agreement is also easily copied. Thus, frequential copying may result in the increased or reduced use of number morphemes. Under foreign influence, e.g. in exile situations, the use of number after cardinals can shift in either direction, depending on the situation. Among her Turkish informants living in Germany, Yıldız (1986: 105–6) notes a strong orientation towards the German plural system (*üç kız kardeşlerim* 'my three sisters', *ilk iki seneler* 'the first two years').

Concerning the linguistic specification of actants and other entities, tendencies to simplify compete with tendencies to clarify. East Old Turkic often had the freedom not to express referents that were apparent from the context or situation. In many standardized Turkic languages, this liberty has partially been replaced by pedantry – the principle of clarity usually prevailing over simplicity. Selective copying takes place in this area, too, especially in the pronominal syntax. Turkic makes rather limited use of anaphora to denote actants whose referents are recoverable from the contextual-situational conditions, e.g. Turkish *Geliyor* '[He, she, it] is coming'. As a rule, discourse introduction requires explicit signaling of the referent concerned: a preverbal subject pronoun usually introduces a new topic.

With regard to anaphora, language contact frequently results in over- and undermarking. Frequential copying may increase or inhibit the use of anaphoric units. Initially, this only violates the norms of discourse pragmatics. Many languages in contact with Turkic exhibit more explicit pronominal referencing than Turkic. Certain Anatolian Turkish dialects, which are probably varieties of the shift type, exhibit overmarking most likely resulting from Greek influence. For the dialects of the Trabzon region, see Brendemoen 1993. Turkish children and adolescents growing up in northwestern Europe are prone to an increased use of anaphora, evidently under the influence of the surrounding majority languages. Yıldız' informants, second-generation Turks living in Germany, often employ personal pronouns that are not necessarily required in Turkish (Yıldız 1986: 105); Aytemiz (1990: 75–6, 129 ff.) also registers this common 'type of error'. Some of Menz' informants also tend to employ a pronominal subject even when they are not introducing new information or establishing contrast to a different first actant (Menz 1991: 46–7). Such usage can mislead the listener, e.g., into expecting a change of subject. A tendency towards 'hypercorrectness' is also visible in the use of pronominal objects, e.g. *Polisler /.../ onu başkanı sandılar, sonra onu /.../ hapis ettiler* 'The police thought he was the leader, then they locked him up' (Menz 1991: 46–7). Pfaff has discussed similar phenomena in a number of contributions (e.g. Pfaff & Savaş 1988). For the discrepancies in the use of pronouns between children growing up in the Netherlands and their peers in Turkey, see Verhoeven 1987 and Schaufeli 1990.

3.5.1. Word order patterns

Word order patterns have often been copied in Turkic language contact situations. The leftbranching sentence syntax mentioned above is one of the fundamental typological features of the Turkic languages. According to this pattern, the syntactically subordinate constituent is preposed to the head. Thus, dependents precede their heads. The predicate core (usually a predicate verb) occupies the final position, complements and free adverbials preceding it: adjective, genitive and participial attributes in front of their heads, adverbials of degree ahead of their adjectives. The typical word order in many contact languages of Turkic greatly differs from the Turkic pattern. In Persian, attributes follow their heads; in Slavic languages and in Greek the predicate verb as a rule precedes the direct object, the genitive attribute follows its head, etc.

Before concluding that foreign influence has resulted in copied word order patterns, however, one must take account of the language-internal variational possibilities already present. Every language has several ordering patterns interacting and competing with one another. Simplistic divisions into, e.g., SOV and SVO languages do not mirror linguistic reality. In Turkic, too, which, as noted, is listed among the 'rigid' so-called SOV languages (Greenberg 1966: 79), the final position of the predicate core constitutes the norm which is systematically deviated from. In the colloquial language especially, these deviations fulfill sentence-perspective functions (Johanson 1977; Erguvanlı 1984). Thus, for example, the predicate core does not always occupy the final position in the sentence. However, it should be kept in mind that the presence of this kind of language-internal variation by no means rules out the possibility of foreign influence. On the contrary, it can facilitate influence if analogous features are involved.

There are numerous unmistakable examples of copied combinational patterns. For the older Turkic languages, see *inter alia* Menges 1968: 182 ff. In Turkic spoken-languages in the Balkan areal, constant copying has restructured the word order to such an extent that, for example, complements and free adverbials generally follow the predicate core. Gagauz, in particular, imitates the rightbranching order of the surrounding Slavic languages and Romanian (Dmitriev 1939; Hetzer 1983: 28). Although Afghan Uzbek has largely maintained the head-final word order pattern, its adverbials mostly follow the predicate core as well (Reichl 1983: 492). Similar influence from German is said to be perceptible in the Turkish spoken in Germany (Yıldız 1986: 104). Of all Turkic languages, Karaim is once again the most extreme: the predicate core generally occupies the same positions as in the respective Slavic contact languages.

Indefinite articles and numerals are always prepositive in Turkic. In the spoken languages, the adjective attribute is also relatively stationary, while the genitive attribute sometimes enjoys greater mobility. We find postpositive attributes in some Turkic translation texts, such as the Hebrew-influenced Karaim Bible translation. Spoken Karaim also has postpositive genitive attributes typical of the Slavic languages.

A number of Turkic languages have copied Persian so-called *iżāfat* constructions, in which the head is connected to the postpositive attribute by *-i* and both constituents are usually of Arabic or Persian origin. Yet cases where such constructions have penetrated Turkic spoken languages involve not so much copied combinational patterns as they do whole globally copied complexes that are treated as lexical or phraseological units. Mixed *iżāfat* constructions only occur when the overall extent of copying is extreme. Doerfer (1988a: 99) illustrates how they are gradually encroaching on Khalaj, e.g. *balu'x-i diyär* 'other village'. In her materials from the Azerbaijanian urban dialect of Tebriz, Kıral (1991: 15) registers only one mixed copy, namely *balï γ-e maxsus* 'the special fish [a goldfish characteristic of the New Year's celebration]'. By contrast, prepositional elements have been copied that were, so to speak, extracted from Persian prepositional phrases containing *iżāfat* constructions. Thus, for instance, the entire prepositional phrase *dar mored-e* 'in respect of' is applied to Turkic material: *dar mored-e bu* 'in respect of that' (Kıral 1991: 14). Numerous Turkic languages have long displayed similar reinterpretations of partial *iżāfat* constructions; according to current knowledge, one such case is the type *ba^{c}ż-ï*... 'a part of...' > *bazï* 'some, certain' that also combines freely with Turkic nouns (Turkish *bazı çocuklar* 'certain children').

The reverse is true in northern Tajik, which, under Turkic influence, has developed prepositive attributes. For example, the combinational pattern of the genitive construction: genitive attribute (= possessor) + basic constituent (= possessed item) + possessive suffix 3.p. (*muallim-ä kitåb-äš* 'the teacher's his/her book') has obviously been copied from Uzbek.

The head-final word order of Turkic proves quite stable. Whether as a result of Turkic influence or not, this feature clearly possesses attractiveness in surrounding languages as well. Persian is an SO language also, and the unmarked word order in all sentences is subject-adverb-object-verb (Windfuhr 1990: 532). The adoption of head-final order has often led to simplification through *stabilization*. While in Old Armenian the predicate verb occupied a relatively free position, in Western Armenian it is usually sentence-final – probably due to Turkic influence. Attributes tend towards similar simplification. In Old Armenian, genitive and adjective attributes were pre- or postpositive; in Western Armenian they can only be prepositive. Since this development already commenced in Middle Armenian, however, it can hardly be attributed to Turkic influence, see 4.2 below. In Old Mongolian the adjective attribute could be postpositive; in modern Mongolian it is exclusively prepositive (Doerfer 1963: 87). So Mongolic and Turkic have converged in this respect too. In Anatolian Greek, the genitive attribute now also occurs only before its head. If B influence generated these phenomena, it has led to underdifferentiation, i.e. a reduction of the previously richer A word-order devices. Therefore, it is conceivable that immigrant Turkish, due to the influence of German, which allows far fewer word order variants to modify the sentence perspective, does not take advantage of the rich possibilities that Turkish offers in this regard (Johanson 1993b).

Quite a few details remain to be worked out in connection with copied word order patterns. The order of constituents is often susceptible to influence, without the latter having especially far-reaching effects on the grammatical system. Whether a head is pre- or postposed may depend on its complexity, among other things; cf. Behaghel's (1932) 'Gesetz der wachsenden Glieder', i.e. the tendency to order constituents according to their increasing complexity.[11] Excessive weight is often avoided in the prefield of the head. Hence, head-final languages tend to place certain constituents postpositively; in other words, they allow a certain amount of 'constituent leaking' beyond the head. A long, successive development of this kind might eventually, as has happened in Karaim, lead to a considerable relaxing of the head-final word order. As Dik states: 'The Prefield is universally less hospitable to complex material than the Postfield. Prefield languages may thus be expected to possess strategies for relieving the Prefield of excessive complexity.' A conceivable result might be 'a Prefield-derived SVO language, i.e. an SVO language which still has a number of Prefield properties' (Dik 1989: 350–1). Karaim seems to be a Turkic language which fits this description.

Pre- and postpositive relational particles present a special case. As mentioned, in line with its leftbranching sentence syntax, Turkic employs postpositions. As morphosyntactic heads, they occupy the final position in their postpositional phrases and function as grammatical relators. Postpositions belong to the stable elements that are continuously renewed by means of the grammaticalization of independent lexemes.

As for the position of the relational particles vis à vis their nominal groups, one pattern can hardly be said to be more attractive than the other. In a head-final language, postpositions are more natural and more probable (for SOV languages, see Greenberg 1966:

79), yet by no means compulsory. Persian, for instance, places the predicate core in the final position while, at the same time, using prepositions. One type of word order change does not necessarily entail others. The transition from prepositive to postpostive relative clauses (see below) is not, as Greenberg's (1966) typological laws suggest, automatically connected with a transition from postpositions to prepositions or from pre- to postpositive attributes. In light of the evolution of prepositions in Karaim, Reichl (1983: 492) considers whether in the future Afghan Uzbek will evolve in a comparable direction. Based on the unpredictable sociolinguistic factors involved in linguistic development, however, he ultimately dismisses this consideration on the grounds that it is speculative and unfounded.

In spite of typologically relative attractiveness, postpositional languages occasionally copy prepositions and prepositional languages, postpositions. (For the structural equivalence of pre- and postpositions, see 1.4, point 21 above.) The development from prepositions to postpositions is characteristic of several Near Eastern languages (Vogt 1945: 223). Turkic influence has been assumed to have caused Western Armenian to develop in such a way. However, postpositional constructions are already found in Old Armenian. Their subsequent development may have been reinforced and intensified through contact with Ottoman (Hovdhaugen 1976: 154).

Karaim has copied prepositional patterns, in particular from Slavic. It features globally copied prepositions that govern Turkic cases, *do* 'before', *po* 'through', etc., e.g. *po dunyanï* 'through the world'. Slavic combinational patterns have also been copied so that Turkic postpositions are now used prepositionally, e.g. *uturu t'än'rig'a* 'towards God'. This process takes place in part by grammaticalizing the possessed item in genitive constructions with postpositive genitive attributes, e.g. *alnïnda X-nïn* 'in front of X' (= 'on the front side of X'; normal Turkic *X-nin alnïnda*). Other languages also offer examples of this kind of copying that proceeds regardless of surface-structural incompatibility. Recall, for example, the abovementioned prepositions copied from prepositional phrases containing *izāfat* constructions and applied to Turkic material, e.g. *dar mored-e bu* 'with regard to that'.

At times, we observe transitional stages from post- to prepositional patterns. Thus, the copy of a B phrase containing a B relator might be assigned an A relator. In Afghan Uzbek dialects, prepositional phrases exist which comprise both a globally copied Tajik preposition with case government and postpositive Uzbek case marking (Boeschoten 1983). This type is also common in spoken southern Azerbaijanian. A globally copied Persian prepositional phrase can be inserted into a slot requiring a Turkic case marker or postposition, e.g. *xårič äz šährdä* 'outside the city'; cf. Persian *xārej az šahr* Kıral 1991: 14). Here, the prepositional phrase is combined with a partially homofunctional postpositive marker from A. Not the entire copied preposition is functionally redundant, but only the locative component assigning it an adverbial role. Hence, this is not a duplication of function. An example with a copied prepositional phrase and a Turkic postposition is *dar hadd-e özünä g'örä* 'according to his own limitations'; cf. Persian *dar hadd-e xodeš* Kıral 1991: 20). The structural properties of the B original have been so extensively replaced that the copy can function with ease in the A grammar.

Analogous structures are found in northern Tajik varieties, e.g. expressions such as *äz såät-i du-dän* 'from two o'clock on' (Rastorgueva 1963: 78). Here, the Uzbek ablative *-dan* is used together with the Iranian preposition *äz*. In their own fashion, these structures contribute to Uzbek–Tajik convergence (cf. Boeschoten 1983). But in this case, the process moves in the opposite direction: A Turkic ablative function marker has been copied, rendering that component of the indigenous preposition functionally redundant which allows the preposition to assume an adverbial function. Thus, different copying processes have produced similar results.

3.5.2. Clause subordination

The Turkic syntax of clause embedding employs prepositive infinitizations. The predications destined for embedding as constituent clauses are nominalized or rendered nonfinite in another way, specifically by means of various verbally derived nominal, adjectival (participial) and adverbial (converbial) predicator suffixes. As the latter can also serve as subjunctors, Turkic constituent clause construction is 'synthetic'. Although the predicator suffixes occupy the position of the aspect-tense-mood morphemes within the morphological word, they do not convey the inventory of the main clause predicators, but rather a more restricted specific inventory.

In functional terms, these infinitizations largely correspond to constituent clauses with free subjunctors (conjunctions or relative pronouns and adverbs) that resemble main clauses and are typical of contemporary European languages. Nonetheless, numerous Turkic languages spoken in the vicinity of Iranian or Slavic languages have also long displayed postpositive clauses akin to Indo-European subordinate clauses inasmuch as they are shaped like main clauses (with typical main clause predicators) and equipped with free junctors.

Traditionally this type of clause-combining has been construed as a tendency to imitate Indo-European subordinate clauses, i.e. as copied rightbranching Iranian and Slavic constructions. As illustrated above, it may be possible to speak of them as mixed copies made up of combinational patterns + function words. The geographic distribution of the copies (Turkestan, Iran, the Balkans) clearly points to Iranian and Slavic influence. The occasional doubts whether Turkic constructions of this kind developed from contact with Indo-European languages, in my opinion, spring from an erroneous interpretation of the copying processes concerned.

On the other hand, it would be fundamentally misleading to describe this syntactic influence on Turkic, as has often been done, as the intrusion of subordinative constructions. Turkic is equipped with its own means of subordination that differ from the copies of Indo-European subordinate clause constructions. Below, we shall take a look at some of the restrictions involved.

In several Turkic languages, the repeated copying of combinational patterns has led to the dominance of imitated postpositive subordinate clauses. In some areas, they have greatly repressed the genuine Turkic constituent clauses. For the southeastern European areal, see Pokrovskaja 1977, for the Turkic dialect of western

Bulgaria, see Kakuk 1960, for Afghan Uzbek, see Reichl 1983. As noted, the latter author suspects that 'the imitation of the Persian subordinate clause' prompted the retreat of the corresponding Turkic subordinate constructions; this he terms 'one of the most striking cases of interference in the syntactical sphere in Afghan Uzbek' (Reichl 1983: 490–1). As Comrie (1981a: 85) notes, the minor Altaic languages that evolved under heavy Russian influence display a particularly pronounced tendency to copy Russian subordinate clause types.

Interestingly, prepositive subordinate clause patterns frequently met the resistance of Indo-European-oriented normative grammarians. Soviet Turcologists repeatedly attempted to 'perfect', 'modernize' or 'normalize' the grammar of Turkic languages by increasing the use of Indo-European, i.e. Russian, subordination devices (see, e.g., Baskakov 1960; 1969). I called attention to Eurocentric prejudices of this kind some time ago (Johanson 1975a). More than a few European Turcologists labored under the assumption that Turkic subordinate clause types deviating from those of their native tongues were semantically vague due to their insufficiently 'progressive' morphosyntactic structures. Even today one encounters such attempts to equate linguistic expression with mental processes. Some views maintain that languages develop in this respect from more primitive conditions via increasingly progressive stages until they reach the highest level, represented by the European subordinate clause.

Thus, for example, the language of the Turkic inscriptions is considered to represent a less evolved stage than more heavily European-influenced Old Uyghur.[12] Over time, certain Turkic languages, foremost Chagatay, are alleged to have appropriated subordinate clause syntax equal to the Indo-European type. Hanser (1974: 157), according to whom linguistic development would seem to go from the implicit to the explicit, from the synthetic to the analytic state, does acknowledge that this development has been more or less radically rescinded in modern Turkic literary languages. Nevertheless, he states that at least Gagauz, which he describes as having developed a complete system of explicit subordinate clauses, has reached the possible final stage. This supposedly ideal state, from which, e.g., Yakut and many other Turkic languages are still far removed, inspires the author to pose the hopeful rhetorical question whether Gagauz is developing in a linguistically progressive direction (Hanser 1974: 203).

Furthermore, it is often claimed that the Turkic devices of clausal subordination are unstable for psycholinguistic reasons. In terms of production and perception, they are said to be difficult to process, difficult to acquire and correspondingly susceptible to influence (Slobin 1986). One area where their instability is claimed to be clearly visible is child language acquisition. Boeschoten attests that Turkish clausal subordination is psycholinguisitically complicated: 'the hypotactic clauses of standard Turkish are difficult, relatively speaking, in speech production and reception' (Boeschoten 1990b: 44). Verhoeven & Boeschoten (1986: 247–8) and Schaufeli (1990: 4) observe a reduced usage of nonfinite verb forms in children of various ages compared to monolingual children in Turkey. Menz (1991: 64) also detects among her informants – adolescents growing up in Germany – a preference for shorter sentences with analytic structures, above all in relative clause constructions, less so in converbial clauses.

One difficulty is attributed to the fact that Turkic constituent clauses do not have the 'canonical' clause structure characteristic of main clauses (Slobin 1982). Above, it was mentioned that subordinate clauses deviate from the internal morphosyntax typical of main clauses. As I have emphasized in other works, however, Turkic constituent clauses do possess several 'canonical' qualities (Johanson 1975a; 1975b; 1991c). They are not subject to any specific word order rules as apply, e.g., to English subordinate clauses. Often they resemble main clauses so closely that the only difference lies in the choice of nonfinite predicator. The use of Turkic nonfinite forms is easier, moreover, inasmuch as the inventory of choices is smaller than the inventory of finite verb forms (see Csató 1990).

For a long time, leftbranching clause subordination has been regarded as psycholinguistically unattractive since it allegedly strains the mind more than the rightbranching type. Concerning the production of sentences, Yngve declares: 'It is clear that as regressive structures grow longer, they require more memory; but progressive structures do not' (Yngve 1961: 134). Later, similar disadvantages were discovered with respect to the comprehensibility of leftbranching structures. One of the psychological implications of Turkic sentence structure appears to be that the speaker must plan ahead the sentence together with all its details, while the listener, at times, has to remember long, encapsulated modifications until the element that is being modified is finally mentioned (Johanson 1975b). For the psychological consequences of leftbranching Turkic sentence structure, see also Forster 1966. Nowadays, however, these interpretations are often rejected; Frazier & Rayner (1988), for example, assert that 'left-branching per se does not give rise to substantial processing complexity'.

Yet speakers whose first language chiefly employs rightbranching clause subordination often encounter particular difficulties with what Wendt (1961: 200) describes as sentence constructions that only make sense after the last word has been uttered. He goes on to say that this kind of system makes Turkish an extremely difficult language to learn for anyone whose native language is unfamiliar with such constructions. This trivial fact may also have informed many a European's opinion of Turkic clause subordination techniques.

According to some psycholinguists, what ultimately speaks against the Turkic constituent clause is its synthetic structure. Even Turkic children are said to favor analytic forms, choosing, when possible, analytic paraphrasing in order to avoid prepositive relative clauses.

We shall return to some of these reservations below.

Finally, the purported instability of the Turkic devices of clause subordination is also claimed to be visible in linguistic history. The copying of Indo-European subordinate patterns would thus manifest a tendency towards the analytic construction type. Regressive clause subordination, on the other hand, is believed to be rarely ever copied by other languages. According to Slobin (1982; 1986), the avoidance of the Turkic type of subordination and the successful efforts to emulate the Indo-European subordinate clause type reflect deep-rooted tendencies of Turkic which are firmly based on psycholinguistic principles. In my opinion, this supposed major tendency in the evolution of Turkic languages must be called into question; at the very least, it should be considerably refined and relativized.

3.5.3. Constituent clauses and copied clause-combining patterns

Turkic *nominal action clauses* are based on verbal noun forms (action nouns, verbal abstracts) and can operate as complement clauses, i.e. as actants of a governing predicate core, e.g. Turkish *gel-eceğ-in-e* ('come' + prospective + possessive 3.p.sg. + dative) *emin-im* ('sure' + copula 1.p.sg.) 'of her/his future coming I am sure' = 'I am sure s/he will come'. Now, many Turkic languages have constructions that are held to be alternative expressions modeled on Indo-European patterns, e.g. Turkish *eminim* ('sure' + copula 1.p.sg.) *ki* ('that') *gelecek* ('come' + prospective) 'I am sure that s/he will come', instead of *geleceğine eminim*.

Earlier we also noted the 'short' complement clauses based on verbal nouns (infinitives) unmarked by a personal suffix, e.g. *çalışmak* in *Çalışmak istiyor* ('want' + present) 'S/he wants to work'. Their first actant is referentially identical to the first actant of the governing (often modal) lexeme. Especially in the Balkan areal, where the absence of infinitives is characteristic, this construction is often lacking. Instead, one encounters copied patterns such as 'she wants that she may work', i.e. with final optative modal units. Instead of constructions such as 'to work I began', we find patterns in the sense of 'I began that I may work'. Gagauz, which, under the influence of its surroundings, has adopted the Balkan type of sentence construction plan (without infinitive) (Hetzer 1983: 26), regularly displays complexes such as *bän istäyim qonušim sänin qarïnlän* 'I would like to talk to your wife' (lit: 'that I may talk ...') (Pokrovskaja 1977). Similar patterns are found in the dialect of the Balkan Roma described by Matras (1990), e.g. *ben istedim koyim* 'I wanted to live'. The situation in Persian-influenced varieties is comparable; for instance, Azerbaijanian *istir öldürä* 'he wants to kill [him]'.

Whether the patterns with postpositive clauses are more attractive per se than the prepositive complement clauses is dubious. Consider

Frazier & Rayner's conclusion that leftbranching in itself does not considerably complicate processing – a result which 'completely undermines the hypothesis that natural languages develop discontinuous constituents to offset the (perceptual) complexity of leftbranching constructions' (Frazier & Rayner 1988: 274). It is true that the greater Turkic areal provides evidence of spoken-language tendencies towards a less intensely integrating clause syntax.[13] Nevertheless, the tendencies that exist in certain areas of intense contact to copy prepositive constructions are by no means typical of the main bulk of Turkic languages. Indeed, they are even entirely atypical of most modern standard languages, including standard Turkish. As noted, the production of nonfinite forms is eased by the fact that the choice is limited to a small number of forms. Postpositive constructions can certainly relieve the verbal prefield of overly long, complicated modifications (see below). However, most contemporary Turkic languages do not take real advantage of this psycholinguistically plausible, simplifying function. Constructions of the type Turkish *şunu düşünüyorum ki ...* 'the following is what I think: ...' occur in many spoken languages; but the clauses that follow them are much too modest in length and/or complexity to be comparable, e.g., to constructions such as *I think that ...* Too often, judgments on the difficulty of Turkic complement clauses prove to be the prejudices of non-native speakers. Thus, it is even claimed that in relation to *eminim ki gelecek,* the short and clear clause *geleceğine eminim* is 'the more complicated but true Turkish way of expressing the same thought as that expressed in the other sentence' (McCarthy 1970: 129).

Turkic relative clauses, actor clauses, are based on deverbal adjective forms, i.e. participles, and can function as adjectives ('adnominally', as participial attributes) or as nouns ('nominally', without a nominal head). A construction such as *yanan evler* corresponds to both 'burning houses' and 'houses that burn/are burning' (see 1.4, point 18). In addition, many Turkic languages also display patterns resembling Indo-European relative constructions with postpositive relative clauses, in which the postpositive predications bear main clause predicators. These patterns are usually explained as copies of foreign combinational patterns.

Frequently they are introduced by a general relative particle in the form of either a global copy or an indigenous unit onto which the combinational features of foreign relative particles have been transferred. Occasionally a pronominal or pro-adverbial element (with or without general relative particle) also occurs, signaling referential identity with one of the constituents of the head. As a rule, this process takes place under conditions largely mirroring those of the 'donor language'.

According to the normal Turkic pattern, a first actant which is identical to the referent of the head cannot be expressed by a subject or subject marker, e.g. Turkish *evi* ('house' + accusative) *satan* ('sell' + participle) [*adam*] ('man') 'the [man] selling the house'. In copied patterns, on the other hand, this referential identity is realized by means of relative words (e.g. interrogative words such as *kim* 'who', *nä* 'what', *ani* 'what, which'), cf. Gagauz *Götüreyim o adama, ani evi sattï bana* 'I'll take it to the man who sold me the house' (Pokrovskaja 1966: 136; cf. Menz 1999: 84–91).

If the first actant of the relative clause is not identical to the referent of the head, the normal standard Turkish pattern denotes it by means of a subject marker on the predicator, while the second actant remains unexpressed, e.g. *sattığı* ('sell' + participle + possessive 3.p.sg.) [*ev*] ('house') [the house] that he is selling/ sold'. However, most Turkic languages less distinctly mark relative clauses whose first actants and heads are not referentially identical, using one and the same relative predicator in both cases, e.g. *-gän.*

Conversely, in copied patterns nonfirst actants of the relative clause that are referentially identical to the head are marked by a general relative particle, a special relative pronoun/pro-adverb or a combination of both. The following is an example from the Azerbaijanian urban dialect of Tebriz: *bu sohbät k'i män eliräm* 'this speech that I am making (Kıral 1991: 42). In the next example, from a dialect of the Balkan Roma, the second actant appears as the direct object denoted by a special relative pronoun: *eski konušma ne onlar konušular* 'an old language that they speak' (Matras 1990).

The structure of Turkic relative clauses is regarded as complex, rather nontransparent and difficult to process. This is especially true of Turkish relative clauses, due, for one, to the usually compulsory choice between two different relative predicators. In the speech production of monolingual Turkish children, relative clauses appear late, after age 5, and still remain rare at 8 to 9 years of age; they are often misunderstood in comprehension tests (Slobin 1986). Bilingual children (of the second immigrant generation) also seem to acquire them late (Pfaff 1988a; 1988b).

Structural factors of this type are believed to explain why in the course of linguistic history Turkic relative clauses have repeatedly been replaced by other types. Afghan Uzbek, which has otherwise retained the head-final pattern, appears to have all but lost its prepositive relative clauses (Reichl 1983: 492; cf. Boeschoten 1983: 49). For Khalaj, see Doerfer 1988a: 232. Today in the urban dialect of Tebriz, the use of *-dik* constructions is uncommon and considered strange (Kıral 1991: 37). Similar developments have occurred in other languages typologically related to Turkic; for the displacement of the Dravidian relative participle by a Hindi construction in Gondi, see Sridhar 1978: 205. These phenomena add relevance to the question whether Turkish relative clause syntax will undergo a comparable metamorphosis, e.g. in the contact situation in Germany. All such considerations, however, should not obscure the fact that diachronically the Turkic relative clause type has *grosso modo* remained quite stable.

Turkic converbial clauses, adverbial action clauses, are based on deverbal adverbial forms. As satellites, they can modify predications or parts of predications, e.g. Turkish *gülümseyerek oturdu* 'smiling, he sat down'. Some converbs, particularly the *-p* converb (which in Turkish has the shape *-(y)Ip*) serve the purpose of so-called verb serialization, a process by which predications are 'strung together' in a clause.

Now, many Turkic languages also have combinations of predications that express similar semantic relations but use free junctors. However, the sequence of the predications is reverse and both are marked by main clause predicators. These mostly temporal, purposive and causal combination types are also considered to be copies of foreign patterns. They are present in large numbers in the old high literary languages, Chagatay, Ottoman, etc., in contemporary standard languages such as Uzbek and Azerbaijanian, as well as in all Persian-influenced spoken language varieties; see, e.g., the Uzbek purposive clauses with the junctors *ki* and *tå ki*, copied from Persian, plus optative-imperative predicators, or the temporal clauses with *vaxti* 'as, when', *qabl äz ink'ä* 'before', *tå* 'until', etc. in Iranian Azerbaijanian (Kıral 1991; 2001). Usually a decrease of prepositive converbial clauses is concomitant; for the situation in Afghan Uzbek, see Reichl 1983.

The verb serialization devices of some Turkic languages have suffered more or less heavy losses. An extreme example of this is Kashkay, which has forfeited the *-p* converb along with all of its typical constructions. The loss of virtually all Turkic verb serialization processes is clearly a result of the Iranicization of Kashkay, i.e. the absence of equivalent devices in Persian (Soper 1987: 396 ff.).

In other Turkic languages as well, e.g. in Turkish, the verb serialization devices have eroded. Instead of *-p* converb + head, coordinative structures are more often used to express a close sequence of events; we shall return to this phenomenon. Contemporary Turkish is even said to exhibit an overall decline in the use of prepositive adverbial action clauses. According to Wurm (1987: 44), young Turks less and less frequently use certain nonfinite verb forms that were still quite common in Turkey 50 years ago. He contends that this phenomenon is particularly visible in metropolitan areas such as Istanbul, and attributes it to increasing Western influence (especially of the German [sic] language and culture) on many Turks. A speaker under this kind of influence is allegedly prone to say *odaya girdim ve oturdum* (with a free junctor and two main clause predicators) 'I entered the room and sat down', rather than the traditional *odaya girip oturdum*. Wurm claims that this reduction is particularly prevalent in Turkish spoken in the European diaspora (cf. however Menz 1991: 77) and diagnoses this replacement or limited use of nonfinite forms as a symptom of linguistic simplification.

All testimonies of weakness and decay notwithstanding, Turkic converbial clauses have held their ground well overall. Psycholinguistically, these types do not seem to present very great difficulties. Watters has shown (1987, in connection with the clause-combining theory of Foley & van Valin's [1984] 'role and reference grammar') that temporal converbial forms in *-ince* and *-irken* are already used by 2-year-olds, while *-ip* forms are acquired somewhat later. Forms in *-erek*, however, do not appear before age 9. For the acquisition and use of converbs to express temporal concepts, see also Slobin 1988.

The alleged unattractiveness of Turkic converbial clauses is additionally disproved by the fact that they have played a remarkably central syntactic role throughout language history. This type of converbial clause is characteristic of Central and Southeast Asian languages in general and can be considered a large-area phenomenon. For the copulative converb characteristic of the Altaic languages and for the 'popularity' of deverbal adverbs in the Ural-Altaic languages, see also Fokos-Fuchs 1962: 105 ff. Converbial constructions have proven attractive in the Slavic group as well; Russian in particular shows a predilection for them. Tajik has largely copied the Uzbek mechanisms of verb serialization (see Perry 1979; Soper 1987: 284 ff.); these copies are based on the aforementioned morphological unit consisting of the preterite stem + *-ä* (e.g. *kärdä* from *kärdän* 'do, make'). In Persian the converbial function of this form is quite restricted (see Lazard 1957b: 162).

In my opinion, the Turkic converbs and their related techniques indeed possess attractive features. Soper asks 'whether verb serialization has any inherent attraction over non-serialization, such as uniformity of grammatical marking, morphological transparency, etc.' (Soper 1987: 328). He answers to the negative, asserting that if such a mechanism were attractive, it could be expected to resist influence: the loss of verbal serialization in Kashkay under Persian influence, however, proves the opposite. But Soper's remarks have little to do with the concept of attractiveness applied in the present study. As we have seen, this concept in no way implies that attractive features cannot be lost under strong foreign influence.

Turkic converbs undoubtedly possess a number of advantages. They are monofunctional in that they establish unequivocal relationships between formal and functional classes. While many Turkic predicators can be used individually for several (finite and nonfinite) predication types, in most Turkic languages the predicators of the adverbial action clauses represent clearly defined classes of prototypical markers.

A further reason for the durability of the converbial clauses, I believe, is inherent in their structure. Relatively long and complex converbial clauses are also frequently used in Turkic spoken languages. This circumstance, which from a psychological point of view may seem astonishing, is explained in part by their external structure, which is especially amenable to the requirements of the spoken language. Converbial clauses usually begin like main clauses, they have nominative subjects[14] and closely resemble the main clause form in other ways as well; for instance, they exhibit no specific word order patterns. The speaker can begin a 'canonical' clause, proceed through it normally and not until the end, at the predicator, decide whether to end it as a main clause or continue it as a complex clause by means of infinitization (Johanson 1975b). Von der Gabelentz (1901: 418) already described how this special feature of the Uralic and Altaic languages gives the speaker the possibility to wait until uttering the verbal form to decide whether to end the sentence or to put it into some kind of relation with the following one. This feature explains the correlation between the dominance of converbial clause-combining patterns, on the one hand, and head-final word order, on the other. Thus Turkic converbial clauses do not require any special planning that would cause difficulties in the immediate speech situation.

Yet there is a further essential factor explaining the remarkably long chains of complex converbial clauses in some older or scarcely Europeanized Turkic languages. Successively staggered, long prepositive constituent clauses are only difficult to produce and interpret when they are true satellites, i.e. when they semantically *modify* the given head. Predications that follow one another as narratively equal content units, on the other hand, present a much lesser strain, even when they occur in long chains.

In my opinion, Turkic converbial narrative clause complexes found in older stages of the language are often misinterpreted.[15] There, converbial suffixes are postpositive relational elements with progressive reference, each suffix signaling a semantic relationship with the predication following it. 'Modification' is not structurally coded in these converbial subjunctors, but instead merely constitutes a possible interpretation in certain contextual-situational conditions. In terms of their narrative value, converbial clauses are often equal to their heads. An East Old Turkic sentence such as *qïšlap sü tašɤqaδəməz* does not primarily render 'After we had wintered, we went into battle', but rather 'We wintered and [then] went into battle'. The widespread assumption among Turcologists that the *-p* converb always expresses an attendant circumstance is entirely unfounded. In later linguistic stages, however, converbial subjunctors increasingly tend to semantically modify their respective heads. Many Turkic languages have moved in the direction of modern European languages, where subordination strongly covariates with modification. For example, French and Russian text construction patterns have been copied onto Turkic subordination systems. This development has led to a kind of degeneration of the converbial syntax. Since long chains of prepositive modifying constituent clauses are difficult to process, the clause chains based on converbs have disappeared from the normal registers of many Turkic languages.

In modern European languages, which lack constructions that are catenated according to the Turkic type, text construction patterns with main clause sequences play an essential role in narrative texts. Such patterns have widely been copied into Turkic or reinforced by means of frequential patterns. However, languages employing rightbranching subordination devices can construct postpositive nonmodifying, propulsive (plot-advancing) constituent clauses, whereas the Turkic copies as a rule cannot. It was precisely this kind of function that the narrative clause complexes based on converbs so nicely accommodated.

In some Turkic languages, another method of connecting semantically related (also nonmodifying, propulsive, etc.) main clauses with other main clauses was or still is performed by connectors of the *kim/ki* type. These too are postpositive relational elements that refer forwards, signalizing a semantic relationship with the next predication. It is interesting that their role mostly corresponds to the role of the converbial suffixes discussed above. We shall return to this point.

3.5.4. Implications of the copied patterns

As noted, the word order in nonfinite clauses is less free than in finite clauses. In turn, certain nonfinite clauses allow a choice between a genitive or nominative subject that is motivated by the sentence perspective (often important for the interpretation in respect of specificity), e.g. in nominal action clauses such as *su-yun* ('water' + genitive) *ak-tığ-ı* ('flow' + verbal noun + possessive 3.p.sg.) 'that [the] water flows' versus *su ak-tığ-ı* 'that water flows'.

However, genitive subjects are considered to be an unattractive feature that also causes difficulties during language acquisition. Slobin (1986) notes that clauses containing a genitive subject are difficult to comprehend, and that Turkish children have problems with the case marking when they begin to use subordinative constructions. They are 'reluctant to interpret a sentence-initial noun in the genitive as an agent' (Slobin 1986). The replacement of genitive subjects by nominative ones also occurs in Turkish exile varieties, possibly as an effect of simplifying foreign influence. In the materials collated by Menz (1991) on Turkish spoken by young second-generation Turkish immigrants in Germany, the genitive marking is only omitted in necessitative constructions such as *o* (instead of *onun*) *da gelmesi lazım* 'and he must come'. The author attributes this phenomenon to copied German combinational patterns; in German these kinds of sentences are constructed with the verbs *müssen* or *sollen* and their subjects are always in the nominative (Menz 1991: 37). Note that the same phenomenon occurs as a syntactic innovation in other Turkic languages as well, where the source of possible influence is often obscure; see, e.g., Karakalpak constructions such as *biz* (instead of *biziŋ*) *awïlγa baruwïmïs kerek* 'we must go to the village' (Baskakov 1960: 30). Similar Crimean Tatar relative constructions, e.g. *o közlägän yoldžu* instead of *onïn közlägän yoldžusï* 'the traveler he is expecting', are ascribed to Uzbek influence (Çeneli & Gruber 1980: 42).

Combinational copies employed in sentence construction are occasionally linked to the use of a certain mood. For the use of mood under Persian influence, see Menges 1968: 183–4. Above, I referred to the copies of purposive adverbial clauses with the optative/imperative, common in some Turkic languages; cf. also the use of the conditional, e.g. in generalizing relative clauses such as (*ol*) *kim kälsä* 'who[ever] may come'. These constructions are not held to be genuinely Turkic. In fact, Menges (1983) suspects an old Altaic influence behind the loss of the subjunctive as a subordinative mood in Slavic. In exchange, numerous Turkic languages later copied Slavic combinational patterns linked to specific moods of subordination. Thus in Gagauz the Turkic optative is frequently used like the subjunctive in Bulgarian, e.g. *isterim -äyim* 'I want to X', *var nicä -äyim* 'I can X' or *läzïm -äyim* 'I must X'; cf. Bulgarian *iskam, moga, trjava da* + subjunctive (Pokrovskaja 1977).

In older developmental stages especially, the Turkic languages show few free junctors and, above all, no subjunctors.[16] Menges (1983; 1987) even attributes the absence in Old Slavic of the conjunctions necessary for subordination to Altaic influences. He explains the loss of the Indo-European relative pronoun the same way.

The Turkic languages have also globally copied many Iranian, Arabic, Slavic and other free junctors and used the copies productively (see, e.g., Mansuroğlu 1955). The junctor *ki,* copied from Iranian, is the most widespread of these, serving everywhere as a very general kind of connector with a broad functional scope (Johanson 1975a). These functional properties also apply to Modern Persian *ke*, which seems to correspond to three Middle Persian junctors, *kē* 'who, which', *kā* 'if', *kū* 'where'. Even contemporary Turkish almost exclusively employs copied free junctors: *ne ... ne* 'neither... nor', *çünkü* 'as, for', *gerçi* 'though', *eğer* 'if', etc. As for the Turkic languages under Russian influence, Baskakov describes an 'increase in the number of various auxiliary words, in particular of conjunctions, of which there were remarkably few in the old language' (1960: 30). The same is true of many non-Turkic languages; for the Zyryan conjunctions copied from Russian, see Schlachter 1974. Karaim displays a number of globally copied Slavic junctors, e.g. *i* 'and', *bo* 'for' *nim* 'before', *no* 'but' and *to* 'so'.

A great many selective copies of foreign junctors can also be found in early developmental stages. The Turkic particles *onto* which the respective combinational features were copied were chiefly interrogative pronouns and interrogative adverbs. This phenomenon is already attested in Old Uyghur (Gabain 1950: 19). In several older Turkic languages *kim*, for example, is used mainly as a junctor of relative and complement clauses. Grönbech (1936: 54) construes this early usage of *kim* as a syntactic borrowing from Indo-Iranian. Slobin's claim, on the other hand, that the old Turkic use of interrogative pronouns as conjunctions was brought about 'first under Mongol influence, and then strengthened by Iranian influence' (Slobin 1986: 281) seems unlikely. In numerous younger Turkic languages, such as contemporary Balkan Turkic, various interrogative pronouns and interrogative adverbs operate as junctors. In Gagauz we find *ani* 'that', *angi* 'which', *aniki* 'so that', *acan* 'when', *necinki* 'because', etc.; only a few free junctors were globally copied into this language (see Gajdardži 1981). Karaim has preserved *kim* 'that, because' and employs the particle *da* 'also' as a conjunction of the Slavic type ('and, as'). A large number of Turkic languages under Russian influence use 'relative pronouns' in accordance with combinational patterns copied from that language.

Constructions that appear to be imitated subordinate clauses of the conjunctional type occur in various older Turkic languages such as Uyghur, Chagatay and Ottoman; even today they are typical of the most deeply Iranian- and Slavic-influenced languages. (For Ottoman, see Bulut 1997.) If they are indeed imitations of Indo-European hypotaxis, there are at least significant differences between the originals and their copies. Although some of the globally and selectively copied junctors may constitute subordinative conjunctions in the donor languages, their copies are subject to restrictions in the recipient languages that preclude structural equality. In Turkic, subordinative conjunctions remain 'foreign bodies, inadmissible [...] to the basic structure' (Johanson 1975a: 105). At the same time, the fact that the Turkic copies are not subordinative does not mean that they are not 'Turkic'. By definition they are A elements; it is only certain unreproduced features of the B models that are 'foreign'.

For example, clauses introduced by *kim* and *ki* are not embedded predications in the manner of prepositive Turkic constituent clauses.

For one thing, the latter accompany their matrix predications when these predications are infinitized, i.e. embedded in superordinate predications. The *kim/ki* clauses are not integrated in this way, but instead represent a kind of external relative conjuncts (similar to the Latin *coniunctio relativa*), which, despite even the closest semantic relationship, are not constituent clauses in the morphosyntactic sense. Even as intraposed predications, they remain parenthetical insertions that are not integrated into the Turkic subordination structure.

Even if connective elements such as *ki* and *kim* can be explained as global or selective copies of foreign models, the question remains whether they entered Turkic by way of foreign clause-combining patterns. As noted, a combinational pattern that is the copy of a certain clause-combining type can also encompass a simultaneously copied conjunction. The copying of clause construction patterns containing junctors of this kind may constitute an old language-contact phenomenon. In order to solve these questions, the presumed Indo-European donor languages must also be evaluated. The model conjunctional constructions may already have been 'vague' structures that consequently do not allow us to judge with certainty whether the connector in question had subordinative power, which of the two connected clauses it belonged to, etc. Such problems are familiar from the older developmental stages of many Indo-European languages. In the course of the 'Gliederungs-verschiebung' described by Paul (1909: 299), transitory stages may arise which are difficult to characterize. During such a transition, a particle belonging to main clause 1 serves initially as a 'connecting unit' to main clause 2; then it evolves into a subjunctor, i.e. signals the formal dependence of the second clause and is interpreted as a part of it. At any rate, whenever possible, the features of the presumed models must be taken into account. This applies, for example, to the morphosyntactic features of Persian *ke* clauses. When it is stressed that in Turkic, *ki* is not integrated into the postposed clause (unlike a subordinative *that* or a relative pronoun in English), then it must be added that the same is of course true of the Persian conjunction.

The conjunctional clause types in question may have emerged from a fusion between 'originally' Turkic patterns and patterns acquired later on. All Turkic languages have asyndetically connected predications, with main-clause-external postposed additions (e.g. Mundy's [1955] 'sentence-plus' phenomena) or intraposed parenthetical insertions. These too do not represent subordinations that are integrated as constituent clauses. But it is in these very constructions that a general connecting *kim/ki* element can serve to underline the semantic bond between the predications.

Above, I indicated that connectors such as *kim/ki* have the ability to connect semantically closely related – also nonmodifying or propulsive – predications with main clauses; thus they play roles that can also be assumed for converbial junctors. The latter particles are elements with a progressive referential direction. They stand between sentence-hierarchically independent (and often also narratively equal-ranking) predications, connecting them as junctors. In some ways (in terms of intonation and pausing), they can be interpreted as part of predication 1, although they do not merge with its predicator. Nor have they usually become subjunctors marking the embedding of predication 2 as a constituent of predication 1.

Therefore, the discussed prepositive infinitizations and the post- and intrapositive clauses with free junctors are generally not competing subordination types, but rather, discrete text construction devices that can compete when both are present in the discourse. (We shall return to the pragmatic aspects of this competition.) Of course, this rule does not exclude the possibility of postpositive modifying main clauses evolving into subordinate clauses in a sentence-syntactic system that is radically changing. In Turkic languages relatively faithful reproductions of subordinate clauses of the modern European type can also develop.

Karaim actually has rightbranching clause subordination, with conjunctions and relative words introducing constituent clauses and predicators that show a morphology typical of main clause predicators. Consider the sentence *Tutasen* ('you are holding') *kołunda* ('in your hand') *burunhu* ('first') *jomakny* ('story'; acc.) *kajsy* ('which') *cykty* ('has appeared') *karaj sezinde* ('in the Karaim language') 'You are holding in your hand the first story that has appeared in the Karaim language' (Mardkowicz 1930). This is a rather exact reproduction of Slavic word order and hypotaxis. Compare the normal Turkic word order, e.g. in Turkish *Elinde* ('in your hand') *Karay dilinde* ('in the Karaim language') *çıkan* ('appearing') *ilk* ('first') *hikâyeyi* ('story'; acc.) *tutuyorsun* ('you are holding').

The Karaim situation represents a rare exception among Turkic languages. It can only be explained by prolonged and intense contact or strong non-Turkic substratum or a combination of both. As mentioned, leftbranching clause subordination is often particularly difficult for speakers of rightbranching languages. This circumstance could play an important role in the evaluation of cases where, conceivably, a non-Turkic group shifted to Turkic and the result of their imposition continues as a substratum influence. Even in the case of Karaim, however, it is impossible to distinguish between the results of substratum influence and those of an intense adoption process that occurred in favorable conditions.

3.5.5. Attractiveness of leftbranching clause subordination

Concerning the issue of attractiveness, we have seen that constituent clauses of the Turkic type are often misunderstood, while the advantages of postpositive additions are exaggerated. Thus McCarthy (1970: 129–30) maintains that the use of conjunctions in Turkish 'helps to break up long sentences into subordinate parts'. The introduction of *ki*, he contends, 'has helped to simplify the long, involved sentences of Ottoman Turkish and brought Modern Turkish and many Western languages a little closer together – a helpful step for simultaneous translators and for students, both Turkish and foreign, learning each other's language' (McCarthy 1970: 129). These statements contain several errors. First, it is precisely the Turkish constituent clauses that are true 'subordinate parts' in the sentence. Second, *ki* clauses and similar conjunctional clauses were present throughout almost the entire history of the Ottoman language but have become atypical of the modern Turkish standard language. Hence, not very many modern-day simultaneous translators could have possibly benefited from them.

Leftbranching clause subordination of the Turkic type proves far from unattractive. Even Karaim, like other Turkic languages, has retained verbal nouns, participles and converbs, using them to construct the predicate cores of subordinate clauses. Thus it has not evolved as far as certain other languages which are claimed to have relinquished their native subordinative mechanisms as a result of language contact. Menovščikov (1969: 124 ff.) describes how northern Asiatic Eskimo languages that have copied Chukchi functional words, e.g. conjunctions, have at the same time partially abandoned their own means of subordination, e.g. converbs.

Several languages in contact with Turkic exhibit copied Turkic combinational patterns. The development of prepositive subordinate clauses is a specific example of the typological convergence of Persian with Turkic (Doerfer 1967: 59). Tajik is rather extreme in this regard as well. It has developed an infinitizing clausal subordination system according to the head-final norm, and, e.g., copied several patterns from Uzbek participial and infinitive syntax. Thus the Tajik participle in *-gi* is used syntactically much like the Uzbek *-gän* participle. Apart from postpositive patterns (with *izāfat*), we also find prepositive ones, e.g. *xåndä-gi kitåb* 'the book (that was) read' (lit.: 'the read book'); cf. Uzbek *oqi-γan kitåb*; Benzing (1954) states that the use of the participle in *-dagi* almost completely matches that of the Turkic participle in *-gän*. Prepositive adverbial clauses that correspond to Turkic converbial clauses are already found in Sogdian (Johanson 1993d). They are particularly frequent in modern Tajik. The participle consisting of the preterite stem and the suffix *-ä* has been activated after the pattern of the Uzbek *-ib* converb, and occurs above all adverbially in spoken Tajik, e.g. *kärdä* 'having done'. The use of this form often corresponds to that of the *-ib* converb, e.g. *Väy därrå bästä kūčä räft* 'Having closed the door, he went onto the street' = 'He closed the door and went onto the street' (Kerimova 1966: 227). Benzing also points out that Turkic influence is detectable in Tajik *åmädägiš* 'since he has come'. This form (*-dägi* participle = Turkic *-gän*, *-š* possessive suffix = Turkic *-i*) is equivalent to Kirgiz *kelgäni*, while the corresponding form in other Turkic languages is the converb in *-gäli* (Benzing 1954).

Turkic prepositive participial clauses have also been copied in Anatolia. Kurdish shows mixed copies that are based on the globally copied Turkic modal word *gäräk* 'necessary' and have replaced older auxiliary verb constructions. These copies developed after an older verb denoting 'must' (reconstructable as **wiyān* for Kurmanji) had been enlisted for the future tense and lost its necessitative meaning (Cabolov 1978: 66). Western Armenian not only forms 'analytic' constituent clauses with conjunctions and relative pronouns, but also Turkic-type 'synthetic' ones based on participles and verbal nouns. For instance, Western Armenian has a prepositive relative clause construction clearly influenced by Turkic, e.g. *ajs dun-ə šin-oγ džardarabed-ə* 'the architect building this house' (Feydit 1948: 126; literally 'the this house building architect'). Here, the Armenian present participle is used similarly to Turkish *-en*; cf. *bu evi yapan mimar*. Also possible are relative clauses with the participle in *-adz* + head + possessive subject marker, e.g. *dzn-adz deγ-s* 'the place where I was born' (cf. the similar widespread Turkic pattern, e.g. Kumyk *tuwγan yerim*), *kats-adz küγ-s* 'the village where I am going/went'. When this type of relative clause has a subject, it takes the genitive, according to the Turkic pattern, e.g. *im des-adz dun-s* 'the house that I see/saw'. Moreover there is a converb that is constructed of a nonfinite form, the infinitive, by means of the instrumental and is used like the Turkish *-erek* converb, e.g. *krelov* 'writing' (cf. Turkish *yazarak*). Even Anatolian Greek, whose relative clauses are usually postpositive, occasionally displays prepositive relative clauses of modest complexity, e.g. *kʼát ira perí* 'the boy I saw' (relative subjunctor + 'I saw' + 'boy'); cf. Turkish *gördüğüm oğlan* (Dawkins 1916: 201).

It would seem, then, that leftbranching clausal subordination is only cumbersome when the constituent clause is rather complex. A more general, natural principle might be at work here, whereby longer elements tend to be postposed. Above, I considered whether the position of the dependent might be related to its degree of complexity and whether excessive weight in the prefield of the head is generally avoided. By postposing heavy constituents, a head-final pattern can be successively relaxed. In terms of the placement of constituent clauses, Karaim has developed into a 'postfield' language which has preserved certain 'prefield' traits. By the same token, languages using prepositive adjectives, but normally displaying postpositive relative clauses can also admit uncomplicated prepositive relative clauses under foreign influence. Pre- and postpositive relative clauses differ significantly from one another in many languages, the prepositive ones in particular usually being less complex.

Thus the often-voiced contention that prepositive constituent clauses with clause-final junctors are generally unattractive is far from convincing. On the contrary, for example, the prepositive type of connected direct speech closed by free junctors of the type *teyin, diän, dep, diye*, etc. 'saying' has actually proven extraordinarily attractive. It is attested in almost all Turkic languages since the Old Turkic period – one exception being Kashkay, which, under intense foreign influence, has relinquished its converbs and therefore has no counterpart to this type. As noted, these units are quotation particles used to convey speech and thought. Secondarily, however, they also function as subjunctors marking purposive clauses and action-motivating causal clauses, cf. the above-cited Turkish optative satellite clause *ev yansın diye* 'so that the house will burn' ('the house will burn saying'). The evidently 'genuinely Turkic' subjunctors placed at the end of such subordinate segments have remained very stable in the Turkic languages; they are also retained in exile situations (see Boeschoten 1990b: 42 ff.). In addition, they have obviously been the models of selective copies into other languages. For the late Sogdian item *w'β-ky* 'saying', which is used much like Old Uyghur *tep*, see Sims-Williams & Hamilton 1990 and Johanson 1993c. In Tajik, *guftä* is used to end direct speech, according to the pattern of the Uzbek converbial form *deb* 'saying' (Doerfer 1967: 56).

Chapter 4

GENERAL AND AREAL TENDENCIES

4.1. General tendencies

I shall now briefly summarize the main results so far. Many of the Turkic characteristics described in the first chapter are identical to the generally attractive features which were discussed in connection with their relative significance for the susceptibility to influence in contact situations. Turkic languages display a remarkably large amount of presumably attractive qualities. The examination of Turkic–non-Turkic convergence, based on examples drawn from different areas, has shown that convergence almost always involves simplification, i.e. the acquisition of those features which are relatively attractive in each case. This applies to the foreign structural elements copied into Turkic as well as the Turkic elements serving as models for copying. Even in the most prolonged and intense of contact situations, for the most part attractive qualities have been copied and unattractive ones replaced.

In language contacts, the Turkic structure appears to have often set the direction of change. This is quite possibly the reason why Turkic has frequently been so aggressive and expansive even though its speakers have not always had the sociopolitical upper hand. But one must beware of jumping to conclusions. Even if the straightforward cases of Turkic–non-Turkic convergence primarily involve the acquisition of features considered typically Turkic, the resulting structural similarities cannot always automatically be attributed to copying from Turkic.

When dealing with these issues, one must avoid circular reasoning. Much convergence lies too far in the past, which prevents us from determining the source of potential influence. But even in more recent and better documented instances, the question of foreign influence is in principle often difficult to answer. If generally attractive qualities indeed exist, and if Turkic exhibits a conspicuously large amount of them, then it follows that it will often be impossible to distinguish Turkic influence from general developmental tendencies. Even in cases where the diachronic linguistic processes are otherwise relatively transparent, it is often difficult to determine whether individual simplifying innovations constitute copies from contact languages or so-called 'drift' and 'spontaneous convergence'. In the latter case, many linguists speak of the effects of a 'universal grammar', attributing the preference for less 'marked' structures to congenital biological mechanisms. They contend that innovations are essentially the result of certain universal natural processes not being suppressed.

What then is influence and what is 'spontaneous' convergence when Persian or other languages move towards the Turkic linguistic type? Is Turkic being copied or are general tendencies independent of Turkic at work? Not every development towards 'easier' structures can be explained as the result of copying. Some developments, for example, are so widespread that it is impossible to trace them back to a certain origin and interpret them as the undeniable results of contact. Frequently, general principles seem to come into play to the effect that linguistic developments result in structures that are so natural, easy to produce and perceptually salient that they occur independently of one another in a wide variety of languages. Many of the processes portrayed above through which non-Turkic languages appear to have typologically approached Turkic may represent cases of 'natural' convergence with no direct copying involved.

Thus although, for example, the morphological structure of many languages in contact with Turkic has approached the Turkic type, it cannot be irrefutably claimed that this convergence was contact-induced. As noted, morphologically, Persian is an atypical Iranian language: 'it has almost completely lost the inherited synthetic nominal and verbal inflection and their inflectional classes' (Windfuhr 1990: 530). However, this process commenced very early on (in the late Old Persian era). Something similar may be true of the Turkic-like morphological structure of Armenian.

Convergence towards a 'natural constituent structure' may be dictated by universal ordering principles, independent of Turkic influence. Grammatical reductions, such as restrictions on the formal inventory, may go back to erosion tendencies independent of B. Without foreign influence, analytic constructions evolve into synthetic ones, and synthetic constructions are replaced by analytic ones. For example, the Mongolian type *nidün minu* 'my eyes' may have become Khalkha Mongolian *nüdemin* (fusion of head and possessive marker) without Turkic influence. Many other examples were cited above, among them the widespread phenomenon that with causatives formed from transitive verbs the first actant of the transitive verb is expressed by a dative complement. According to Hovdhaugen (1976), most of the Western Armenian morphological and syntactic features reminiscent of Turkic are attributable to independent developments brought on by old inner-Armenian structural tendencies, among them the pronounced 'agglutinating' tendency.

An instructive example is the use of forms of the verbs of speech as quotation particles and subjunctors. Such developments (ranging from forms of the verb 'say' and the like to conjunctions) have taken place independently of one another in a wide variety of languages: in many southern Asian languages, in Indo-Aryan, in Dravidian, in African languages, in pidgins and creoles, etc. The phenomenon is considered to be a trait of the 'Indian *Sprachbund*', adopted from Dravidian languages; in the Atlantic creoles it is usually traced back to African origins. In light of the large diffusion of this very natural development, it is difficult to pinpoint copying processes in individual cases. While Tajik *guftä* (see 3.5.5 above) was most probably copied from Uzbek, no corresponding Turkic source can be reliably assigned, e.g., to Mongolian *kemen* 'saying' (Khalkha *gedz(i)*, etc.). Ebert (1991) uses Chamling to illustrate the gradual evolution from a verb of speech to a conjunction. Like Turkic, Chamling is an SOV language and therefore places reported speech in the object position before the verb. For a comparable pattern in Amharic, see Gragg 1972.

The same considerations apply to the allegedly simplifying influences on Turkic. When certain varieties use or increase the frequency of postpositive clauses with main clause predicators (e.g. *ölmüş* in Turkish *baktım [ki] ölmüş* 'I looked and saw that he had died', literally: 'I looked: he obviously has died'), this is not necessarily the result of copied combinational and frequential patterns. Boeschoten correctly warns against 'invoking interference of the 'Indo-European' type as an explanation for the development of psycholinguistically easier structures' (Boeschoten 1990b: 44).

Certain positions taken in the debate on grammatical copying are dictated by higher-level considerations of a universalistic or other nature.[1] I cannot discuss the details here. Let me only reiterate that a 'natural' tendency can evidently be more or less *reinforced* by contact-related influence. A general tendency towards a certain structure, which, because it is general, is already latently present in A, can be strengthened by means of contact with B, which already possesses the structure. Consequently, the introduction of the structure in A is facilitated or accelerated. Thus we must supplement the simple question 'copying or independent tendency?' by the further alternative 'or a tendency reinforced by the contact language?'.

In the latter case, the tendency is the factor that paves the way for the innovation, while the language contact triggers it. There is no reason, as so often happens, to view the 'secondary', triggering function as insignificant. As noted, I also speak of 'copying' in this case, specifically, of copying processes that have been prepared by the 'naturalness' of corresponding diachronic tendencies. At times it is even questioned whether a B structure can exert any influence at all on A if the structure does not agree with 'natural' principles. For the prerequisite congruency with natural acquisition processes, see, e.g., Andersen 1989: 386.

4.2. Sources of areal tendencies

When certain developments have taken a similar course within a certain area, one often speaks of 'general areal tendencies' or even *Sprachbund* phenomena. Such designations naturally raise the issue of the origin of these tendencies. Here, we encounter the same fundamental problems as with strictly bilingual interactions, the difference being that with *Sprachbund* phenomena the issues of successive multi-layered influence are much more complex. If a certain development transcends a given areal, then the same categorical objections leveled against the assumption of contact-related influence arise as elaborated above. Nonetheless, the very issue of linguistic universals makes it essential for linguists to conduct empirical areal-typological investigations in order to learn to possibly distinguish areal-specific processes from those of a more general nature.

Regarding the tendencies of the linguistic development in Anatolia, for example, we are faced with complicated questions. As Hovdhaugen (1976) indicates, some of the phenomena found in the Inner Anatolian Greek dialects may have emanated from general tendencies in the linguistic development that took place in Anatolia. But where did these areal tendencies originate? Whereas the Turkic-like structural peculiarities of certain Anatolian Greek dialects are usually attributed to Ottoman influence, Hovdhaugen even wonders whether they might derive from contacts with Armenian. After all, some of these characteristics – tendencies towards 'agglutination', possessive suffixes, loss of adjective inflection, prepositive attributes, etc. – occur in Armenian as well. In addition, as we have seen, Hovdhaugen rejects the possibility of deep Turkic influence on the Anatolian Greek dialects. However, the contact between Armenian and Greek in Anatolia is generally held to have been limited to lexical copying.

Where, then, do the Turkic-like features of Western Armenian have their roots? Western Armenian morphosyntax is considered to have been heavily influenced by Ottoman. An important argument *against* Ottoman structural influence is the fact that there are no clear cases of phonological influence, above all, however, that

Western Armenian displays remarkably few Turkic loanwords. This contradicts the scale of adoption, on which lexical influence normally occupies the first place. In the absence of lexical global copies, the possibility of deeper structural influence appears slight. According to Hovdhaugen, Western Armenian and Ottoman Turkish are structurally less similar than is generally presumed. He contends that in many respects Western Armenian has gone its separate way, over time actually becoming less similar to Turkish than it was during previous developmental stages.

We must undoubtedly posit rather old interactions for some of the similarities discussed above. This applies, among others, to the still unanswered question concerning the typological affinities between the Altaic and Uralic languages. We shall return to the issue of Turkic–Mongolic relations below.

Many old 'tendencies' that have contributed to convergence may be 'general' merely in the sense that their sources are unknown. We have seen that some of the central questions regarding early Turkic–Persian convergence remain unanswered as well: The loss of the Old Iranian gender distinctions also took place during the late Old Persian period (Windfuhr 1990: 541). The debate over Turkic influence on the evolution of the Tajik grammatical system has legitimately called into question whether certain correspondences should be viewed as direct copies from Uzbek. However, the controversy has also included some undeniable cases of copying from Turkic. For a long time, indigenous Soviet Tajik linguistics showed a strong tendency to conceal the linguistic relationships between Tajik and Uzbek. Benzing (1954) remarks that Rastorgueva's (1952) description of nonlexical influence on Tajik makes not the slightest mention of Uzbek. Compare Soper's comment regarding the treatment of the evidential (indirective) meanings of several Tajik verb forms: 'It seems as if it has been decided that the hearsay mood in Northern Tajik based on the old perfect form has developed without a decisive influence from Uzbek' (Soper 1987: 90).

As far as the convergence of common Slavic with the Turkic type is concerned, Menges (1983) reckons with early, mostly fundamental Altaic influences, predating the development of the individual historical Slavic languages. In certain cases for which chiefly late Turkic influence has been presumed, we may have to posit much older influences; see, e.g., the remarks concerning Bulgarian evidentials (indirectives) above (3.4). As noted, the Russian predilection for converbial constructions may also be related to a large-area tendency, in this instance reinforced by Turkic.

As for the origin of the Turkic-like traits of Armenian, the situation is again fraught with difficulties. Some of these phenomena were already present in Old Armenian, e.g. postpositional constructions. Without engaging in a critical evaluation of the presumed South Caucasian substratum, let us keep in mind that, e.g., Georgian, too, has postpositions. If Armenian displays a morphological structure very similar to the Turkic type, it is also true that the development leading to this similarity began relatively early. Similarities with Turkic are first encountered in Middle Armenian, a western variety of Armenian that attained significance in the Cilician empire from the twelfth century on. Hovdhaugen considers it impossible that such phenomena could have resulted from Turkic influence. Instead he explains the morphological and syntactic affinities as mostly brought about by 'the independent development of ancient structural tendencies within Armenian itself' (Hovdhaugen 1976: 158). He contends that if one were unfamiliar with the Middle Armenian material, one would be inclined to overestimate Turkic influence. The fact that Anatolian Armenian dialects developed similarities to Turkic before Turks entered the respective contact areas can therefore only be attributed to 'a curious coincidence of unknown causes' (Hovdhaugen 1976: 158). Thus, he asserts, the loss of case and number inflection and the stable prepositive position of the adjective attribute can hardly go back to Turkic influence, since both phenomena already appear in Middle Armenian (cf. Karst 1901: 392–3).

All the same, we cannot exclude older influences from Turkic varieties or non-Turkic varieties of the 'Turkic type'. Following the Turkish conquest of Anatolia, some of the earlier acquired features of Western Armenian may have been reinforced and stabilized by the prolonged and intensive contact with Ottoman. In certain cases, on the other hand, this reinforcement is less apparent. Not even the Western Armenian relative clause construction based on participles bears witness to sustained influence from Ottoman. Feydit (1948: 306, fn. 1) assures us that this use of participles, which is absent in the classical language, is nothing but a 'calque' of the same forms of the Turkish verb. Hovdhaugen (1976: 157) sees them as 'a clear case of Turkish influence'. However, the patterns differ from each other. When the first actant of a Turkish relative clause is not referentially identical to the head, the possessive suffix denoting the first actant is attached to the participial segment (e.g. *git-tiğ-im köy* 'the village I went to'). In Western Armenian, however, the possessive personal suffix is affixed to the head: *kats-adz küy-s*. This 'seule différence' (Feydit) is not to be underestimated. Although the marking of the nucleus to which the dependent clause refers is the norm in the majority of Turkic languages (*bar-γan awl-ïm*, etc.), it is not typical of Turkish.

In many ways, the Western Armenian development seems to follow a Modern Persian rather than a Turkish pattern. All three languages exhibit parallel developments in the aspect-tense systems, e.g. renewal of the present and imperfect tenses. Whereas the Turkish present tense renewal employs a postverb (converb + *yorï-r* 'runs' > *-iyor*), Western Armenian makes use of a method conspicuously similar to that of Modern Persian. In both Modern Persian and Western Armenian the high-focal present was renewed by means of a prepositive unit that evolved into a prefix (Persian *mi-*, Western Armenian *gə*), while the prefixless old present became the subjunctive form. Both languages renewed the high-focal imperfect in the same way. We find similar patterns in Kurdish, where present and imperfect are signaled by a prefix (e.g. Kurmanji *di-*). The Eastern Armenian present and imperfect renewal, on the other hand, have taken a different course. There, the equivalent of Western *gə sirem* 'I love' is *sir-um e-m*, which consists of a converb (< locative form) + 'I am' (cf. Turkish *-mek-te-yim*).

The Western Armenian perfect in *-er em* (perfect participle + 'I am') also bears similarities to the Modern Persian perfect (aorist stem + *-e* + *-am* 'I am'). Kurdish structures its perfect forms similarly, namely on the basis of the perfect participle (in Kurmanji in *ī*, otherwise in *-ū*), e.g. Kurmanji *k'ät-ī* 'fallen', *k'äti-mä* 'I have fallen'. Compare similar Turkic constructions such as Azerbaijanian *-miš* + *-äm* and Turkish *-miş* + *-im*. The Turkish form, however, is clearly indirective, whereas in Modern Persian, Kurdish and Azerbaijanian (under Persian influence) the perfect also functions as a nonevidential postterminal past. Western Armenian adheres to the Modern Persian–Kurdish pattern in this respect also. According to Feydit (1948: 132), the Western Armenian perfect sometimes conveys a slight notion of doubt, e.g. *kərer e* 'he has, it seems, written'.

Consequently, it is not improbable that other Western Armenian structural features reminiscent of Turkic are actually imitations of Persian patterns. And thus we have returned to the more general, underlying question of Turkic–Persian convergence.

Above, I presumed that actional postverbial constructions became widespread as a result of language encounters. But where should we seek their point of departure? Perhaps in Iranian also, where they have existed for a long time? The secondary use of converbs for postverbial constructions may be a typically Turkic phenomenon, yet it is by no means an exclusively Turkic one. We can observe that outside the Central Asian–Turkic areal these sorts of patterns occur, for example, also in southern Asia, predominantly in Indo-Aryan (e.g. Urdu) and in Dravidian. Comparable patterns appear neither in the Iranian Pamir languages nor in Pashto, but we do find them northwest of the Pamir mountains in Tajik, in a form less similar to the northern Indo-Aryan patterns than the Turkic ones. Tajik postverbial constructions display unmistakable Uzbek features; it must be considered as proven that they constitute a case of Turkic influence (see Rastorgueva 1964; Perry 1979). Rastorgueva (1964: 132) illustrates how, in Tajik dialects spoken in the proximity of Turkic-speaking areas, postverbial constructions are most heavily represented, while they occur either less frequently or not at all in more distant dialects. Soper (1987: ch. 2) sees a correlation between the degree of Uzbek influence on various Tajik dialects and the number of 'complex verb constructions' or their level of integration in the grammars of the respective dialects. Thus the copying path is clear here. Similar postverbial constructions in

Khwarezmian may also go back to the progressively strong Turkic influence to which Iranian Khwarezm was exposed from the eighth century on.

Mari has obviously also copied its postverbial constructions from neighboring Turkic languages. In Finno-Ugric languages, which are located further away from Turkic-speaking areas, postverbial constructions are either less prevalent (Udmurt) or nonexistent (Zyryan); see Serebrennikov 1960: 265, 275.

The fact that some geographically limited problems involving contact-induced influence can be considered solved does not, of course, mean that the question concerning the origin of the respective phenomena has been answered. The wide diffusion of similar verb complexes in other regions remains enigmatic. Maybe, as Masica has suggested, they are 'a speech fashion that spread at a time when northern India was in close contact with Central Asia, perhaps from the former to the latter' (Masica 1976: 185).

Reflections of this kind take us back far in time to prehistorical glottogenetic processes. Numerous other structural features portrayed here as typical of the Turkic languages are similarly widespread. As noted repeatedly, remarkable structural isoglosses link Dravidian to languages of the Altaic type, although no corresponding direct language contact has probably taken place for at least three millennia. The present study cannot discuss the large-area structural parallels: the well-known similarities between Turkic and languages of the 'Indian', 'Ethiopian' and 'Japanese–Korean' *Sprachbund*; so-called 'Ural-Altaic', 'Indo-Altaic' congruencies, etc. Many of these irrefutable parallelisms constitute correlative bundles of associated structural features. Some of them may exclusively derive from 'natural' tendencies; others presuppose an areal basis. At times, the similarities are so pronounced that they cannot possibly be the result of momentary adstratum influence. Once again, I should like to stress that typological parallelisms do not necessarily imply genetic relationship and that, moreover, the main genetic hypotheses are highly controversial. If, for instance, Japanese and Korean, whose genetic relationship has not been established, are very similar today and exhibit typically 'Ural-Altaic' syntactic features, this might be the result of early continental contacts between them as well as interactions with older forms of Tungusic and Mongolic (perhaps also Gilyak).

4.3. Early leveling of Turkic?

What is decisive for us, however, is that Turkic is exceptionally rich in the presumably attractive features discussed. Since the earliest phases of its documentable history, it has possessed a structure that has often determined the direction of change. This is presumably one reason why Turkic has been so expansive in language contact situations, provided the social conditions were not too much to its disadvantage.

This raises the question: What kind of language is it that displays such a high degree of regularity and simplicity? In the course of its known history, Turkic has repeatedly erased the traces of old irregularities, replacing them by new standardizations. Regardless of the natural historical divergence of the Turkic languages, leveling due to *koinéization* frequently occurred. In the process, the vestiges of many earlier differences were deleted. The demographic shifts during the Mongol era, when Turkic was the language that became extraordinarily widespread, had a particularly leveling effect on the language. In light of the great number of attractive features the Turkic languages have in common, the question even seems justified whether the earliest known form of Turkic might in fact have been a type of koiné.

Koinés are known to typically develop towards the 'natural', to simplify by abolishing or altering 'marked' structures. On the one hand, certain complicated elements are lost even when they are present in all of the varieties contributing to the koiné. On the other hand, elements of minority varieties can survive if they are linguistically easier (Trudgill 1986: 126). Sustained contacts between mutually comprehensible prehistoric Turkic varieties of comparable prestige may have produced language forms that allowed members of various tribal confederations to communicate because regional differences had been leveled and marked variants had largely disappeared. Thus a balanced and 'progressive' type of

Turkic could have developed that, by contrast to the contributing varieties, was extremely regular and simple. From a typological point of view, its status would be comparable *mutatis mutandis* to the status progressive Manchu holds among the Tungusic languages.

An assumption of this kind, although it cannot be further argued within the scope of the present study, could also be fruitful for the problem concerning the genetic relatedness of the Altaic languages. The circumstance that Mongolic has converged with Turkic rather than moved away from it by way of divergence – which is usual among related languages – would thus not necessarily be an argument against the Altaic hypothesis.

As Doerfer has emphasized in various contexts, the early Altaists were only familiar with the developmental stages of progressive languages such as Turkic, Manchu and modern Mongolian. This led them to misconstrue the situation, i.e. to overestimate the similarities. Since they did not know archaic languages such as Old Mongolian and Evenki, they were not aware that the differences between the languages under comparison had been greater in earlier developmental stages. It is undeniable that gradual divergence is characteristic of related languages; the further back one traces their developments, the more similarities one finds. The convergence of Mongolic with Turkic thus constitutes a development in the opposite direction. At first sight, it appears to be comparable to Persian–Turkic convergence, which has been visible since the Middle Persian era and has culminated in modern northern Tajik. Doerfer views the Turkic–Persian development as being parallel to that of Turkic–Mongolic. As noted, he considers northern Tajik a Turkic language *in statu nascendi* that illustrates how the apparent relatedness of Turkic and Mongolic (and Tungusic) may also have once evolved (Doerfer 1967: 67).

The relatively recent convergence of certain Mongolic languages with Turkic, however, does not prove that Mongolic and Turkic were originally far apart and moved closer together only later as a result of sustained historical contact. If the earliest Turkic known to us really is the result of a leveling koinéization, then we can only expect Old Mongolian to reflect an older developmental state. In the course of ensuing contact-related developments, individual Mongolic languages may have gradually moved in the direction of this 'progressive' type.

Let us tentatively assume that Turkic and Mongolic once shared the abovementioned 'exclusive' vs. 'inclusive' distinction (see 3.4). Modern Mongolian can be shown to have dropped this old difference (Doerfer 1963: 87). A corresponding loss may have occurred earlier in Turkic, leaving behind traces in the peripheral languages Yakut, Sayan Turkic and Turkmen (Schönig 1987). Thus it is possible that Mongolic subsequently moved closer to Turkic in this respect. This development is more plausible by far than the one alluded to above, namely that those peripheral Turkic languages copied the 'exclusive' vs. 'inclusive' distinction independently of one another from various contact languages.

Now, the supposed relations between the postulated Turkic koiné and the oldest known form of Modern Persian are also interesting. The latter developed in the northeastern part of the Iranian area, becoming the language of the Eastern caliphate in the eighth century and replacing Sogdian as the lingua franca of trade in Transoxania and along the Central Asian trade routes. It evidently did not evolve directly from a Sassanid Middle Persian basic dialect to a standard language. Rather, it was already at its inception a morphologically and lexically eclectic medium used by Iranians and non-Iranians alike, an Islamic-Iranian language of communication employed by various language groups in the respective border areas (Utas 1991). The earliest Modern Persian differs from Sassanid Middle Persian, among other things, in terms of its morphological regularization, e.g. the restructuring of the verbal system. Thus, early Modern Persian development already displays conditions probably not unlike those of Turkic. Even if the exact Turkic contribution to the oldest form of Modern Persian remains unknown, it is certain that initial leveling provided the conditions conducive to an increasingly close Turkic–Modern Persian symbiosis.

4.4. Similarities in the most stable substructures

If the Altaic languages are genetically related, then the period when they comprised a linguistic community must belong to the distant past (see Róna-Tas 1986; cf. Johanson 1991a: 121). Such a remoteness in time implies that their divergencies have progressed too far and their language contacts have been too diverse for a large amount of easily discernible similarities to have survived until today. As we have seen in the course of this exposition, all structural features are more or less susceptible to contact-related influence; none appears to be absolutely inalienable.

If at all, genetic affinities are to be sought in the most conservative and most stable parts of the languages in question. Let us then turn our attention to those factors that were *less probably* caused by copying or general developmental tendencies. In the oldest evolutionary stage known to us, Turkic already exhibits a strikingly complex verbal system. Evidently it was never subject to any significant leveling. In all genuinely Turkic languages, the system has either remained virtually intact or its complexity has even increased. By contrast, other languages have hardly copied from this system. We have seen that Persian, Mongolic and other varieties acquired numerous attractive features, probably for the most part under Turkic influence. Complicating features, on the other hand, were seldom acquired, neither by means of copying from Turkic languages nor otherwise. Unlike Turkic declination, Turkic conjugation, due to its complex structures, has found few imitators.

The existence of such a complex verbal system might, as noted, be considered indicative of genetic continuity. It has, in fact, remained intact even in extremely heavily foreign-influenced languages such as Karaim and Chuvash. We might therefore expect to find old, inherited similarities precisely in this complex. Certain parts of the Turkic verbal system are apparently more stable than others, specifically the inflectional categories close to the primary stem, e.g. the markers forming secondary verbal stems and used to denote actionality and diatheses. Among their characteristics are an internal position, a high degree of cohesion, firm incorporation into the complex lexicosyntactic combinational system, and an often central role which also concerns sentence hierarchy. It appears that these features are most resistant to the kinds of restructuring processes that occur in every verbal system. As far as we know, they have not been copied. Even if the sequence of inflectional morphemes within a word does not always reflect the chronology of their development, these Turkic suffixes can be said to be very old. Several noticeable irregularities bear witness to this fact, e.g. irregularities among the lexically motivated allomorphs of the causative suffixes. These irregularities, too, were later partially leveled, albeit to a lesser extent than those of other morphemes. The traces of old differences are more tangible here than elsewhere. (Cf. Johanson 1999c; 2000d.)

When, in this innermost and most stable area of verbal morphology, we encounter systematic correlations among languages – in part material and semantic similarities between certain morpheme categories, in part analogous complex combinational patterns – then these congruencies can be considered convincing evidence of genetic relationship.

Consequently, even the *traces* of such systematic correspondences deserve more attention than some other similarities. We must, for example, question whether it is merely a matter of coincidence that the most conclusive parallels between the possibly genetically related Altaic languages are found precisely in their verbal stem morphology. Ramstedt (1912) already collated a number of potentially related markers of secondary verbal stems in various Altaic languages, eight of which Poppe (1973) later attempted to reconstruct. Ramstedt placed a great deal of importance on these and other morphological affinities. In his 'Introduction to Altaic linguistics' he asserts that the facts of the grammatical – especially morphological – stock and its developmental direction provide much more reliable clues to the genetic question than all the phonetic phenomena taken together (1957: 15). Miller says of the secondary verbal-stem markers: '[...] these cognate morphemes are to be seen operating in precisely the arbitrary (but not random) fashion that, given the assumptions of the comparative method, argues most strongly in favor of genetic relationship [...] Borrowing [...] by Mongolian from Turkic and then by Tungus from

Mongolian, is out of the question, once we inspect the forms and their functions within the morphology' (Miller 1991; cf. 1990).

If this is true, the Tungusic languages would have to be considered particularly archaic in respect of their verbal systems, as they possess a considerably larger amount of actionality markers and combinations of actionality markers close to the primary stem than other Altaic languages. In Turkic most of the actionality markers would have been lost early on or become unproductive as a result of lexicalization. This would have generated the need to renew a number of them using the postverbial technique. In the course of Turkic–Mongolic language contacts, this method would then have been adopted by the Mongolic languages as well.

Drawing a wider circle, we discover that, among the morphological similarities between Dravidian and the Altaic languages, it is precisely the suffixes of voice (passive, causative, medium, cooperative, etc.) that exhibit particularly distinct parallels to their Turkic equivalents.

In a similar fashion, an 'inclusive' vs. 'exclusive' distinction might have belonged to the old affinities. In Tungusic, this distinction is alive and well today, while younger Mongolic languages show only remnants of it. In the Turkic languages still containing traces of the distinction, as we have seen, it can hardly be considered a result of contact-induced copying. The feature is probably too unattractive to have been 'contagious'. More conceivably, it was later relinquished also by languages that had originally shared it, leaving traces only in less progressive varieties.

In this context, it is certainly a thought-provoking fact – and one worthy of attention in typological discussions of the genealogical and contact-linguistic type – that the Dravidian conjugation also has an 'inclusive' vs. 'exclusive' opposition and that it denotes this opposition by virtue of a corresponding distinction on the personal pronoun of the 1.p. plural. Note that here too the inclusive form consists of a combination of the exclusive and a 2.p. personal element.

These speculations, like others, must remain unresolved here. Nonetheless, it is clear that these kinds of features specifically, be they ever so residual, are criterial for the problem of genetic relationship. The purpose of these remarks has been not so much to answer individual diachronic questions as to indicate the complex underlying causal interactions. By taking these interactions into account, diachronic linguistic investigations will be able to achieve new, concrete solutions. In general as well as Turkic linguistic history, simplifying statements must make way for differentiated argumentation.

As noted at the outset of this study, we still lack sound, empirically proven hypotheses to explain the diachronic processes in question.[2] More exact methods must be applied in the attempt to determine the regularities of contact-induced change. The most pressing desideratum is first to establish broad areal typologies that especially take those peripheral areas into account where new structures develop in language contact.

NOTES

Notes to Chapter 1

1 This makes contact-linguistic investigations of the development of contemporary Turkish spoken in Germany and other Western European countries all the more urgent (Johanson 1988b; 1991b).
2 Written Greek was not widely known here; influence was most profound in villages without Greek schools.
3 It is usually assumed that over the centuries Anatolian Greek influenced co-areal Turkish almost exclusively in the lexical domain (see also Johanson 1990c). Hovdhaugen (1976: 160) finds no evidence of phonological, morphological or syntactic influence from Greek or Armenian in the Turkish literary language. He does, however, point out that the dialects have not yet been examined in this light.
4 Paul (1909: 394) speaks of phonic 'substitution', when an A speaker in imitating B pronunciation employs the closest correspondences in his native tongue instead of the foreign sounds. The different types of 'integration', i.e. adaptation to the basic code, should not be confused with habitualization or conventionalization (see below), although they may on occasion empirically coincide.
5 They have a comparable effect in the case of imposition. In second language acquisition, 'homogene Hemmung' [homogeneous inhibition] allegedly constitutes the greatest and most frequent difficulty (Juhász 1970: 99). In this context, according to Auburger (1983: 5), underdifferentiations can be more persistent than overdifferentiations.
6 There are no objective criteria for determining the 'foreignness' of copied elements in the A system. Descriptive analysis cannot systematically discern 'foreign elements' from nonforeign ones; structural criteria, such as the results of adaptation or the lack thereof,

are rarely unequivocal. Thus, assessments of foreignness are mostly subjective and/or based on etymological knowledge.
7 See Tietze 1964 for Persian derivational suffixes in Turkish and Azerbaijanian; for frequent Altaic derivational suffixes in Persian, see Doerfer 1963: 32 ff.
8 Thus the Greek consonant alternations $\gamma \sim y$, $k \sim k^{1'}$, $x \sim x^1$ have close Turkish equivalents; cf. Hovdhaugen 1976: 145.
9 This notation has been misunderstood to the effect that *Bugün geliyorsunuz* is 'elliptical' and that *Siz* would be 'redundant', e.g. from a pragmatic point of view. This is certainly not my opinion.
10 For East Old Turkic (including Old Uyghur) word formation, see Erdal 1991.
11 Turkic thus fulfills Greenberg's (1963) stipulation that a language possessing tense, aspect and mood inflection also has person and number inflection. The generativist literature usually refers to subject markers as 'agreement markers' (because they signal agreement between the 'subject' and its head). According to my conception of grammar, they signal, without being subjects themselves, person and number of the first actant of the predication, regardless of whether or not the first actant is realized in the clause (see Johanson 1990b).
12 I avoid the term 'agglutination' because it is ambiguous and usually encompasses at least three characteristics: juxtaposition, highly synthetic structure and predictable morphemic variation.
13 This simplified description does not include language-specific variations.
14 Occasionally case forms can also constitute the derivational base. For example, nominalizing suffixes (such as Turkish *-ki*) can be attached to locative and genitive suffixes and then be extended by means of denominal suffixes.
15 The literature in English often employs the term 'explicator' (and 'explicator compounds'), but, unfortunately, too frequently also uses the misleading designation 'aspect auxiliary'.
16 Cf. Ross's (1982) observations about 'cool' languages, which can omit a participant when this participant can be considered as understood.

Notes to Chapter 2

1 To be distinguished from code frequency in the terms of the functional load (Martinet 1955: 78–9).
2 As Doerfer (1988b: 67 ff.) notes in reference to the lexicon, a frequently used word is usually also a well-known word, whereas not every well-known word is also frequently used.

3 Some linguists even profess that only internal change leads to simplification, while foreign influence increases a grammar's 'markedness', thus being the principal cause of complications in the system (Bailey 1973; Traugott 1973).
4 I cannot address the question here whether foreign influence has a 'negative' or 'positive' effect. According to Slobin (1986), syntactic influence has helped the Turkic languages enrich their available means of expression.
5 In child language, the substitution of fricatives by plosives is 'natural', whereas the opposite tends to be true of language change. Thus [p], one of the most easily acquired and most stable sounds, is frequently altered in diachronic language change. Many processes characteristic of child language apparently result from limited muscular or retention capacity.
6 For the Turkic typological characteristic of maintaining clear morpheme boundaries, see Johanson 1974a: 82 ff., 1979b: 136 ff.
7 Concerning the lexicon, see Doerfer 1988b and the comments in Johanson 1989b.
8 However, he points out that extreme differences can make acquisition so difficult that certain 'interference' patterns become habitualized.
9 Cf. Haugen 1950b: 'Some languages import the whole morpheme, others substitute their own morphemes.' For the inadequate use of the term 'substitution' in this context, however, see 1.3.2 above and Johanson 1993b.
10 In cases such as this, Haugen (1950b) prefers to speak of 'systematic fragments' rather than coexisting systems.
11 Hovdhaugen would even compare this influence with Arabic–Persian influence on Ottoman. However, as Brendemoen (1999: 357–8) rightly points out, there is vast dialectal variation as to the degree of Turkish influence in Cappadocia. In some southern villages, the Turkish impact has been extremely strong at all linguistic levels. Hovdhaugen's claim is thus not valid for these villages.
12 Deeters (1927: 57 ff.) differentiates between the 'mixed language E' resulting from adoption and the 'mixed language T' resulting from language shift.
13 Berta assumes a similar development in the wake of the language shift that took place among the Khazar-speaking Kabars, who joined up with the Hungarian tribes in the ninth century (Berta 1997: 305).
14 During this period, Khwarezm also blossomed as a center of Turkic literary activity.

Notes to Chapter 3

1 However, originally Arabic words were often copied from Persian, where some of these adaptations had already taken place.
2 Cf. McCarthy (1970: 65): 'it was largely due to French influence that this phoneme has a firm place in both Turkish phonology and orthography'.
3 In Halich Karaim we find [ö] > [ä] and [ü] > [i]; in Trakai Karaim [ö] and [ü] are retracted except initially. Nevertheless, the principles of sound harmony are maintained (see Csató & Johanson 1996 and Csató 1999). Similar sound-harmonic conditions obtain in Gagauz, and may also be assumed for old Armenian-Kipchak. Hamp's analysis of palatalization and sound harmony in Karaim appears to be inaccurate (Hamp 1976).
4 Referring to Paul (1909: 400), Doerfer (1963: 86) compares this state of affairs with the frequent copying of inflectional endings in Romani, another language spoken by nomads.
5 We do not know, however, whether *-säm* already followed the possessive suffix in Volga Bulgar.
6 Pronominal predicators are normally unaccentable, i.e. they cannot carry the high pitch, e.g. *-siniz* in Turkish *geli'r-siniz* 'you (will) come'. Compare, however, exceptions such as Uzbek *kelir-si'z*.
7 Similar phenomena also occur in diaspora varieties; Menz (1991: 52 ff.), e.g., cites instances of double causative marking.
8 However, the Turkish children growing up in the Netherlands, examined by Boeschoten & Verhoeven (1986), did not display typical signs of influence on the verbal system, i.e. no disruptions of the inflectional or conjugational systems, etc.
9 Although I agree neither with the author's description (pp. 213 ff.) nor with his analysis of the Kashkay system (p. 362), I must refrain from providing a critical evaluation here.
10 For the influence of the translations from Persian on the development of Ottoman in the fourteenth to fifteenth century, see Römer 1981.
11 According to another Behaghelian 'law', for reasons of perceptual psychology, more important information follows less important information.
12 According to von Gabain's (1961: 69) psychologizing interpretation, the still 'form-deficient' Turkic inscriptions allegedly bear witness to a 'collective consciousness'; in Uyghur she finds that this condition has been replaced by 'a harmonious composition of coordination and subordination'.
13 In written Turkish, *-me*, for example, which occurs as a predicator of complement clauses, is significantly more frequent than in the spoken language (Hřebíček 1978).

14 Certain other nonfinite clauses require the choice between a genitive and nominative subject, which is determined by the sentence perspective; see 3.5.4.
15 It is probable, if not empirically provable, that Turkic hypotaxis developed from parataxis and that the contemporary clause combinations developed from main clause sequences. In light of several text-construction properties of Turkic converbs, one might speculate whether the old, etymologically no longer analyzable converbial suffixes evolved from particles that originally stood between two predications and were later reinterpreted as belonging to the first (or merged with the first predication's clause-final predicator). This development would differ from that of European languages, where the cataphoric element came to be assigned to the second predication (e.g. *thereafter* > *whereafter*). Turkic thus would have developed a subjunctor marking the embedding of the first predication as a constituent of the second, whereas in European languages the second predication became embedded in the first. If Turkic evolved in this manner, then we must assume successive connection shifts and probably also transitional phases in which it would be hard to determine to what extent the junctor was already embedded in the preceding predication, whether it already possessed subordinating power, etc.
16 The term *subjunctor* designates subordinative relators for predications, i.e. grammatical markers that introduce or end embedded clauses, connect them with basic segments (heads) and signal their semantic functions. Free subjunctors are subordinative particles (e.g. subordinative conjunctions and relative words). For free Turkic postpositive subjunctors of the type *dep, diye*, see 3.5.5.

Notes to Chapter 4

1 Fokos-Fuchs, who is eager to use syntactic affinity as a proof of genetic relatedness and, correspondingly, tries to reduce the role of grammatical copying, asserts that even substantial changes in the area of syntax that would seem to have developed under foreign influence are in fact the results of internal developments in the language in question (Fokos-Fuchs 1962: 125).
2 Cf. Best & Kohlhase (1983), who also advance arguments in favor of applying the methods of probability calculus.

REFERENCES

Adamović, M. (1983) Der tschuwaschische Plural in -*sem*. *Finnisch-Ugrische Mitteilungen* 7/1983, 21–7.
Aksu-Koç, A.A. & D.I. Slobin (1985) The acquisition of Turkish. In: D.I. Slobin (ed.) 1985, *The crosslinguistic study of language acquisition. 1. The data*, 839–78. Hillsdale.
Andersen, R.W. (1984) The one to one principle of interlanguage construction. *Language Learning* 34/1984, 77–95.
—— (1989) The 'up' and 'down' staircase in secondary language development. In: N. Dorian 1989, 385–94.
Appel, R. & P. Muysken (1987) *Language contact and bilingualism*. London.
Auburger, L. (1983) Grundstrukturen der Mehrsprachigkeit. In: P.N. Nelde (ed.) 1983, *Theorien, Methoden und Modelle der Kontaktlinguistik*, 1–17. Bonn.
Aytemiz, A. (1990) *Zur Sprachkompetenz türkischer Schüler in Türkisch und Deutsch.* (= *Europäische Hochschulschriften*, 21:90.) Frankfurt & Bern, etc.
Bailey, C.-J. (1973) *Variation and linguistic theory*. Arlington.
Bakaev, Č.X. (1973) *Jazyk kurdov SSSR. Sravnitel'naja xarakteristika govorov*. Moskva.
Baskakov, N.A. (1960) *The Turkic languages of Central Asia: problems of planned culture contact. The Turkic peoples of the USSR: the development of their languages and writing*. Oxford.
—— (1966) O nekotoryx tipologičeskix izmenenijax v sintaksise sovremennyx tjurkskix literaturnyx jazykov. *Tjurkologičeskij sbornik*, 1966, 17–23. Moskva & Leningrad.

—— (1969) *Osnovnye processy vnutristrukturnogo razvitija tjurkskix, finno-ugorskix i mongol'skix jazykov.* Moskva.

Bátori, I. (1979) Russen und Finnougrier: Zweisprachigkeit und sprachliche Interferenz. In: P.S. Ureland (ed.) 1979, *Standardsprache und Dialekte in mehrsprachigen Gebieten Europas*, 1–26. Tübingen.

Bazin, L. & J. Feuillet (1980) L'opposition constation / non-constation en turc et en bulgare. *Zeitschrift für Balkanologie* 16/1980, 9–15.

Bechert, J. & W. Wildgen (1991) *Einführung in die Sprachkontaktforschung.* Darmstadt.

Behaghel, O. (1932) *Deutsche Syntax. 5. Wortstellung, Periodenbau.* Heidelberg.

Benzing, J. (1953a) *Einführung in das Studium der altaischen Philologie und der Turkologie.* Wiesbaden.

—— (1953b) Remarques sur les langues tongouses et leurs relations avec les autres langues dites 'altaïques'. *Ural-Altaische Jahrbücher* 25, 109–18. [Also in: L. Johanson & C. Schönig 1988, 42–51.]

—— (1954) Review of Rastorgueva 1952. *Zeitschrift der Deutschen Morgenländischen Gesellschaft* 104/1954, 231. [Also in: L. Johanson & C. Schönig 1988, 165.]

—— (1959) Das Tschuwaschische. In: J. Deny et alii 1959, 695–751.

Bereczki, G. (1988) Geschichte der wolgafinnischen Sprachen. In: D. Sinor (ed.) 1988, *The Uralic languages. Description, history and foreign influences*, 314–50.

Berta, Á. (1997) Review of Johanson 1992. *Turkic Languages* 1/1997, 302–7.

Best, K.-H. & J. Kohlhase (eds) (1983) *Exakte Sprachwandelforschung. Theoretische Beiträge, statistische Analysen und Arbeitsberichte.* (= *Göttinger Schriften zur Sprach- und Literaturwissenschaft*, 2.) Göttingen.

Bethlenfalvy, G. et alii (eds) (1992) *Altaic religious beliefs and practices.* Budapest.

Bickerton, D. (1980) Decreolisation and the creole continuum. In: A. Valdman & A. Highfield (eds) 1980, *Theoretical orientations in creole studies*, 109–27. New York.

—— (1981) *Roots of language.* Ann Arbor.

Boeschoten, H.E. (1983) *Usbekisches aus Aibak (Samangan).* Utrecht.

—— (1990a) *Acquisition of Turkish by immigrant children. A multiple case study of Turkish children in the Netherlands aged 4 to 6.* Tilburg.

—— (1990b) Turkish in the Netherlands: patterns of change over generations. In: B. Brendemoen 1990, 39–48.

—— & L.Th. Verhoeven (1986) Turkish language acquisition of Turkish children in the Netherlands. In: A. Aksu & E. Erguvanlı (eds) 1986, *Proceedings of the Second Conference on Turkish Linguistics*, 269–80. İstanbul.

REFERENCES

Boretzky, N., W. Enninger & Th. Stolz (eds) (1996). *Areale, Kontakte, Dialekte. Sprache und ihre Dynamik in mehrsprachigen Situationen.* (= *Bochum-Essener Beiträge zur Sprachwandelforschung*, 24.] Bochum.

Borovkov, A.K. (1952) Tadžiksko-uzbekskoe dvujazyčie i vzaimootnošenija uzbekskogo i tadžikskogo jazykov. *Učenie Zapiski Instituta Vostokovedenija*, 4, 165–200. Moskva.

Boyle, J.A. (1966) *Grammar of modern Persian.* Wiesbaden.

Brands, H.W. (1973) *Studien zum Wortbestand der Türksprachen. Lexikalische Differenzierung, Semasiologie, Sprachgeschichte.* Leiden.

Brendemoen, B. (1987) Turkish in Europe – some aspects of semantic transfer. [Lecture manuscript.] (Turkish version: Kuzey-Batı Avrupa Türkçesi'ne ödünç yolu ile giren yabancı kaynaklı deyimler. *Dilbilim Araştırmaları* 1992, 19–24.)

—— (ed.) (1990) *Altaica Osloensia.* Oslo.

—— (1992) Some remarks on the vowel harmony in a religious dialect text from Trabzon. In: G. Bethlenfalvy et alii 1992, 41–57.

—— (1993) Pronominalsyntax in den türkischen Schwarzmeerdialekten – syntaktische Innovation oder Archaismus? In: J.P. Laut & K. Röhrborn 1993, 51–73.

—— (1999) Greek and Turkish language encounters in Anatolia. In: B. Brendemoen et alii 1999, 353–78.

—— E. Lanza & E. Ryen (eds) (1999) *Language encounters across time and space.* Oslo.

Bulut, Chr. (1997) *Evliya Çelebis Reise von Bitlis nach Van.* (= *Turcologica*, 35.) Wiesbaden.

Bybee, J.L. (1985) *Morphology. A study of the relation between meaning and form.* Amsterdam & Philadelphia.

Cabolov, R.L. (1978) *Očerk istoričeskoj morfologii kurdskogo jazyka.* Moskva.

Clyne, M. (1987) Constraints on code-switching. How universal are they? *Linguistics* 25, 739–64.

Coetsem, F. van (1988) *Loan phonology and the two transfer types in language contact.* Dordrecht & Providence, R.I.

Comrie, B. (1981a) *The languages of the Soviet Union.* Cambridge.

—— (1981b) *Language universals and linguistic typology. Syntax and morphology.* Oxford.

Csató, É.Á. (1990) Non-finite verbal constructions in Turkish. In: B. Brendemoen 1990, 75–88.

—— (1996) Some typological properties of North-Western Karaim in areal perspectives. In: N. Boretzky et alii 1996, 68–83.

—— (1999) Syllabic harmony in Turkic: The evidence of code-copying. In: B. Brendemoen et alii 1999, 341–52.

—— (2000) Some typological features of the viewpoint aspect and tense system in spoken North-Western Karaim. In: Ö. Dahl 2000, 671–99.

—— & L. Johanson (1996) Zur Silbenharmonie des Nordwest-Karaimischen. *Acta Orientalia Hungarica* 48/1996, 329–37.
Çeneli, I. & E.A. Gruber (1980) *Krimtatarische Chrestomathie aus Gegenwartstexten*. Wiesbaden.
Dahl, Ö. (ed.) (2000) *Tense and aspect in the languages of Europe*. Berlin & New York.
Dankoff, R. & J. Kelly (1982) *Compendium of the Turkic dialects by Mahmud al-Kashgari*. 1. Harvard.
Dauzat, A. (1938) *Les patois, évolution, classification, étude*. Paris.
Dawkins, R.M. (1916) *Modern Greek in Asia Minor. A study of the dialects of Sillí, Cappadocia and Phárasa with grammar, texts, translations, and glossary*. Cambridge.
Deeters, G. (1926) Armenisch und Südkaukasisch. Ein Beitrag zur Frage der Sprachmischung. 1. *Caucasica* 3/1926, 37–82.
—— (1927) Armenisch und Südkaukasisch. Ein Beitrag zur Frage der Sprachmischung. 2. *Caucasica* 4/1927, 1–64.
Demir, N. (1992) Zur Verwendung der Hilfsverbverbindung *-ip dur-* in einem anatolischen Dialekt. In: G. Bethlenfalvy et alii 1992, 89–95.
Deny, J. (1921) *Grammaire de la langue turque (dialecte osmanli)*. Paris.
——, K. Grønbech, H. Scheel & Z.V. Togan (eds) (1959) *Philologiae Turcicae Fundamenta*, 1. Aquis Mattiacis.
Dik, S.C. (1989) *The theory of Functional Grammar. 1. The structure of the clause*. (= *Functional Grammar series*, 9.) Dordrecht.
Dmitriev, N.K. (1939) Gagauzskie ètjudy. In: *Učenie zapiski Leningradskogo gosurdarstvennogo universiteta*, ser. filologičeskix nauk, vyp. 1: 20/1939, 3–27. [Also in: N.K. Dmitriev 1962, *Stroj tjurkskix jazykov*, 251–70. Moskva.]
Doerfer, G. (1963) *Türkische und mongolische Elemente im Neupersischen. 1. Mongolische Elemente im Neupersischen*. (= *Akademie der Wissenschaften und der Literatur. Veröffentlichungen der Orientalischen Kommission*, 16.) Wiesbaden.
—— (1967) *Türkische Lehnwörter im Tadschikischen*. (= *Abhandlungen für die Kunde des Morgenlandes*, 37,3.) Wiesbaden.
—— (1988a) *Grammatik des Chaladsch*. (= *Turcologica*, 4.) Wiesbaden.
—— (1988b) *Grundwort und Sprachmischung. Eine Untersuchung an Hand von Körperteilbezeichnungen*. (=*Münchner Ostasiatische Studien*, 47.) Stuttgart.
—— (1993) Das Suffix *-mlš* áls Lehnelement. In: J.P. Laut & K. Röhrborn 1993, 87–92.
Dorian, N. (1981) *Language death. The life cycle of a Scottisch Gaelic dialect*. Philadelphia.
—— (ed.) (1989) *Investigating obsolescence. Studies in language contraction and death*. (=*Studies in the social and cultural foundations of language*, 7.) Cambridge.

REFERENCES

Drimba, V. (1973) *Syntaxe comane*. București & Leiden.

Đurovič, L'. (1988) The concept of diaspora language. *Diaspora languages in Western Europe* (= *Slavica Lundensia*, 12), 7–9. Lund.

Džangidze, V.T. (1978) *Ingilojskij dialekt v Azerbajdžane* (*Voprosy grammatičeskoj i leksičeskoj interferencii*). Tbilisi.

Ebert, K.H. (1991) Vom Verbum dicendi zur Konjunktion. Ein Kapitel universaler Grammatikentwicklung. In: W. Bisang & P. Rinderknecht (eds) 1991, *Von Europa bis Ozeanien – Von der Antonymie zum Relativsatz* (= *Arbeiten des Seminars für Allgemeine Sprachwissenschaft der Universität Zürich*, 11), 77–95.

Eckmann, F.R. (1977) Markedness and the contrastive analysis hypothesis. *Language Learning* 31/1977, 315–30.

Enç, M. (1986) Topic switching and pronominal subjects in Turkish. In: D.I. Slobin & K. Zimmer 1986, 195–208.

Erdal, M. (1991) *Old Turkic word formation. A functional approach to the lexicon.* (= *Turcologica*, 7.) Wiesbaden.

Erguvanlı, E.E. (1984) *The function of word order in Turkish grammar*. Berkeley & Los Angeles & London.

Faingold, E.D. (1989) *The case for fusion: (Jewish) Ladino in the Balkans and the Eastern Turkish Empire.* (= *Arbeiten zur Mehrsprachigkeit*, 36.) Hamburg.

Feydit, F. (1948) *Manuel de langue arménienne (Arménien occidental moderne)*. Paris.

Fokos-Fuchs, D.R. (1962) *Rolle der Syntax in der Frage nach Sprachverwandtschaft mit besonderer Rücksicht auf das Problem der ural-altaischen Sprachverwandtschaft*. Wiesbaden.

Foley, W. & R. van Valin (1984) *Functional syntax and universal grammar*. Cambridge.

Forster, K.I. (1966) Left-to-right processes in the construction of sentences. *Journal of Verbal Learning and Verbal Behavior* 5/1966, 285–91.

Frazier, L. & K. Rayner (1988) Parametrizing the language processing system: left- vs. right-branching within and across languages. In: J.A. Hawkins (ed.) 1988, *Explaining language universals*, 247–79. Oxford.

Gabain, A. von (1950^2) *Alttürkische Grammatik*. Leipzig.

—— (1961) *Das uigurische Königreich von Chotscho 850–1250.* (= *Sitzungsberichte der Deutschen Akademie der Wissenschaften zu Berlin. Klasse für Sprachen, Literatur und Kunst* 1961:5.) Berlin.

Gabelentz, G. von der (1901) *Die Sprachwissenschaft*. [Reprint Tübingen 1972.]

Gajdardži, G.A. (1981) *Gagauzskij sintaksis. Pridatočnye predloženija sojuznogo podčinenija*. Kišinev.

Givón, T. (1971) Historical syntax and synchronic morphology: an archaeologist's field trip. *Chicago Linguistic Society* 7/1971, 349–415.

—— (1979) Prolegomena to any sane creology. In: I.F. Hancock (ed.) 1979, *Readings in creole studies*, 3–35. Ghent.
Gragg, G.B. (1972) Semi-indirect discourse and related nightmares. *Chicago Linguistic Society* 8/1972, 75–82.
Grannes, A. (1978) Le redoublement turc à M initial en bulgare. *Linguistique balkanique* 21/1978, 37–0.
—— (1988) Influence turc sur le bulgare. *Centre des Études Balkaniques. Inalco. Bulletin de liaison* 7/1988, 3–20. Paris.
Greenberg, J. (1963) Some universals of grammar with particular reference to the order of meaningful elements. In: J. Greenberg (ed.) 1963, *Universals of language*, 73–133. Cambridge.
—— (1966) *Language universals*. The Hague.
Grönbech, K. (1936) *Der türkische Sprachbau*. Kopenhagen.
Hamp, E.P. (1976) Palatalization and harmony in Gagauz and Karaite. In: W. Heissig et alii (eds) 1976, *Tractata Altaica*, 211–3. Wiesbaden.
Hanser, O. (1974) Türkischer Satzbau. Die Nebensatzgrammatik des Türkischen, untersucht an ausgewählten Beispielen. *Wiener Zeitschrift für die Kunde des Morgenlandes* 65–6/1973–4, 155–218.
Haugen, E. (1950a) Problem of bilingualism. *Lingua* 2/1950, 271–90.
—— (1950b) The analysis of linguistic borrowing. *Language* 26/1950, 210–31.
—— (1969) On the meaning of bilingual competence. In: R. Jakobson & Sh. Kawamoto (eds), 1969 *Studies in general and oriental linguistics: presented to Shirô Hattori on the occasion of his sixtieth birthday*, 219–29. Tokyo.
—— (1972) *The ecology of language*. Essays by Einar Haugen. Selected and introduced by A.S. Dil. Stanford.
—— (1973) Bilingualism, language contact, and immigrant languages in the United States: a research report, 1956–70. In: Th.A. Sebeok (ed.) 1973, *Current trends in linguistics,* 10:1, 505–91. The Hague & Paris.
Hayasi, T. (2000). Lexical copying in Turkic: The case of Eynu. In: A. Göksel & C. Kerslake (eds) (2000), *Studies on Turkish and Turkic languages* (= *Turcologica*, 46), 433–9. Wiesbaden.
Hetzer, A. (1983) Wortkundliche Probleme bei Sprachbünden unter besonderer Berücksichtigung des südosteuropäischen Areals. *Zeitschrift für Balkanologie* 19/1983, 16–47.
Hockett, C.F. (1958) *A course in modern linguistics*. New York.
Hoenigswald, H.M. (1989) Language obsolescence and language history: matters of linearity, leveling, loss, and the like. In: N. Dorian 1989, 347–54.
Hovdhaugen, E. (1976) Some aspects of language contact in Anatolia. *Working Papers in Linguistics from the University of Oslo*, 7, 142–60.
Hřebíček, L. (1978) The Turkish language reform and contemporary grammar. (The difference between the spoken (S) and written (W) texts

on the level of grammatical morphemes.) *Archív Orientální* 46/1978, 334–7.
Jakobson, R. (1932) Zur Struktur des russischen Verbums. *Charisteria Guilelmo Mathesio*, 74–84. Pragae.
—— 1938) Sur la théorie des affinités phonologiques des langues. *Actes du Quatrième Congrès International de Linguistes*, 48–59. Copenhague.
Jansen, B., J. Lalleman & P. Muysken (1981) The alternation hypothesis: acquisition of Dutch word order by Turkish and Moroccan foreign workers. *Language Learning* 31/1981, 315–36.
Jensen, H. (1931) *Neupersische Grammatik*. Heidelberg.
—— (1959) *Altarmenische Grammatik*. Heidelberg.
Johanson, L. (1969) Review of Menges 1968. *Orientalia Suecana* 17/1968 (1969), 171–80.
—— (1971) *Aspekt im Türkischen. Vorstudien zu einer Beschreibung des türkeitürkischen Aspektsystems.* (= *Acta Universitatis Upsaliensis. Studia Turcica*, 1.) Uppsala.
—— (1974a) Sprachbau und Inhaltssyntax am Beispiel des Türkischen. *Orientalia Suecana* 22/1973 (1974), 82–106. [Also in: L. Johanson 1991c, 1–25.]
—— (1974b) Review of Weiers 1972. *Acta Orientalia [Havniæ]* 36/1974, 459–72.
—— (1974c) Review of Brands 1973. *Orientalia Suecana* 22/1973 (1974), 198–210.
—— (1975a) Some remarks on Turkic 'hypotaxis'. *Ural-Altaische Jahrbücher* 47, 104–18. [Also in Johanson 1991c, 26–70.]
—— (1975b) Fiilimsi önermelerin görevleri üzerine. *I. Türk Dili Bilimsel Kurultayına sunulan bildiriler 1972*, 525–29. Ankara.
—— (1976a) Zum Präsens der nordwestlichen und mittelasiatischen Türksprachen. *Acta Orientalia [Havniæ]* 37/1976, 57–74. [Also in Johanson 1991c, 99–116.]
——(1976b) Das tschuwaschische Aoristthema. *Orientalia Suecana* 23–4/1974–75 (1976), 106–58. [Also in Johanson 1991c, 117–69.]
—— (1976c) Review of Drimba 1973. *Orientalistische Literaturzeitung* 71/1976, cols 585–90.
—— (1977) Bestimmtheit und Mitteilungsperspektive im türkischen Satz. *Zeitschrift der Deutschen Morgenländischen Gesellschaft*, Suppl. III:2, 1977, 1186–1203. [Also in Johanson 1991c, 225–42.]
—— (1978a) Die Ersetzung der türkischen -*t*-Kausativa. *Orientalia Suecana* 25–6/1976–7 (1978), 106–33. [Also in Johanson 1991c, 170–97.]
—— (1978b) Türkçede önceden kestirilemez nitelikteki alomorflar. *Türk Dili Araştırmaları Yıllığı-Belleten 1977* (1978), 121–6.
—— (1979a) Die westoghusische Labialharmonie. *Orientalia Suecana* 27–8/1978–9 (1979), 63–107. [Also in Johanson 1991c, 26–70.]

—— (1979b) *Alttürkisch als 'dissimilierende Sprache'.* (= *Abhandlungen der Akademie der Wissenschaften und der Literatur, Mainz, Geistes- und sozialwissenschaftliche Klasse* 1979:3.) Wiesbaden.

—— (1981) *Pluralsuffixe im Südwesttürkischen.* (= *Abhandlungen der Akademie der Wissenschaften und der Literatur, Mainz, Geistes- und sozialwissenschaftliche Klasse* 1981:9.) Wiesbaden.

—— (1986a) Reproduktion,Widerstand und Anpassung: Zur lautlichen Iranisierung im Türkischen. In: R. Schmitt & P.O. Skjærvø (eds) 1986, *Studia Grammatica Iranica*, 185–201. München.

—— (1986b) Zur Konsonantenstärke im Türkischen. *Orientalia Suecana* 33–5/1984–6, 195–209. [Also in Johanson 1991c, 84–98.]

—— (1988a) Grenzen der Turcia. Verbindendes und Trennendes in der Entwicklung der Türkvölker. In: U. Ehrensvärd (ed.) 1988, *Turcica et Orientalia*, 51–61. Stockholm.

—— (1988b) Zur Entwicklung türkeitürkischer Varietäten in Nordwesteuropa. *Turkish in North-West Europe Newsletter* 1/1988, 3–8.

—— (1988c) Iranian elements in Azeri Turkish. In: E. Yarshater (ed.) 1988, *Encyclopædia Iranica*, 3, cols 248b–51a. London & New York.

—— (1989a) Review of Ureland 1987. *Nordic Journal of Linguistics* 12/1989, 93–4.

—— (1989b) Review of Doerfer 1988b. *Acta Orientalia* (Copenhagen) 50/1989, 174–8.

—— (1990a) Studien zur türkeitürkischen Grammatik. In: Gy. Hazai (ed.) 1990, *Handbuch der türkischen Sprachwissenschaft.* 1, 146–278. Budapest.

—— (1990b) Subjektlose Sätze im Türkischen. In: B. Brendemoen 1990, 193–218.

—— (1990c) Review of Chr. Tzitzilis, 1987, Griechische Lehnwörter im Türkischen (mit besonderer Berücksichtigung der anatolischen Dialekte). *Oriens* 32/1990, 454–6.

—— (1991a) Zu den Grundfragen einer kritischen Altaistik. *Wiener Zeitschrift für die Kunde des Morgenlandes* 80/1990 (1991), 103–24.

—— (1991b) Zur Sprachentwicklung der 'Turcia Germanica'. In: I. Baldauf, K. Kreiser & S. Tezcan (eds) 1991, *Türkische Sprachen und Literaturen.* (= *Veröffentlichungen der Societas Uralo-Altaica*, 29), 199–212. Wiesbaden.

—— (1991c) *Linguistische Beiträge zur Gesamtturkologie.* (= *Bibliotheca Orientalis Hungarica*, 37.) Budapest.

—— (1991d) Zur Typologie türkischer Gerundialsegmente. In: T. Tekin (ed.) 1991, *Türk Dilleri Araştırmaları 1991. Researches in Turkic Languages 1991*, 98–110.

—— (1991e) On syllabic frontness oppositions in Turkic. *Varia Eurasiatica*, 77–94. Szeged.

—— (1991f) Review of Doerfer 1988a. *Zeitschrift der Deutschen Morgenländischen Gesellschaft* 141/1991, 185–7.

—— (1991g) Zur Postterminalität türkischer syndetischer Gerundien. *Ural-Altaische Jahrbücher* N.F., 9/1990 (1991), 137–51.

—— (1992) *Strukturelle Faktoren in türkischen Sprachkontakten* (= Sitzungsberichte der Wissenschaftlichen Gesellschaft an der J. W. Goethe-Universität Frankfurt am Main, 29:5), Stuttgart.

—— (1993a) Zur Anpassung von Lehnelementen im Türkischen. In: J.P. Laut & K. Röhrborn 1993, 93–102.

—— (1993b) Code-copying in immigrant Turkish. In: G. Extra & L.Th. Verhoeven (eds) (1993) *Immigrant languages in Europe*, 197–221. Clevedon, etc.

—— (1993c) Graphie und Phonologie im Türkischen: Probleme der Lautharmonie. In: O. Werner (ed.) 1993, *Probleme der Graphie*, 83–94. Tübingen.

—— (1993d) Review of Sims-Williams & Hamilton 1990. *Acta Orientalia* 54/1993, 197–9.

—— (1994) Türkeitürkische Aspektotempora. In: R. Thieroff & J. Ballweg (eds) 1994, *Tense systems in European languages*, 247–66. Tübingen.

—— (1995) On Turkic converb clauses. In: M. Haspelmath & E. König (eds) 1995, *Converbs in cross-linguistic perspective. Structure and meaning of adverbial verb forms, adverbial participles, gerunds*, 313–47. Berlin & New York.

—— (1996a) Terminality operators and their hierarchical status. In: B. Devriendt, L. Goossens & J. van der Auwera (eds) 1996, *Complex structures: A functionalist perspective*, 229–58. Berlin & New York.

—— (1996b) Kopierte Satzjunktoren im Türkischen. *Sprachtypologie und Universalienforschung* 49/1996. 1–11.

—— (1996c). On Bulgarian and Turkic indirectives. In: N. Boretzky et alii 1996, 84–94.

—— (1997) Kopien russischer Konjunktionen in türkischen Sprachen. In: D. Huber & E. Worbs (eds) 1997, *Ars transferendi. Sprache, Übersetzung, Interkulturalität*, 115–21. Frankfurt.

—— (1998a). Zum Kontakteinfluss türkischer Indirektive. In: N. Demir & E. Taube (eds) 1998, *Turkologie heute. Tradition und Perspektive*, 141–50. Wiesbaden.

—— (1998b) Code-copying in Irano-Turkic. *Language Sciences* 20/1998, 325–37.

—— (1999a) Frame-changing code-copying in immigrant varieties. In: G. Extra & L. Verhoeven (eds) 1999, *Bilingualism and migration*, 247–60. Berlin & New York.

—— (1999b) The dynamics of code-copying in language encounters. In: B. Brendemoen et alii 1999, 37–62.

—— (1999c) Cognates and copies in Altaic verb derivation. In: K.H. Menges & N. Naumann (eds) 1999, *Language and literature. Japanese and the other Altaic languages*, 1–13. Wiesbaden.

REFERENCES

—— (2000a) Turkic indirectives. In: L. Johanson & B. Utas (eds) 2000, *Evidential. Turkic, Iranian and neighbouring languages*, 61–87. Berlin & New York.

—— (2000b) Linguistic convergence in the Volga area. In: D. Gilbers, J. Nerbonne & J. Schaeken (eds) 2000, *Languages in contact*, 165–78 (= *Studies in Slavic and General linguistics, 28.*) Amsterdam & Atlanta.

—— (2000c) Viewpoint operators in European languages. In: Ö. Dahl 2000, 27–187.

—— (2000d) Attractiveness and relatedness: Notes on Turkic language contacts. In: J. Good & A.C.L. Yu (eds) (2000) *Proceedings of the twenty-fifth annual meeting of the Berkeley Linguistic Society. Special session on Caucasian, Dravidian, and Turkic linguistics*, 87–94. Berkeley.

—— & É.Á. Csató (eds) (1998). *The Turkic languages*. London.

—— & C. Schönig (eds) (1988) *Kritische Beiträge zur Altaistik und Turkologie.* (= *Turcologica*, 3.) Wiesbaden.

Juhász, J. (1970) *Probleme der Interferenz*. München.

Kakuk, S. (1960) Constructions hypotactiques dans le dialecte turc de la Bulgarie Occidentale. *Acta Orientalia Hungarica* 11/1960, 249–57.

Karst, J. (1901) *Historische Grammatik des Kilikisch-Armenischen*. Straßburg.

Kazakis, K. (1970) The status of Turkisms in the present-day Balkan languages. In: H. Birnbaum & S. Vryonis (eds) 1970, *Aspects of the Balkans. Continuity and change*, 87–116. The Hague & Paris.

Kerimova, A.A. (1966) Tadžikskij jazyk. In: V.V. Vinogradov (ed.) 1966, *Jazyki narodov SSSR 1. Indoevropejskie jazyki*, 212–36. Moskva.

Kiparsky, P. (1973) Phonological representations. In: O. Fujimora (ed.) 1973, *Three dimensions in linguistic theory*, 1–136. Tokyo.

Kıral, F. (1991) = Kıral-Shahidi Asl, F. (1991) *Persische Lehnsyntax im aserbaidschanischen Stadtdialekt von Täbriz*. [M.A. thesis, University of Mainz.]

—— (2001) *Das gesprochene Aserbaidschanisch von Iran: Eine Studie zu den syntaktischen Einflüssen des Persischen*. (= *Turcologica*, 43.) Wiesbaden.

Kissling, H.J. (1960) *Osmanisch-türkische Grammatik*. (= *Porta linguarum orientalium*, N.S., 3.) Wiesbaden.

Koç, S. (ed.) (1988) *Studies on Turkish linguistics*. Ankara.

Lazard, G. (1957a) *Grammaire du persan contemporain*. Paris.

—— (1957b) Caractères distinctifs de la langue tadjik. *Bulletin de la Société de Linguistique de Paris* 52, 117–86.

Laut, J.P. & K. Röhrborn (eds) (1993) *Sprach- und Kulturkontakte der türkischen Völker*. Wiesbaden.

Lewandowski, Th. (1976) *Linguistisches Wörterbuch*. 1. Heidelberg.

Mackey, W.F. (1970) Interference, integration and the synchronic fallacy. In: J.E. Alatis (ed.) 1970, *Bilingualism and language contact*. George-

town University round table on languages and linguistics, 23, 195–227. Washington, D.C.
Mansuroğlu, M. (1955) Türkçede cümle çeşitleri ve bağlayıcıları. *Türk Dili Araştırmaları Yıllığı-Belleten 1955*, 59–71.
Mardanov, Š.K. (1983) O tipax russkix kalek v uzbekskom literaturnom jazyke. *Sovetskaja Tjurkologija* 1983:1, 15–23.
Mardkowicz, A. (1930) *Elijahunun ucuru (jomak)*. (= Bibljoteczka karaimska, 1.) Luck.
Martinet, A. (1955) *Économie des changements phonétiques. Traité de phonologie diachronique*. Berne.
—— (1960) *Éléments de linguistique générale*. Paris.
Matras, Y. (1990) On the emergence of finite subordination in Balkan Turkish. Paper presented at the *5th International Conference on Turkish Linguistics*, London, 15–17 August 1990. [To appear in: H. Boeschoten & L. Johanson (eds), *Turkic languages in contact*.]
Masica, C. (1976) *Defining a linguistic area: South Asia*. Chicago.
McCarthy, K.M. (1970) *The linguistic adaptation of loanwords in modern Standard Turkish*. University of North Carolina at Chapel Hill.
Meillet, A. (1921) *Linguistique historique et linguistique générale*. Paris.
Memetov, A. (1986) Russkie kal'ki v krymskotatarskom jazyke. *Sovetskaja Tjurkologija* 1986:4, 13–21.
Menges, K.H. (1947) *Qaraqalpaq grammar. 1. Phonology*. New York.
—— (1949) Zum Özbekischen von Nord-Afghanistan. *Anthropos* 41–4/ 1946–9, 673–710.
—— (1968) *The Turkic languages and peoples. An introduction to Turkic studies*. (= Ural-Altaische Bibliothek, 15.) Wiesbaden.
—— (1983) Slavisch-altajische Kontakte. *Die slawischen Sprachen* 4/1983, 37–61.
—— (1987) Die Funktion der türkischen Sprache im Balkanraum und ihre mögliche Rolle bei der Formierung der heutigen slavischen Nationalsprachen. In: Chr. Hannick (ed.) 1987, *Sprachen und Nationen im Balkanraum. Die historischen Bedingungen der Entstehung der heutigen Nationalsprachen*. Wien.
Menovščikov, G.A. (1969) O nekotoryx social'nyx aspektax évoljucii jazyka. *Voprosy social'noj lingvistiki*, 110–34. Leningrad.
Menz, A. (1991) *Studien zum Türkisch der zweiten deutschlandtürkischen Generation*. [M.A. thesis, University of Mainz.]
—— (1999) *Gagausische Syntax. Eine Studie zum kontaktinduzierten Sprachwandel*. (= Turcologica, 41.) Wiesbaden.
Miller, R.A. (1990) How dead *is* the Altaic hypothesis? In: B. Brendemoen 1990, 223–37.
—— (1991) Anti-Altaists *contra* Altaists. *Ural-Altaic Yearbook* 63/1991, 5–62.
Moravcsik, E. (1978) Language contact. In: J. Greenberg (ed.) 1978, *Universals of human language*, 1, 93–122. Stanford.

Mundy, C.S. (1955) Turkish syntax as a system of qualification. *Bulletin of the School of Oriental and African Languages* 17/1955, 279–305.

Musaev, K.M. (1984) *Leksikologija tjurkskix jazykov*. Moskva.

Oikonomides, D.Ê (1958) *Grammatikê tês ellênikês dialektu tu Pontu*. Athênnai.

Oksaar, E. (1972) Bilingualism. In: Th.A. Sebeok (ed.) 1972, *Current trends in linguistics*, 9, 476–511. The Hague.

Paul, H. (1909⁴) *Prinzipien der Sprachgeschichte*. Halle a. S.

Perry, J. (1979) Uzbek influence on Tajik syntax: the converb constructions. *The elements. A parasession on linguistic units and levels, including papers from the conference on non-Slavic languages of the USSR*, 448–61. Chicago.

Pfaff, C.W. (1979) Constraints on language mixing: intrasentential code-switching and borrowing in Spanish/English. *Language* 55/1979, 291–318.

—— (1987) Functional approaches to interlanguage. In: C.W. Pfaff (ed.) 1987, *First and second language acquisition processes*, 81–102. Cambridge, Mass.

—— (1988a) Turkish in contact with German: language maintenance and loss among immigrant children in West Berlin. Paper presented at the *Conference on Language Maintenance and Loss*, Noordwijkerhout, 28–30 August 1988. [Manuscript.]

—— (1988b) Linguistic and social determinations of Turkish/German bilingualism of migrant children in Berlin. *Diaspora languages in Western Europe*. (= *Slavica Lundensia* 12), 49–74. Lund.

—— & T. Savaş, (1988) Language development in a bilingual setting: the acquisition of Turkish in Germany. In: S. Koç 1988, 351–86.

Pokrovskaja, L.A. (1966) Gagauzskij jazyk. In: N.A. Baskakov (ed.) 1966, *Jazyki narodov SSSR 2. Tjurkskie jazyki*, 112–38. Moskva.

—— (1977) Razvitie vnutristrukturnyx izmenenij v balkano-tureckix dialektax pod vlijaniem slavjanskix jazykov. *Altaica* (= *Mémoires de la Société Finno-Ougrienne*, 158/1976 [1977]), 213–9. Helsinki.

—— (1978) *Sintaksis gagauzskogo jazyka v sravnitel'nom osveščenii*. Moskva.

Poplack, S. (1980) 'Sometimes I'll start a sentence in English y termino en Español': Toward a typology of code-switching. *Linguistics* 18/1980, 581–618.

—— (1981) Syntactic structure and social function in codeswitching. In: R.P. Durán (ed.) 1981, *Latino language and communicative behavior*, 169–84. Norwood, N.J.

Poppe, N.N. (1973) Über einige Verbalstammbildungssuffixe in den altaischen Sprachen. *Orientalia Suecana* 21/1973, 119–41.

Pritsak, O. (1959) Das Karaimische. In: J. Deny et alii 1959, 318–40.

Ramstedt, G.J. (1912) *Zur Verbalstammbildungslehre der mongolisch-türkischen Sprachen*. (= *Journal de la Société Finno-Ougrienne* 28/1912: 3.) Helsingfors.

REFERENCES

—— (1957) *Einführung in die altaische Sprachwissenschaft*. Bearbeitet und herausgegeben von P. Aalto. 2. (= *Mémoires de la Société Finno-Ougrienne*, 104/2.) Helsinki.
Rastorgueva, V.S. (1952) *Očerki po tadžikskoj dialektologii. Vypusk 1. Varzobskij govor tadžikskogo jazyka*. Moskva.
—— (1963) *Očerki po tadžikskoj dialektologii. Vypusk 5. Tadžiksko-russkij dialektnyj slovar'*. Moskva.
—— (1964) *Opyt sravnitel'nogo izučenija tadžikskix govorov*. Moskva.
Reichl, K. (1983) Syntactic interference in Afghan Uzbek. *Anthropos* 78/1983, 481–500.
Ritter, H. (1921) Aserbaidschanische Texte zur nordpersischen Volkskunde. *Der Islam* 11/1921, 181–212.
Römer, C. (1981) Der Einfluß der Übersetzungen aus dem Persischen auf die Entwicklung des Osmanischen im 14. und 15. Jahrhundert. *Wiener Zeitschrift für die Kunde des Morgenlandes* 73/1981, 89–114.
Róna-Tas, A. (1986) *Language and history. Contributions to comparative Altaistics*. (= *Studia Uralo-Altaica* 25.) Szeged.
Ross, J.R. (1982) Pronoun deleting processes in German. Paper presented at the annual meeting of the Linguistic Society of America, San Diego.
Sapir, E. (1921) *Language*. New York.
Schaufeli, A. (1990) *Turkish in an immigrant setting. A comparative study of the first language of monolingual and bilingual Turkish children*. Amsterdam.
Schlachter, W. (1974) Die koordinierenden Konjunktionen des Syrjänischen als Entlehnungsproblem. *Acta Linguistica Hungarica* 24/1974, 331–6.
Schönig, C. (1987) Diachronic and areal approach to the Turkic imperative paradigm. In: M. van Damme & H. Boeschoten (eds) 1987, *Utrecht papers on Central Asia*. (= *Utrecht Turkological Series*, 2.), 205–22. Utrecht.
Seaman, P.D. (1972) *Modern Greek and American English in contact*. Den Haag.
Seiler, H. (1988) *Die universalen Dimensionen der Sprache: eine vorläufige Bilanz*. (= *Arbeiten des Kölner Universalien-Projekts*, 75.) Köln.
Serebrennikov, B. (1960) *Kategorii vremeni i vida v finno-ugorskix jazykax permskoj i volžskoj grupp*. Moskva.
Setälä, E.N. (1915) Zur Frage nach der Verwandtschaft der finnisch-ugrischen und samojedischen Sprachen. (= *Journal de la Société Finno-Ougrienne* 30/1915: 5.) Helsinki.
Sims-Williams, N. & J. Hamilton (1990) *Documents turco-sogdiens du IXe-Xe siècle de Touen-huang*. London.
Slobin, D.I. (1973) Cognitive prerequisites for the development of grammar. In: C. Ferguson & D.I. Slobin (eds) 1973, *Studies of child language development*, 175–208. New York.
—— (1977) Language change in childhood and history. In J. McNamara (ed.) 1977, *Language learning and thought*, 185–214. New York.

—— (1980) The repeated path between transparency and opacity in language. In: U. Bellugi & M. Studdert-Kennedy (eds) 1980, *Signed and spoken language: biological constraints on linguistic form*, 229–43. Weinheim.

—— (1982) Universal and particular in the acquisition of language. In: E. Wanner & L.R. Gleitman (eds) 1982, *Language acquisition: the state of the art*, 128–70. Cambridge.

—— (1985) Crosslinguistic evidence for the language-making capacity. In: D.I. Slobin (ed.) 1985, *The crosslinguistic study of language acquisition*. 2, 1157–1249. Hillsdale, N.J. & London.

—— (1986) The acquisition and use of relative clauses in Turkic and Indo-European languages. In: D.I. Slobin & K. Zimmer 1986, 273–94.

—— (1988) The development of clause chaining in Turkish child language. In: S. Koç 1988, 27–54.

—— & K. Zimmer (eds) (1986) *Studies in Turkish linguistics*. Amsterdam & Philadelphia.

Soper, J.D. (1987) *Loan syntax in Turkic and Iranian: The verb systems of Tajik, Uzbek and Qashqay*. Los Angeles.

Sridhar, S.N. (1978) Linguistic convergence: Indo-Aryanization of Dravidian languages. *Studies in the Linguistic Sciences* 8/1978, 197–215.

Teodosijeviç, M. (1985) Yugoslavya'da konuşulan Türkçenin sadeleştirilmesi ve eşanlamlı kelimelerin yanlış kullanılması. *Beşinci Milletler arası Türkoloji Kongresi. Tebliğler. I, Türk Dili*, 1, 261–5. İstanbul.

Tesnière, L. (1939) Phonologie et mélange des langues. *Travaux du Cercle Linguistique de Prague* 8/1939, 83–93.

Thomason, S.G. (1980) Morphological instability, with and without language contact. In: J. Fisiak (ed.) 1980, *Historical morphology*, 359–72. The Hague.

—— & T. Kaufman (1988) *Language contact, creolization and genetic linguistics*. Berkeley & Los Angeles & London.

Tietze, A. (1952) Die formalen Veränderungen an neueren europäischen Lehnwörtern im Türkischen. *Oriens* 5/1952, 230–68.

—— (1964) Persische Ableitungssuffixe im Azerosmanischen. *Wiener Zeitschrift für die Kunde des Morgenlandes* 59–60/1963–4, 154–200.

Tietze, A. & O. Ladstätter (1994). *Die Abdal (Äynu) in Xinjiang*. (= Österreichische Akademie der Wissenschaften. Philosophisch-historische Klasse. Sitzungsberichte, 604.) Wien.

Traugott, E.C. (1973) Some thoughts on natural syntactic processes. In: C.-J.N. Bailey & R. Shuy (eds) 1973, *New ways of analyzing variation in English*, 313–22. Washington.

Trudgill, P. (1986) *Dialects in contact*. Oxford.

Uhlenbeck, E.M. (1981) Productivity and creativity. Some remarks on the dynamic aspects of language. In: W. Dietrich & H. Geckeler (eds) 1981,

Logos semantikos. Studia linguistica in honorem Eugenio Coseriu 1921–1981, 3, 165–74. Berlin.

Ureland, P.S. (ed.) (1987) *Sprachkontakt in der Hanse. Aspekte des Sprachausgleichs im Ostsee- und Nordseeraum.* (= *Linguistische Arbeiten*, 191.) Tübingen.

Utas, B. (1991) New Persian as an interethnic medium. In: I. Svanberg (ed.) 1991, *Ethnicity, minorities and cultural encounters* (= *Uppsala Multiethnic Papers*, 25), 103–11. Uppsala.

Venneman, Th. (1973) Explanation in syntax. In: J. Kimball (ed.) 1973, *Syntax and semantics 2*, 1–50. New York.

Verhoeven, L.Th. (1987) Acquisition of spatial reference in Turkish. In: H. Boeschoten & L.Th. Verhoeven (eds) 1987, *Studies on modern Turkish*, 217–30. Tilburg.

—— & H.E. Boeschoten (1986) First language acquisition in a second language submersion environment. *Applied Psycholinguistics* 7/1986, 241–56.

Vočadlo, O. (1938) Some observations on mixed languages. *Actes du Quatrième Congrès International de Linguistes*, 169–76. Copenhague.

Vogt, H. (1945) Substrat et convergence dans l'évolution linguistique. Remarques sur l'évolution et la structure de l'arménien, du géorgien, de l'ossète et du turc. *Studia septentrionalia* 2/1945, 213–28.

—— (1971) *Grammaire de la langue géorgienne.* Oslo.

Watters, J.K. (1987) An investigation of Turkish clause linkage. In: R.D. van Valin, Jr. (ed.) 1987, *Davis Working Papers in Linguistics*, 2, 130–41.

Weiers, M. (1972) *Die Sprache der Moghol der Provinz Herat in Afghanistan (Sprachmaterial, Grammatik, Wortliste).* (= *Abhandlungen der Rheinisch Westfälischen Akademie der Wissenschaften*, 49; *Materialien zur Sprache und Literatur der Mongolen von Afghanistan*, 1.) Opladen.

Weinreich, U. (1953) *Languages in contact. Findings and problems.* (= *Publications of the Linguistic Circle of New York*, 1.) New York.

—— (1958) On the compatibility of genetic relationship and convergent development. *Word* 14/1958, 374–9.

Wendt, H.F. (1961) *Sprachen.* Frankfurt a.M. & Hamburg.

Whitney, W.D. (1881) On mixture in language. *Transactions of the American Philological Association* 12, 5–26.

Windfuhr, G.L. (1990) Persian. In: B. Comrie (ed.) 1990, *The world's major languages*, 523–46. New York & Oxford.

Wurm, S. (1960) Appendix I. In: N.A. Baskakov 1960, 44–58.

—— (1987) Évolution de la langue et déclin culturel. *Diogène* 137/1987, 35–48.

Yıldız, G. (1986) *Untersuchungen zum Sprachgebrauch türkischer Jugendlicher der zweiten Generation in der Bundesrepublik Deutschland.* [M.A. thesis, University of Giessen.]

Yngve, V.H. (1961) The depth hypothesis. In: R. Jakobson (ed.) 1961, *Structure of language and its mathematical aspects*, 130–8. Providence.

Zajączkowski, A. (1932) *Sufiksy imienne i czasownikowe w języku zachodniokaraimskim. (Przycznek do morfologji języków tureckich).* (= *Polska Akademja Umiejętnoci. Prace Komisji Orjentalistycznej*, 15.) Kraków.

INDEX

ablative 16, 24, 82, 108, 116
abstract(ness) 47, 89–90, 98–100
accusative 31, 47, 101–3, 123
acquisition x, 9, 41–2, 45–8, 55, 58, 74, 119, 126, 129, 139, 142, 157, 159
actant 20, 23, 27, 30–1, 89, 104, 107, 110, 121, 123, 141, 146, 158
actionality x, 20, 23, 30, 88, 92–3, 96, 152, 154
action clause 27, 121, 124–5, 127, 129
action noun 27, 121
actor clause 27, 122 (cf. relative clause)
adaptation(al) 9–10, 12, 17, 48, 55, 58–60, 62, 75–6, 157, 160
adessive 108
adjective, adjectival 13, 16, 24–5, 27, 31, 47, 81, 86, 103, 108–9, 111–3, 117, 122, 137, 143, 145
adoption viii, 3, 8–9, 38–40, 43, 47, 50–3, 66–9, 71, 79, 96, 99, 113, 134, 144, 159
adstratum 148
adverb(ial) 25, 27, 40, 79, 96, 111–3, 116–7, 117, 123–4, 125–7, 129, 131, 135
adverbial action clause 27, 124–5, 127 (cf. converbial clause)
adverbialize 20

Afghan Uzbek 7, 18, 112, 115–6, 118, 124–5
African languages 141
agglutinating, agglutination, agglutinative ix, 21, 45–6, 64, 84–5, 92, 141, 143, 158
agreement 25, 31, 47, 108–9, 158
allomorph(ic), allomorphy 21, 45, 51, 66, 82, 89, 91, 96, 153
allophone 14
Altaic xi, 3, 20–1, 25, 65, 74, 76, 80, 95, 98, 107, 118, 126–7, 130, 144, 148, 150, 152–4, 158
Altay Turkic 12, 93, 105, 109
alternation 9
Amharic 142
analogy, analogous 10, 18, 53–5, 80–1, 87, 89, 108, 112, 116, 153
analytic 15, 17, 44, 55, 79, 80, 84, 92, 95–6, 108, 118–20, 136, 141
anaphora, anaphoric 16, 18, 30, 110
Anatolian Greek ix, 6, 7, 13, 16, 59, 62, 64–5, 68, 70, 74, 77–8, 83, 94, 103–4, 113, 136, 143, 157
Arabic vii, 4, 11–2, 14, 59, 75–6, 103, 112, 130, 159–60
areal (contacts, tendencies) 4, 37, 62, 105, 143, 147–8, 155

179

Armenian 7, 8, 74–5, 79, 84, 87–8, 99, 107–9, 113, 115, 136, 141, 143–7, 157
Armenian-Kipchak 160
aspect(ual), aspect-tense viii, 20, 23, 27, 29, 30, 40, 47, 83, 88, 90, 93, 99, 100–1, 117, 146, 158
attractive(ness) viii-xi, 2–3, 41, 43–49, 53–4, 56–9, 63, 73–5, 77–81, 84–5, 88–9, 91, 93, 99, 102, 108–9, 113–5, 121, 126, 129, 134, 137, 139–40, 149, 152
attribute 25, 27, 47, 108–9, 111–3, 115, 122, 125, 143, 145
auxiliary verb 13, 16, 30, 88, 136
Azerbaijanian 4, 7, 8, 12, 61, 70, 79, 81, 90, 113, 116, 121, 123–5, 147, 158

Balkan languages 13, 62, 80, 81, 102, 105, 108
Balkan Turkic 4, 7, 68, 106, 112, 117, 121, 123, 131
Bashkir 67, 105
basic code 9, 11, 61, 62, 70, 71, 75, 157
Black Sea coast 68, 78
block (of structural properties) 9, 12–14, 16, 18, 39, 40, 76
Bulgar 67, 82, 86, 160
Bulgarian 14, 66, 67, 81, 99, 102, 106, 108, 130, 145

cardinal number 25, 109–10
case ix, 11–2, 16, 20, 22–5, 28–9, 44, 46–7, 57, 80–3, 85–8, 101–2, 107–9, 115–6, 129, 145, 158
cataphoric 161
Caucasian 8, 13, 75, 145
causal 28, 124, 137
causative, causativity 20–1, 23, 31, 84, 87–91, 107, 141, 153–4, 160
Central Asia 62, 69, 147–8, 151
Chagatay 106, 118, 124, 131
Chamling 141–2
Chinese 75, 77, 104
Chukchi 135
Chuvash 7, 67, 79, 82, 86, 94, 96–7, 152
clausal, clause x, 11–2, 15–20, 25–8, 30–1, 36, 40, 48, 59, 61–2, 68, 80, 85, 93, 95, 115–37, 142, 146, 158, 160–1
clause-combining 117, 121, 126–7, 132
clause subordination 48, 116–121, 133–7
code 2–3, 9–13, 18–9, 60, 62, 70–1, 75, 81, 157
code copying 1–2, 8–9, 54, 60–1
code switching vii, 9, 35, 56
cohesion 24, 44–5, 52, 80, 85, 88, 90–1, 152
Coman (Cuman) 102, 106
combinational (copy, copying, feature, pattern, property, etc.) 9, 11–3, 15–9, 25, 28, 36, 40, 54–8, 61–2, 79–81, 83–7, 90, 93, 95–7, 103, 105–6, 112–3, 115, 117, 122, 129–32, 135, 142, 152–3
comparison 24, 107–8
comparative 24, 44, 81, 108
compound(ing) 17, 24–5, 30–1, 56, 81, 158
conditional 97, 130
conjugation(al) 20–1, 87–8, 96, 98, 152, 154, 160
conjunctor 28,
conjunction(al) x, 11–2, 17–9, 27–8, 40, 117, 130–6, 141–2, 161
connector 128, 130, 132–3
consonant 14, 31–2, 48, 63, 75, 77–8, 158
constituent clause 18, 27–8, 31, 40, 116–21, 126, 128, 131–7
conventionalized, conventionalization 6, 10, 60–1, 76, 92, 157
converb(ial) x, 23, 27–30, 68, 92–6, 100, 117, 119, 124–8, 133, 135–7, 145–7, 161
converbial clause 119, 124–8, 135
convergence, convergent 10, 14, 60–2, 64, 73–4, 76, 83, 88, 98, 104, 116, 135, 139–41, 144, 147, 150
cooperative 154
copula particle 23, 90, 100
copy(ing) viii-xi, 8–19 et passim
Crimea 69, 70
Crimean Tatar 16, 70, 129

Daco-Rumanian 106
dative 16, 31, 82–3, 107, 121, 141

declination 20–1, 24, 79, 81–2, 152
deep influence 39, 59, 62, 64–5
demonstrative pronoun 25, 40, 80, 102
derivation(al) ix, 11, 22, 81, 83, 103, 158
de-Turkicized xi, 59, 106
diathesis, diathetic x, 15, 20, 23, 40, 84, 88–9, 152 (cf. voice)
direct speech 28, 137
divergence, divergent 3–4, 10, 36, 57, 59–60, 88, 149–50, 152
Dolgan 7, 68
dominance, dominant 2, 5–6, 9, 14, 43, 49, 62, 66, 70, 79, 101, 117, 127
dominated 2, 8, 9
Dravidian 20–1, 25, 124, 141, 147–8, 154
duration (of contact) 5–6, 59–60, 66

East Old Turkic 105, 110, 128, 158
Eastern Turkestan (Xinjiang) 3, 69, 71, 78
embedded, embedding 26–8, 116, 131–3, 161
enclitic 12, 24, 45, 92
English 11, 14, 17, 21, 58, 101, 119, 132
equivalence (position), equivalent 11–12, 14–16, 18, 28, 30, 36, 38, 53–4, 56–7, 60–1, 63, 75, 77, 79–81, 87, 89–90, 101, 115, 125, 135, 146, 154, 158
equative 82
Eskimo 135
Evenki 87, 150
evidential(ity) 21, 29, 67, 99, 144–5, 147 (cf. indirective, indirectivity)
exclusive 105, 151, 154
Eynu 71

finite 17, 23, 68, 83, 93, 101, 104, 126, 129
Finno-Ugric 7, 14, 39, 67, 76–7, 79, 82, 86, 94, 97, 105, 148
focal(ity) 64, 93, 98, 100, 146
frame 11–2, 52, 54, 61
foreignness 157–8
French 11, 16–7, 75, 106–7, 128, 160
frequential (copy, copying, property, quality) 9, 13, 18, 55, 61, 109–10, 128, 142

fusion (of morphemes) ix, 15, 21, 40, 45, 57, 79, 141
future 100, 121, 136

Gagauz xi, 7, 49, 77–8, 107, 112, 118–9, 121, 123, 130–1, 160
gender 13, 25, 31, 47, 64, 104, 108, 144
genetic xi, 3–4, 65–6, 68, 74, 88, 96, 148, 150, 152–5
genitive 21, 25, 29, 31, 51, 101–2, 107, 111–3, 115, 129, 136, 158, 161
genitive construction 25, 113, 115 (cf. possessive construction)
Georgian 8, 99, 145
German 15, 17–8, 47–8, 55, 81, 101, 105, 108, 110, 112, 114, 125, 129
gerund(ial), gerundival x, 18 (cf. converb, converbial)
Gilyak 20, 149
global (copy, copying) viii, 9, 11–4, 16, 18–9, 32, 36, 39–40, 44, 46, 50, 52, 55, 57–9, 61, 67, 75–6, 78–86, 89–90, 103–4, 109, 112, 115–6, 123, 130–2, 136, 144
glottalization 67, 78
grammatical categories 97–105 et passim
grammaticalization, grammaticalized 20, 28, 30, 92, 95, 114–5
Greek viii–ix, 6–7, 11, 13, 16, 37, 56, 59, 62, 64–5, 68, 70, 74, 77–80, 83–4, 89, 94, 101, 103–4, 108–11, 113, 136, 143, 157–8

habitualization, habitualized 10, 60, 157, 159
Halich Karaim 77–8, 160
head 22, 25–8, 30, 84, 93, 111–4, 122–3, 125, 127–8, 136, 141, 146, 158, 161
head-final x, 112–4, 124, 127, 135–6
head-oriented(ness) 22, 26, 29–30, 86
Hebrew 6, 102, 106, 112
high-focal 64, 93, 100, 146
Hindi 124
Hungarian 86, 105, 108, 159
hypotactic, hypotaxis 17, 19, 119, 131, 134, 161

imperative 100, 105, 125, 130
imperfect 99, 146

imperfective 98
imposed, imposition viii, 3, 8, 38–9, 43, 47, 55–6, 66–9, 71, 78, 96–7, 99, 134, 157
inchoativity 88
inclusive 105, 151, 154
indefinite(ness) 98, 102, 103
indefinite case 24, 102
indefinite article 112
indirective, indirectivity 21, 29, 67, 99, 144–5, 147 (cf. evidential, evidentiality)
Indo-Altaic 148
Indo-Aryan 141, 147
Indo-European vii, x, 2, 8, 17–9, 36, 46, 70, 74–5, 80, 84, 105–6, 117–8, 120–2, 130–2, 142
Indo-Iranian 131
infinitive 13, 121, 135–6
infinitization 20, 27, 29, 116–7, 127, 132–3, 135
infix 21
inflection(al) ix, 13, 21–3, 36, 39, 45, 47, 52, 57–9, 65, 78–9, 82–3, 87, 92, 96–7, 104, 108, 141, 143, 145, 152–3, 158, 160
instability 119–20
integration 10–2, 51–2, 60, 92, 147, 157
intensive (adjective) 31, 81
intensity (contact), intensive vii-viii, xi, 5–7, 18, 49–50, 59–60, 62, 67, 69–70, 73, 76, 78, 90, 97, 99, 115, 122, 134, 137, 139, 145
intensity (actionality) 88
interrogation, interrogative 11, 20, 31, 87–90, 97, 123, 131
intraclausal code copying 9, 19
intrapositive 133
intraterminal(ity) 93, 98
intransitivity 88
inventory 16, 100, 117, 119, 141
Iranian vii, 4, 7, 12–4, 60, 65, 69, 71, 74, 76–8, 81, 83, 93, 99, 104, 107, 116–7, 125, 130–1, 141, 144, 147–8, 151
Iranicized, Iranicization 7, 60, 77–8, 125
iterative, iterativity 23, 88

Japanese 3, 20, 25, 148
junctor x, 11, 26–8, 68, 80, 117, 124–5, 130–3, 137, 161
juxtaposing, juxtaposition 15, 21, 40, 45–6, 54, 79, 81–2, 84–5, 91, 158

Karaim vii, xi, 6, 13, 37, 49, 59, 65, 68, 70, 74, 77–9, 81, 85, 96–7, 102, 104, 106–7, 112, 114–5, 130–1, 133–7, 152, 160
Karakalpak 63, 69, 129
Kashkay vii-viii, 7, 63, 68, 78, 83, 90, 94, 101, 125–6, 137, 160
Kazakh 4, 32, 69
Khakas 67, 96, 105
Khalaj 7, 70, 94, 96, 112, 124
Khalkha 81, 87, 94, 109, 141
Khazar 159
Khwarezmian 69, 94, 147–8
Kirgiz 4, 135
koiné(ization) xi, 2, 8, 42–3, 48, 70, 149–51
Koranes 7
Korean 3, 20, 25, 148
Kumyk 136
Kurdish 7, 74, 99, 136, 146–7
Kurmanji 136, 146–7

Ladino 8, 70–1
language maintenance 65–9, 71, 96
language shift 3, 6, 49, 65–6, 68, 70, 97, 159
leftbranching x, 21, 25–6, 28, 48, 93, 111, 114, 119–20, 122, 134–6
leveled, leveling 4, 91, 149, 151–3
lexeme 21, 27–8, 30–1, 44, 79, 86, 92–3, 114, 121
lexical, lexicon 4, 12–8, 21–3, 25, 31, 36, 39–40, 50, 52, 59–62, 65, 67–8, 71, 76, 78, 89–92, 95–96, 104, 112, 143–4, 151, 153–4, 157–9
lexicosyntactic (word-internal) 22, 85–7, 90, 152
lingua franca 151
loan semantics 14
loan syntax 15
loanword 4, 12, 14, 36, 63, 69, 76, 144
locative 22, 29, 82, 116, 146, 158

long(-lasting), long(er)-term, prolonged (contacts) viii-viii, xi, 6–7, 15, 18, 49–50, 62–3, 66, 73, 75–6, 78, 97, 99, 134, 139, 145

Macedonian 7
main clause 26–7, 30–1, 117, 119, 122, 124–5, 127–8, 132–3, 142, 161
Manchu 77, 150
manner of action 20
Mari (Cheremis) 82, 94, 148
marked(ness) 41–4, 52, 54–5, 59, 61–2, 77, 84, 140, 149, 159
material (copy, copying, alteration, change, similarity, property, quality, restructuring, shape) 9, 11–3, 45, 75, 96, 153
medial(ity), medium 20, 23, 88, 154
mixed copy(ing) 18–9, 79–81, 84, 112–3, 117, 136
modal 27, 79, 121, 136
modification (semantic) 21–3, 25–30, 46, 86–9, 92–3, 95, 120, 122, 124, 127–8, 133
Mongolian 15, 74, 87, 94, 102, 104–5, 109, 113, 141, 150–1, 153–4
Mongolic 3–4, 7, 15, 68, 71, 74, 79, 81–2, 84, 88, 94, 104, 113, 144, 149–52, 154
mood viii, 20, 23, 27, 40, 47, 87–8, 98–99, 101, 117, 129–30, 144, 158
morpheme, morphemic viii-ix, 11, 15, 18, 20–1, 27, 32, 35–6, 44–5, 51–2, 54–55, 66, 79–80, 82–85, 87–91, 95–7, 110, 117, 153, 158–9
morphological, morphology ix, 10–3, 17, 21–2, 24, 27, 35, 37, 39–40, 43–7, 51, 54, 58, 60, 64–5, 74, 80–3, 85, 88, 90–1, 95–6, 98, 103, 109, 117, 126, 133, 140–1, 145, 151, 153–4, 157
morphological adaptation, reshaping 12, 58
morphonology 68
morphosyntactic, morphosyntax 12, 20, 26, 28, 30, 35, 39–40, 45, 52, 57, 71, 93, 114, 118–9, 132, 143

necessitative 129, 136
negation, negative 20–1, 23, 79–80, 87–8, 97
nominative 47, 102–3, 109, 127, 129, 161
nominal 20–2, 24–7, 46–7, 81–2, 90, 97, 101, 103, 109, 114, 116, 121–2, 129, 141
nominal action clause 27, 121, 129
nominal phrase/group 25–6, 28, 101, 109, 114
nominalize(r) ix, 116, 158
nonfinite x, 27, 116, 119, 122, 125–6, 129, 136, 161
nonmaterial copying 14
nonmodifying 128, 133
nonpossessive subject markers 90
nontransparent 123
noun 13, 16–7, 23, 25–7, 29, 39, 51, 81–2, 84, 86, 103–4, 113, 121–2, 129, 135–6
number ix, 16, 18, 20, 22, 25, 81–2, 86, 88, 103–4, 108–10, 145, 158

object xi, 24, 31, 102–3, 107, 111, 113, 123, 142
Old Turkic, see East Old Turkic
Old Uyghur 69, 105–6, 118, 131, 137, 158 (cf. Uyghur)
optative 28, 79, 100, 121, 125, 130, 137
Ottoman 6, 11–2, 14, 17, 58, 67, 75, 80, 83, 88, 99, 104, 106, 115, 124, 131, 134, 143–6, 159–60
Ottomanization 67
overdifferentiation 10, 15–6, 157

Pamir languages 69, 147
paradigm 35–6, 40, 79, 83, 89, 91, 100–1, 105
participle, participial x, 13, 18, 23, 25, 27, 94, 100, 105, 111, 117, 122–4, 135–6, 146
particle xi, 11, 23–4, 27–8, 40, 45, 57, 79–80, 83, 89–90, 97, 100, 108, 114, 123, 130–3, 137, 141, 161
Pashto 147
passive, passivity 20–1, 23, 84, 87–8, 154
past (tense) 13, 99, 147
perceptible, perceptibility, perception,

perceptive, perceptual 41–2, 46–7, 54, 57, 85, 119, 122, 140, 160
perfect 93, 98–9, 105, 144, 146–7
perfective 98
peripheral (affix) ix, 23, 46, 85, 89–90, 104
peripheral (language) 7, 95, 151, 155
periphrastic 88
Persian vii-viii, xi, 4, 7, 13, 18, 59, 63, 68–71, 73, 75, 79–81, 83–4, 86, 88, 90, 94, 98–9, 101–3, 106–9, 111–3, 115–116, 118, 121, 125–6, 129–32, 135, 140–1, 144, 146–7, 150–2, 158–60
person(al) (pronoun, suffix) ix-x, 20, 22, 25, 27, 40, 88–9, 104–5, 110, 121, 146, 154, 158
phoneme 52, 76, 160
phonemization 14, 77–8
phonic adaptation, restructuring 12, 48, 75
phonological, phonology 5, 10, 13–4, 19, 21, 24, 29–30, 32, 36–9, 43, 45, 48, 52, 54, 56, 60, 66–7, 69, 75–79, 84, 89, 91, 106, 143, 157, 160
phonotactic adaptation 12, 32, 75
pluperfect 97, 101
plural(ity) 12, 18, 20–3, 25, 32, 44, 51, 80, 82, 86–7, 103–4, 109–10, 154
Pontic Greek 68, 103
possession 29, 107
possessive marker (morpheme, suffix) 16, 19–20, 22–3, 25, 29, 44, 80–1, 84, 86–7, 107, 113, 121, 123, 129, 135, 141, 143, 146, 160
possessive construction xi, 19, 55–6, 113 (cf. genitive construction)
possessive subject marker 136
possibility 20, 79, 87–8
postfield 114, 136
postposed, postpositive 11–2, 17, 21, 28, 48, 55, 112–7, 121–2, 127–8, 132–7, 142, 161
postposition(al) 11–2, 16, 24, 26, 28–9, 40, 57, 83, 92, 114–6, 145
postterminal(ity) 29, 98–9, 101, 105, 147
postverb(ial) 30, 88, 91–6, 146–8, 154

predicate, predicative 11, 23, 93, 111, 113
predicate core 11, 23, 25–8, 30–1, 111–2, 115, 121, 135
predication 20, 25, 27, 29–30, 93, 104, 107, 116, 122, 124, 126–8, 131–3, 158, 160–1
predicator 11, 20, 27, 93, 117, 122–7, 133, 142, 160–1
prefield 114, 122, 136–7
prefix(ing) 21, 30, 57, 81, 85, 146
prenominal x, 26
preposition(al) xi, 11–2, 28, 57, 108, 113, 115–6
preposed, prepositive x, 11, 25, 27–8, 31, 55, 68, 80, 111–3, 115–6, 118, 120–2, 124–5, 127–8, 131, 133, 135–7, 143, 145–6
present (tense) 64, 93, 98, 100, 121, 146
prestige viii-ix, 5, 49, 149
presumptive 100
preterite 94, 126, 135
pro-adverb(ial) 123
progressive, see high-focal
pronominal 30, 79, 110–1, 123, 160
pronoun 19, 25, 28, 30, 40, 79–80, 84, 90, 102, 110–1, 117, 130–2, 136, 154
propulsive (plot-advancing) 128, 133
psycholinguistic(s) 41, 44, 46, 49, 119–22, 125, 142
purpose, purposive 28, 124–5, 130, 137

quantifier 25
quotation particle 20, 137, 141

reciprocal, reciprocity 23, 88
rectum 25, 27
reduplication, reduplicative 31, 81, 85
reflexive, reflexivity 23, 88
regens 25, 27
reinforced, reinforcement xi, 10, 18, 53, 55, 61–2, 91, 106, 108, 115, 128, 142, 145–6
relational particle 11, 28, 57, 114
relative clause x, 17, 19, 27, 80, 115, 119–20, 122–4, 130, 136–7, 146 (cf. actor clauses)
renewal 28, 43, 64, 91, 93, 98, 100, 114, 146, 154

replica syntax 18
reshaping 9, 12–3, 16–7, 32
restructuring 12, 76, 93, 97, 112, 151, 153
rightbranching 26, 93, 112, 117, 119–20, 128, 133–4
Roma(ni) 7, 68, 121, 123, 160
Romanian 112
Russian 12, 14–8, 39, 51, 56, 63, 75–6, 103, 106, 109, 118, 126, 128, 130–1, 145

Salar 7, 104
salience, salient 46, 51, 85, 140
Samoyed 67–8
satellite 25, 27–8, 124, 127, 137
Sayan Turkic 7, 67, 151
scale (of attractiveness, adoptability, stability, etc.) 37–40, 50–2, 59, 65–7, 144
selective copying viii, 9, 13–18 et passim
semantic (copy, copying, feature, property, etc), semantics 9–10, 12–23, 25–8, 30, 36, 39, 45–7, 54, 58, 83, 86, 89–93, 96–9, 101, 103–4, 107, 109, 118, 124, 127–8, 132–3, 153, 161
semantically essential 47, 98–9, 104
sentence perspective 17, 26, 114, 129, 161
serialization 68, 124–6
Shor 105
Siberian Turkic 4, 67–8, 78
simplification 17, 42–3, 45, 47–8, 74–5, 77, 90, 92, 97–8, 104, 109–10, 113, 122, 125, 129, 134, 139–40, 142, 149, 159
singular 18, 25, 103–4, 109
Slavic vii, xi, 4, 6–7, 13, 30, 66–8, 74, 76–81, 85, 98, 103, 107, 111–2, 115, 117, 126, 130–1, 134, 144–5
social (condition, factor, prestige) viii–x, 2–3, 5–6, 9–10, 38, 40, 43, 49–50, 59–62, 66, 70, 149
social dominance 2
socio-(communicative, -cultural, -political) 4, 58, 60, 140
sociolinguistic(s) 7, 37, 59, 115
Sogdian 69, 135, 137, 151

sound harmony 24, 29, 32, 45, 48, 59, 76–8, 160
spontaneous convergence 140
spontaneity 88
Sprachbund 62, 141, 143, 148
stability 37–9, 42, 46–7, 50–3, 66, 82, 85, 90, 104
stabilization 113
structured, structuredness 51–4, 56, 88
structural dominance 2
subject xi, 20, 24–5, 29–31, 101, 103–4, 110, 113, 123, 127, 129, 136, 158, 161
subject marker 20, 23, 27, 90, 104, 123, 136, 158
subjectless 30
subjunctive 100, 130, 146
subjunctor 17, 19, 27–8, 117, 128, 130, 132–3, 136–7, 141, 161
subordinate, subordination, subordinating, subordinative x, 17–9, 25, 27, 48, 68, 111, 116–21, 128–9, 130–7, 160–1
substitution 9, 11, 14, 17, 75, 157, 159
substratum 2–4, 66–9, 75, 78, 96–7, 99, 134, 145
suffix 21 et passim
suffix rank 21, 85, 88
syllabic(ity) 21, 45, 82
syntactic, syntax x, 10, 12–13, 15–8, 20–1, 25–8, 30–1, 36–7, 39–40, 44, 48, 54, 57, 59–60, 62, 64–5, 67–9, 74, 80, 87, 89, 91–3, 95, 98, 101, 103, 105–8, 110, 111, 114, 116–9, 122, 124, 126, 128–9, 131, 133, 135, 141, 145, 148, 157, 159, 161
synthesis, synthetic ix, 15, 17, 19–20, 27, 31, 44, 46, 55, 79–84, 87–8, 90–2, 95–6, 108, 117–8, 120, 136, 141, 158

Tajik viii-xi, 7, 11, 13, 60, 62–5, 69, 74, 77, 79, 81–4, 89–91, 94, 99–103, 106–7, 113, 116, 126, 135, 141, 144, 147, 150
Tatar 4, 7, 15, 67, 94
temporal, tense viii, 13, 20, 23, 40, 64, 88, 90, 93, 98–100, 124–126, 136, 146, 158

INDEX

aspectotemporal 30
terminative 82
Tofan 67–8, 105
Trakai Karaim 160
transparency, transparent 21, 45–6, 58, 73, 79, 82, 89, 126, 140
Tungusic 3, 68, 77, 79, 87, 95–6, 102, 149–50, 153–4
Turkic 3 et passim
Turkic characteristics 19–33
Turkish vii, 3–4, 6–8, 11, 13–25, 27–31, 33, 43, 46, 48, 55–6, 58, 60, 64, 67–8, 75–6, 78, 81–2, 84, 86, 90, 93–5, 97, 99, 100–4, 106–10, 112–4, 119–25, 129–30, 134, 136–7, 142, 144–7, 157–60
Turkicization, Turkicized xi, 7, 60, 69, 96
Turkmen 4, 69, 105, 151
Tuvan 105
typological, typology xi, 2–4, 7–8, 11, 17, 20–1, 37, 42, 49, 53–4, 56–62, 71, 74, 78, 80–2, 85, 87–9, 104, 107–8, 111, 115, 124, 135, 140, 143–4, 148, 150, 154–5, 159

Udmurt 148
unattractive(ness) viii–x, 53, 59, 73, 78, 85, 95, 119, 126, 129, 135, 137, 139, 154
underdifferentiation 10, 15–7, 114, 157
Uralic 4, 21, 127, 144
Ural-Altaic 20, 65, 126, 148
Urdu 147

Uyghur 4, 71, 131, 160 (cf. Old Uyghur)
Uzbek 4, 7, 11, 13, 15, 17–8, 31, 49, 60, 62, 64, 69, 77–9, 83, 94, 99–101, 103, 106, 112–3, 115–6, 118, 124–6, 129, 135, 137, 141, 144, 147, 160

verb(al) ix–xi, 13, 15–7, 20–1, 23, 27–31, 44, 46–7, 64, 67–8, 79–80, 82–3, 87–101, 104–5, 107, 111, 113, 116, 119, 121–2, 124–7, 129, 135–6, 141, 144, 146–8, 151–4, 160
verbal abstract 27, 121
verb-final x–xi
viewpoint 23, 98
voice 20, 154 (cf. diathesis)
Volga (basin, region) 7, 67, 78, 82, 96
Volga Bulgar 82, 86, 160
vowel 31–2, 48, 75–8
vowel harmony 76, 78

Western Turkestan 7, 60, 69
word order x–xi, 15, 17–8, 26, 35–6, 40, 56, 61, 64, 106, 111–6, 119, 127, 129, 134
word structure 18, 21, 79–97, 106

Yaγnåbī 69
Yakut (Sakha) 4, 7, 68, 102, 105, 119, 151
Yellow Uyghur 7, 104
Yenisey-Ostyak 68

Zyryan 12, 130, 148